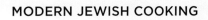
MODERN JEWISH COOKING

MODERN JEWISH COOKING

RECIPES & CUSTOMS FOR TODAY'S KITCHEN

LEAH KOENIG

PHOTOGRAPHS BY SANG AN

CHRONICLE BOOKS
SAN FRANCISCO

Library of Congress Cataloging-in-Publication Data available.

ISBN 978-1-4521-2748-4

Manufactured in China

Designed by Sara Schneider

Prop styling by Glenn Jenkins

Food styling by George Dolese and Elisabet der Nederlanden

10 9 8 7 6 5 4 3 2 1

Chronicle Books LLC

680 Second Street

San Francisco, California 94107

www.chroniclebooks.com

ACKNOWLEDGMENTS

This cookbook, like all books, would not exist without the hard work, patient advice, and genius insights of a whole team of people. Thank you to:

My agent Jenni Ferrari-Adler, who supported and encouraged me in shaping an idea into a proposal.

Bill LeBlond, who originally commissioned the book, my talented editor Sarah Billingsley, who shepherded it along the way, and the whole team at Chronicle Books.

Gabriella Gershenson for contributing the foreword and being a regular source of inspiration.

Kate Elias who helped me edit the manuscript, and whom I'm thrilled to have as both a friend and now a professional collaborator.

The incredible photography and design team, including Sang An, George Dolese, and Sara Schneider. It is an honor to see how my recipes and words came alive under your creative care.

The many friends and family who helped test, taste, and tweak recipes along the developing process: Anna and Naf Hanau, Anya Rous, Dan Steingart and Rachel Kort, Devorah and Manor Klein Lev-Tov, Elizabeth Lambshead and Brett Mullin, Ellen Smith Ahern and Chris Ahern, Matt Carl, Eve Stoller and Chris Chavez, Eric Gold, Tamar Kornblum, Michael Kodransky, Stephen Klein, Hannah Giles and Preston Demouchet, Judith Belasco and Mark Berkowitz, Dana Dasch and Philippe Gerschel, Julie Dawson and Benjy Fox-Rosen, Chani and Eden Pearlstein, Liz Alpern, Liz Fisher and Jeremy Brown, Daniel Zana and Yaffa Vinikoor, Aliyah Vinikoor, Carol Koenig, Ora Fruchter and Bradford Jordan, Temim Fruchter, Dasi Fruchter, Sruly Lazaros and Shai Fuller, Russ Agdern and Marisa Harford.

Rozanne Gold, who offered invaluable insights at a critical moment in the book's development.

My parents Carol Koenig and Richard Koenig, my brother Seth, my in-laws Rena and Chaim Fruchter, and my sisters-in-law Temim, Ora, and Dasi, for their support.

And finally, to baby Max, the best thing I ever made, and Yoshie Fruchter, whose love for kasha varnishkes and potato kugel is unmatched, for being my partner in all adventures large and small.

CONTENTS

10   FOREWORD

12   INTRODUCTION

CHAPTER ONE
BREAKFAST

22   Apple and Honey Granola

23   Black Pepper and Pistachio Granola

24   Matzo Granola with Walnuts and Coconut

26   Lemon and Rose Water Scones

28   Spicy Cheddar Biscuits

31   Sour Cream Coffee Cake with Pecan Streusel

33   Pumpkin–Chocolate Chip Muffins

34   Cinnamon-Sugar Apple Pancakes

36   Savory French Toast with Seared Tomatoes and Za'atar Butter

38   Baked Tomatoes and Eggs

40   Shallot, Leek, and Ginger Omelet

41   Mozzarella, Tomato, and Basil Frittata

42   Three-in-One Matzo Brei

44   Smoked Salmon Hash with Lemon-Mint Vinaigrette

45   Home Fries with Smoked Paprika

46   Roasted Garlic–Potato Blintzes

49   Orange-Scented Cheese Blintzes

51   Apple-Cranberry Chremslach

CHAPTER TWO
SALADS AND SPREADS

54   Spring Pea Salad with Browned Butter Vinaigrette

55   Sugar Snap Pea, Corn, and Basil Salad

56   Tomato Salad with Fried Capers

57   Watermelon Israeli Salad

58   Carrot Salad with Mint and Dates

60   Romaine Wedge Salad with Buttermilk Dressing

61   Avocado–White Bean Salad with Basil-Mint Pesto

62   Grilled Pear, Fennel, and Toasted Walnut Salad

67   Roasted Beet Salad with Preserved Lemon

68   Roasted Bell Pepper and Black Olive Salad

69   Red Cabbage and Beet Slaw with Caramelized Walnuts

70   Matbucha

71   Heirloom Tabbouleh

72   Fattoush

73   Supremely Creamy Hummus

74   Hummus im Basar

76   Chopped Chicken Liver

77   Vegetarian Chopped "Liver"

CHAPTER THREE

SOUPS

80 20 Cloves of Garlic Borscht

81 Sourdough Gazpacho

82 Tomato-Chickpea Soup with Spinach

84 Butternut Squash and Pear Soup

86 Creamy Sorrel Soup with Harissa

88 Rustic Vegetable Soup with Dill Dumplings

90 Wild Mushroom and Barley Soup

91 Chorizo, Tomato, and Cabbage Soup

93 Classic Chicken Soup

94 Spicy Ethiopian Chicken Stew

95 Goulash

96 Black Bean–Sweet Potato Chili

CHAPTER FOUR

VEGETABLES

100 Garlic-Marinated Zucchini

101 Grilled Zucchini with Balsamic Dressing

102 Sautéed Green Beans with Labneh and Sliced Almonds

105 Puréed Carrots with Orange and Ginger

106 Lemon-Caper Smashed Potatoes

107 Pan-Roasted Turnips

108 Roasted Delicata Squash with Thyme Bread Crumbs

109 Miso-Roasted Asparagus

111 Roasted Eggplant and Tahini Crostini

113 Balsamic-Roasted Mushrooms and Corn

114 Roasted Broccoli with Shallots and Lemon

115 Roasted Cauliflower and Red Onion

116 Fried Cauliflower with Creamy Cilantro Sauce

118 Sephardi Leek Patties

119 Potato Latkes with Apple-Date Chutney and Cinnamon Sour Cream

124 Beet Latkes with Chive Goat Cheese

126 Fried Green Olives

127 Potato-Leek Kugel

128 Butternut Squash Kugel with Crispy Shallots

130 Fennel Gratin

132 Mango-Ginger Tzimmes

133 Caraway Cabbage Strudel

CHAPTER FIVE

NOODLES, MATZO, GRAINS, AND BEANS

138 Creamy Noodles with Lemon, Mint, and Chives

139 Sweet Noodle Kugel with Dried Cherries and Figs

142 Kasha Varnishkes

145 Beef Kreplach with Ginger and Cilantro

147 Savory Matzo Farfel

148 Parsley Matzo Balls

149 Jalapeño-Shallot Matzo Balls

150 Dolmades

152 Dilled Rice with Lima Beans

153 Saffron Rice Pilaf

154 Bukharian Beef and Carrot Rice Pilaf

156 Mamaliga

157 Pine Nut and Scallion Couscous

158 Couscous with Winter Squash and Chickpeas

161 Toasted Almond Israeli Couscous

162 Bulgur with Walnuts and Pomegranate

164 Farro Salad with Corn and Jalapeño

165 Ful Medames with Poached Eggs

168 Vegetarian Porcini and Farro Cholent

170 Slow-Cooker Spiced Beef and Chickpea Stew

CHAPTER SIX

FISH, CHICKEN, AND MEAT

174 Tilapia in Spicy Tomato Sauce

175 Baked Sole with Bitter Greens

176 Grilled Salmon with Orange and Herbs

177 Greek Goddess Salmon

178 Brown Sugar–Citrus Gravlax

182 Gefilte Fish in White Wine–Herb Broth

186 Moroccan Chicken with Preserved Lemons

187 Apple Cider–Braised Chicken

188 Roast Chicken with Fennel and Orange

190 Rosemary-Maple Roast Chicken

191 Chicken Schnitzel with Caper Vinaigrette

194 Steak and Za'atar Fajitas

197 Red Wine and Honey Brisket

199 Spicy Chorizo and Red Pepper Penne

200 Pomegranate Molasses Meatballs

202 Mushroom-and-Beef-Stuffed Peppers

CHAPTER SEVEN

VEGETARIAN MAINS

206 Breaded Eggplant and Tomato Stacks

207 Sweet Potato–Scallion Frittata

208 Spinach Shakshuka

210 Spiced Lentil Patties

213 Porcini-, Tomato-, and Kale-Stuffed Peppers

215 Grilled Portobellos with Herbs and Mozzarella

216 Mushroom–Goat Cheese Tart

218 Baked Ziti with Caramelized Cherry Tomatoes

221 Spinach-Matzo Lasagna

223 Cinnamon-Roasted Seitan and Onions

224 Panfried Tofu Steaks with Shallot Gravy

CHAPTER EIGHT

BREADS AND PASTRIES

233 Classic Challah

236 Challah with Sautéed Leeks and Thyme

238 Pumpkin-Apple Challah

240 Homemade Bagels

242 Pletzels

245 Spinach and Cheese Bourekas

246 Butternut Squash and Sage Bourekas

248 Peach and Raspberry Tart

250 Chocolate-Raspberry Babka

254 Bittersweet Glazed Sufganiyot with Peanut Butter Cream

CHAPTER NINE

COOKIES, CAKES, AND OTHER SWEETS

259 Sweet Hamantaschen

    261 Lekvar

    262 Golden Apricot Filling

    263 Chocolate–Poppy Seed Filling

264 Savory Hamantaschen

    266 Sweet Potato–Parmesan Filling

    267 Tomato-Beef Filling

271 Chocolate-Almond-Hazelnut Horns

274 Chocolate-Almond Meringues

276 Rugelach Two Ways

278 Walnut Mandelbrot

279 Coconut Macaroons

280 Rhubarb-Oatmeal Crumble Bars

282 Chocolate Cupcakes with Apricot Jam Frosting

284 Orange-Glazed Cornmeal Cake

286 Honey-Cinnamon Pound Cake

287 Passover Pear Cake

288 Plum-Almond Cake

290 Upside-Down Apple Cake

292 Kabocha Squash–Chocolate Chip Cake

294 Chocolate-Banana Bundt Cake

295 Ricotta–Vanilla Bean Cheesecake with Raspberry Sauce

300 Chocolate Chip Cheesecake with Caramel Whipped Cream

302 Lemon Cheesecake with Almond Shortbread Crust

303 Jeweled Rice Pudding

304 Caramel-Chocolate Matzo Clusters with Pistachio

306 Tahini, Roasted Fig, and Pistachio Sundaes

307 Maple-Cardamom Roasted Pears

308 Chocolate-Dipped Figs

309 Chocolate-Strawberry Egg Cream

CHAPTER TEN

FILLINGS AND EXTRAS

312 Rosemary-Roasted Garlic for Challah

313 Cinnamon-Honey Tahini Spread

314 Cream Cheese Many Ways

316 Ashkenazi Charoset

317 Sephardi Charoset

318 Schmaltz and Gribenes

319 Creamy Horseradish Herb Sauce

320 Preserved Lemons

322 Spicy Dill Pickles

323 Baharat

CHAPTER ELEVEN

THE HOLIDAYS

326 Shabbat

329 Purim

330 Passover

333 Shavuot

334 Rosh Hashanah

336 Yom Kippur

338 Sukkot

340 Hanukkah

342 SOURCES

344 INDEX

FOREWORD

GABRIELLA GERSHENSON,

FOOD FEATURES EDITOR AT *EVERYDAY WITH RACHAEL RAY* MAGAZINE

When I first got to know Leah, we were working together at *Saveur* magazine—I was starting there as an editor, and she was filling in for our research chief. We quickly became co-conspirators and friends, recognizing a shared predilection for cute pastry chefs and frequent snack breaks to the staff kitchen. We also bonded over our shared love of Jewish food, from the fragrant, nutty spice za'atar to the more old-fashioned but decidedly delicious farmers' cheese.

During our brief time working together, Leah was immersed in all things Jewish. She was working on *The Hadassah Everyday Cookbook*, the official cookbook of the vaunted Hadassah Jewish women's organization. Meanwhile, I was gearing up to write my first feature story for the magazine about revisiting Riga, Latvia, with my parents, who hadn't been back since they left during the first wave of Jewish migration in the 1970s. Writing such a personal story requires a good sounding board, and I regularly turned to Leah for advice. The conversations would often turn to my grandmother and the role she played in instilling my love for

Jewish traditions through the foods that she made. Though I was concerned that I was boring Leah, I couldn't help but notice how intently she listened.

Fast forward a few years. Leah has now written her *second* book on Jewish food, *Modern Jewish Cooking*, which comes as no surprise to me. The fact that it serves as a definitive handbook of holiday favorites and excellent classic dishes—noodle kugel? cheese blintzes? borscht? check, check, check—as well as everyday foods that embrace Jewish flavors beyond Europe, is not surprising either. Leah crafted these recipes not only for her readers but to explore her own roots, and to create her own traditions, too.

She approaches the Jewish food canon with a keen sense of perspective. After all, for thousands of years, Jews have been a wandering tribe of people without a homeland. Food-wise, that means that you end up eating a lot like your neighbors. In America, for example, we might view Eastern European food as Jewish food; but, in reality, Jewish food is polyglot. Which is why, in *Modern Jewish Cooking*, you'll find a Mideast-inflected almond-date smoothie and Sephardi leek patties alongside Yiddishe kasha varnishkes (toasted buckwheat and bow-tie noodles) and American egg creams.

As for her timing in writing *Modern Jewish Cooking*, Leah's could not have been better. As she explores in her introduction and the personal and historical sidebars scattered throughout the book, now may be the best moment in modern history to rediscover Jewish food. This is a boom time for the cuisine, filled with hip, urban entrepreneurs rolling up their sleeves and making everything from artisanal gefilte fish to raw sesame halvah and hand-rolled bagels. Ethnic foods used to be something that our parents and grandparents hid in hopes of assimilating and thriving in society. Now, it's the thing that sets us apart and makes our contribution unique.

Reading and cooking through her book, it is clear that Leah celebrates Jewish cuisine as a living, breathing thing. In many ways, she hews to tradition—you will find killer recipes for matzo brei and hamantaschen. She's also included a chapter that explains the significance of the major Jewish holidays and the symbolic foods associated with them. But, like many contemporary cooks, Leah is committed to seasonality, and that sensibility finds delectable expressions in her recipes. For Sabbath dinner menus, for instance, she suggests Pumpkin-Apple Challah in the winter, Creamy Sorrel Soup with Harissa in the spring, Sourdough Gazpacho in the summer, and Rosemary-Maple Roast Chicken in the fall.

As ideal as this cookbook is for the starter Jewish kitchen, it's just as wonderful for everyday eating, no matter what your background is. Who wouldn't want to tuck into a melty Mozzarella, Tomato, and Basil Frittata for breakfast, dive into crispy Chicken Schnitzel with Caper Vinaigrette for lunch, have a sweet slice of Kabocha Squash–Chocolate Chip Cake as an afternoon snack, or some tender Grilled Salmon with Orange and Herbs for dinner? With this comprehensive and thoughtful cookbook, Leah has created so much more than a primer. She has written a work that can be passed down from parent to child, or simply be an inspiration for dinner tonight. It's up to you.

INTRODUCTION

Growing up, I could have really used a *bubbe* (Yiddish for "grandmother"). Being raised in a Jewish home, I was exposed early on to the joys of briny corned beef and fluffy matzo balls swimming in chicken soup. But while I loved the way these foods tasted, the secrets of how to make them remained a mystery.

My bubbe, Bessie Sparber, passed away years before I was born. One of those intuitive, shoot-from-the-hip Jewish cooks, she used a juice glass to measure sugar and had a sixth sense for how to make a dish smell, feel, and taste just right. But she never had the opportunity to beckon me into the kitchen as only a grandmother can. And I never had the pleasure of standing next to her, one hand tucked protectively in her apron pocket, watching while she cooked. I inherited her name (my middle name is Bess), but not her recipe for gefilte fish. And while my mom can turn out a superbly juicy brisket and ethereal applesauce-topped potato latkes, it never occurred to me as a kid or a busy teenager to ask her how.

When I finally found my way to the stove as a senior in college, I started cooking macaroni and cheese, stir-fries, and oatmeal-raisin cookies—foods more reflective of my American upbringing than my Jewish one. Then Rosh Hashanah rolled around. And Hanukkah, Purim, and Passover after that. On my own for these holidays for the first time, I found myself wishing I had the recipes for the dishes I grew up eating fixed in my culinary muscle memory. Instead, I was standing at the bottom of what felt like a mountain of history, tradition, and knowledge, looking up at an intimidating climb.

So I took a deep breath and started cooking. I scoured cookbooks and looked online for recipes that evoked the tastes I loved. On weekends, my friends and I would gather in one of our tiny Brooklyn kitchens with the ingredients for bagels or rugelach spread out before us on the counter. After much trial, plenty of error, and occasional frantic phone calls to my mom, I began to build a repertoire of classics—cheese blintzes, garlicky borscht, and mushroom-barley soup that stuck warmly to my ribs on chilly winter nights.

A few years later I met my boyfriend, now husband, Yoshie Fruchter. When we began hosting Shabbat dinners together in our apartment, I added new recipes to the mix. Jewish food sometimes gets dismissed as being lackluster or too heavy for today's palate. But the tender challah emerging from my oven and the chicken soup bubbling on the stove were every bit as fragrant and satisfying as I remembered.

While learning these recipes, I began to feel something slowly building along with a newfound sense of cooking confidence: Freedom. Because I had not inherited specific recipes, I felt free from any pressure to simply copy what I was taught, and free to improvise and add my own personality. I was creating my Jewish repertoire from scratch, and doing it in my twenty-first-century kitchen filled with vegetables from the farmers' market and a sauce-splattered laptop that played music while I chopped. There, I could incorporate ingredients that fell outside the Eastern European repertoire I inherited, and cook in a way that felt true to my life. I could bake an old-school honey cake one night and then stir sautéed jalapeño and shallots into matzo balls the next. Because in my modern Jewish kitchen, there was room for both. It was a hugely empowering time for me both personally and gastronomically. And my story is just one of many.

Historically speaking, Jewish cooking has had a tendency to focus on the past. To yearn for what was, hold tightly to tradition, and strive to capture times gone by through food. But we are in the midst of an exciting sea change. Over the last decade, a new crop of restaurateurs and food purveyors has begun to breathe new life into Jewish cuisine (see pages 181 and 185). They are bringing an artisanal sensibility to the delicatessen, reinventing classic Eastern European dishes, and exploring the bold cuisines of Israel and the Middle East (see page 64). Meanwhile, a small but growing generation of young Jewish farmers (see page 85) has reconnected to the notion that the Jewish relationship with food begins not at the stove or the table, but in the field.

Like me, these chefs, business owners, and farmers keep a loving eye on tradition—Jewish food simply makes no sense without it. And yet, they are not afraid to infuse history with a sense of innovation—to incorporate global flavors and fresh, seasonal ingredients into the mix. They care deeply about culinary heritage, but understand that in order for the Jewish kitchen to thrive in the twenty-first century and beyond, it cannot be static. It must be vibrant, exciting, and ever evolving.

I wrote *Modern Jewish Cooking* for the next generation of Jewish cooks. My hope is that it makes the dishes from the past feel accessible and relevant, while leaving room for experimentation and personal expression. I hope that it upends every stereotype of Jewish food as bland, outdated, or exclusive and encourages you to cook these amazing foods for the people you love.

Anyone who craves the briny, creamy, tangy, crisp, and soul-satisfying flavors of Jewish cuisine is invited to take part in this journey. Whether you grew up eating Jewish food or not, whether you have kneaded challah dough zero times or one hundred, whether you have never been to a seder or lead one every year, now is the time to connect, explore, and dig in.

ASHKENAZI, SEPHARDI, MIZRAHI: MANY CULTURES, ONE CUISINE

When Americans think about Jewish cuisine, they tend to think about Eastern European comfort food, and the cured meats and pickles of the delicatessen. But throughout history, Jews have been a wandering people, which means the Jewish kitchen spans not just centuries but continents. (Although I admit, if there is an Antarctic Jewish culinary heritage, I have not yet heard about it!)

As an American with ancestors from Lithuania and Russia, my own orientation to Jewish cuisine skews heavily in that direction. But it is only one part of the story. Throughout this book, you will notice that I refer to three broad categories of Jewish cultures: Ashkenazi, Sephardi, and Mizrahi. Each category represents an amalgam of many different countries that collectively make up the sum of the Jewish people worldwide. Following is a rundown.

Ashkenazi Jews largely hail from Russia, Poland, Lithuania, Romania, and other Eastern European countries. The category also includes Jews from Central European countries like Germany, Austria, and Hungary, as well as France. The majority of Ashkenazi Jews lived in relatively cold climates and developed a hearty peasant cuisine that they took with them when they moved en masse to America between 1840 and 1920. (Israel, South Africa, and Australia are also home to sizable Ashkenazi populations.) For much of the last two centuries, mainstream American Jewish culture has been strongly Ashkenazi identified. It is from these roots that iconic foods like bagels, pastrami, matzo balls, brisket, babka, schmaltz, chopped liver, and gefilte fish entered the country's cuisine.

Sephardi Jews trace their ancestry to the Iberian Peninsula, specifically Spain and Portugal. After the Spanish Inquisition in the fifteenth century, these Jews scattered to other parts of the world, including Italy, Latin America, North Africa, and the Middle East. Sephardi Jews hailed from warmer climates and typically had access to a greater variety of ingredients than Ashkenazi Jews. As a result, they developed a diverse and flavorful cuisine based around fresh produce, olive oil, and spices. Stuffed vegetables, the use of pine nuts and raisins as both a savory garnish and in desserts, fish simmered in tart sauces, and savory pastries like bourekas are all typical of Sephardi cuisine.

Mizrahi Jews are a more recently defined category and include Jews who trace their ancestry to Middle Eastern countries like Syria, Iran, Lebanon, Egypt, Yemen, and Iraq. Gastronomically speaking, there is a lot of overlap between Sephardi and Mizrahi cuisines, as both are centered in Mediterranean climates. Mizrahi Jews are known for using a diverse array of spices and spice blends, as well as condiments like the fiery Yemenite hot pepper and cilantro sauce called s'chug.

There are other Jewish communities that do not fit easily into these three categories. They include the Jews of Ethiopia, the Bukharian Jews (and Jews living in other parts of Central Asia), and Indian Jews. Each group has its own unique take on Jewish cooking and adds different flavors and customs to the melting pot.

Overall, the categories are far from perfect. Too often, the subtle differences between countries and communities get lost or muddled under the larger blanket labels. And yet one thing is clear: Jews are a wandering people who have settled in virtually every corner of the world. So use these labels as guides, but take them with a grain (or perhaps a pinch) of salt.

A NOTE ON KEEPING KOSHER

This cookbook is kosher, but it isn't. Let me explain. The word *kosher* refers to the Jewish dietary laws that stem from the Torah and that have, throughout history, guided the way Jewish people eat. There are many minutiae involved with keeping kosher (which means "fit" in Hebrew). Here are the basic laws:

- Certain animal species, most notably pigs, shellfish, and some birds, are prohibited, as is any mammal that does not both chew its cud and have cloven hooves.

- Permitted birds and animals must be slaughtered in accordance with Jewish law.

- The consumption of blood is prohibited.

- Milk and meat cannot be cooked together in the same dish or served at the same meal.

Along with the holidays and festivals, kashrut (the kosher laws) exists at the heart of Jewish cuisine. The laws have helped shape and define Jewish cooking and have added sacred beauty and significance to what it means to eat as a Jew. And yet, while all the recipes in this cookbook follow the kosher laws, I do not really think of it as a "kosher" cookbook.

Jewish cuisine today remains intrinsically tied to kashrut, but it also transcends it. One does not have to keep kosher or even be Jewish to make, eat, or connect with these food traditions. My life is a case in point. Growing up, my family did not observe the kosher laws, and my father's side of the family is not Jewish. And yet our kitchen was regularly filled with foods that felt, smelled, and tasted Jewish. Long before kashrut came into my life in any practical way, these foods were a core part of my identity.

So yes. This cookbook is kosher in both spirit and practice. And if you use it, you will be cooking kosher food. But more important, I hope cooking from it leaves you feeling more connected—to family, friends, community, history, or simply a beautiful meal.

STOCKING YOUR KITCHEN LIKE A GROWN-UP

Back when I first started cooking in my early twenties, I used to think that the tools I used did not really matter. In many respects, that is true. With fresh ingredients and a creative spirit, you can make many wonderful meals with minimal gear. Throughout history, Jewish cooks have done just this, nourishing their families using glasses as makeshift measuring cups and relying on creaky, unpredictable ovens—all without an electric mixer or immersion blender in sight.

As I have made cooking a more integral part of my life, my mind has changed. I am absolutely not suggesting that you need to go out and purchase an entire kitchen's worth of top-of-the-line gear or stock your drawers with a bunch of random, one-use gadgets. But over time, my experience has been that having the right tools can make cooking more adventurous and more consistently successful. So whether you are just getting started as a cook or have been at it for years, here are some kitchen must-haves that will give you the confidence and freedom to play in the kitchen.

FOOD PROCESSOR. If I had to pick one kitchen appliance to bring with me to a desert island, it would be a food processor. They are just so useful, particularly with Jewish cooking. They are instrumental in making creamy hummus and smooth kreplach dough. They quickly chop nuts and chocolate for babka and rugelach, and mash cooked vegetables into smooth purées. Swap the regular blade for the shredding blade and you shave 20 minutes off potato latke and kugel prep. Have I convinced you yet? Believe me, I guard the limited work space of my kitchen fiercely, but my food processor—and I have a large one, not the mini version—is worth the footprint.

ELECTRIC MIXER. Yes, you can mix cookie and cake batters and whip egg whites by hand. But electric mixers make these jobs significantly easier and more pleasant. With any luck, I will one day have a KitchenAid stand mixer, which is the time-tested, categorical best in its class. But alas, they are expensive and take up far too much counter space for me to justify buying one at this stage of my life. If you can, go for it! Otherwise, a smaller handheld electric mixer that comes with both regular beaters and an egg whisk does the job well, and it can also fit snugly inside a cabinet.

GRILL PAN. Grill pans are not nearly as popular as they should be. The cast-iron or heavy-metal pans have a series of ridges across the bottom, which mimic the grill marks and smoky flavor you get from cooking over a gas or charcoal grill. They are great for grilling indoors on your stovetop during the colder months. And for an apartment dweller like me who only dreams of having a backyard to grill in, they are useful year-round.

INSTANT-READ THERMOMETER. Thermometers are an indispensable tool for any cook or baker who wants to know precisely when to take a loaf of bread, roast chicken, or side of beef out of the oven. Digital instant-read thermometers, which record a food's internal temperature in seconds, are the best, quickest, and most accurate of their kind.

KITCHEN SCALE. American cooks are slowly coming around to the kitchen scale (a tool already widely used in other parts of the world), and I could not be happier about it. Using a digital kitchen scale adds a simple precision to your cooking and baking that you cannot get from measuring cups or spoons. They are also super-useful for weighing produce. My understanding of what two medium potatoes looks like may be different from yours—and that can impact a final dish. But 2 lb/910 g of potatoes is something we can all agree on.

PASTRY BRUSH. When I was first learning how to cook, pastry brushes seemed fancy and unnecessary. But the more I cook and bake, the more useful I realize those little kitchen brushes are. They are perfect for spreading egg wash onto challah without ending up with puddles of egg pooling all over the baking sheet. And for delicate jobs like painting butter onto phyllo dough for strudel, there is nothing better.

POTATO MASHER. This handy, inexpensive kitchen tool should really go by another name. It does so much more than mash potatoes! It is great for turning all kinds of cooked vegetables and fruits into purées.

SHARP KNIVES. Cooking is so much faster and more enjoyable when you start with sharp knives. There is no need to spend a fortune on the highest-quality knife set, though if you can afford it, it is a kitchen investment that will serve you well. Outfit yourself with a diverse selection of midpriced knives—a sturdy paring knife for trimming vegetables; small and large serrated knives for peeling citrus, and slicing tomatoes, bread, and cakes; and a large chef's knife or two for all your chopping needs. Most important, keep them sharp. Think of it like you think of going to the dentist: Go to a professional sharpener once or twice a year, then use an inexpensive home knife sharpener to help your knives keep their edge in the interim.

KITCHEN HOW-TO'S

I have scattered tips and notes throughout this cookbook—little guides and clarifications that steer you toward success. But certain topics came up so often, I thought it best to gather them together in one handy spot.

BLENDING HOT SOUPS. There are two different ways to blend creamy soups. The first is with an immersion blender, which is also called a stick blender or a hand blender. These useful, easy-to-clean tools can be stuck directly into a pot of hot soup. But as convenient as they are, I often end up with stray chunks of vegetables in my puréed soup. The second option is to spoon the soup into a standard blender, which produces consistently smooth results. If you go this route, work in batches and be careful not to overload the blender. Hot soup expands when you switch the blender on, which can result in a scalding hot mess. So be patient and do not fill the blender more than half full at a time. As you blend, place a kitchen towel on top of the blender lid and press down firmly.

CANNED VS. DRIED BEANS. The recipes in this cookbook call almost exclusively for canned beans. I love cooking with dried beans for their rich flavor, but find that the convenience of canned beans wins out in my day-to-day practice. If you prefer dried beans, or want to experiment with soaking and cooking your own, you have my absolute blessing (and admiration!). Substitute 1¾ cups/430 g of cooked beans for every 15-oz/430-g can. And be sure to reserve the cooking liquid, in case you need it for the recipe.

CUTTING BASIL. Several recipes in this book call for fresh basil leaves to be cut into thin ribbons. The term for this technique is *chiffonade*, and it is simple to do. Start by stacking several leaves on top of each other. Then, starting at one end, roll the leaves tightly like a jelly roll. Finally, use a sharp knife to thinly slice the leaves perpendicular to the roll. You will end up with bunches of fresh, fluffy ribbons that add great flavor to dishes.

GREASING A PAN. As insignificant as it may seem, greasing can mean the difference between a cake or a frittata sliding out of a pan and onto a plate, or getting stubbornly stuck. The simplest way to grease is to use a little more of whatever fat you are using in the recipe itself. If you are baking with butter, rub a little extra around the pan's surface. Using vegetable oil? Take a pastry brush and spread about a teaspoon's worth around the pan.

HOMEMADE MATZO MEAL. Save an extra trip to the grocery store by making your own matzo meal. Break up a few matzo sheets and pulse them in the food processor until they take on a breadcrumb-like consistency.

MEASURING DRY INGREDIENTS. There are two basic ways to measure flour, sugar, and dry grains with measuring cups. The first method, "scoop and sweep," scoops the measuring cup directly into the bag or container and levels off the cup with the blunt side of a butter knife. The second, "spoon and sweep," uses a spoon to fill the cup and then levels it off with a knife. Believe it or not, it can make a difference. I recommend using the spoon and sweep method because it yields more consistent measurements. Scooping tends to pack the ingredient into the cup (particularly flour), so you can end up with more than you want. Neither system is perfectly accurate, which is why I also recommend buying a digital scale to weigh ingredients.

REMOVING CORN KERNELS. Frozen corn is useful during the winter, when corn is out of season. But nothing beats the milky, sweet flavor of in-season corn. To remove the kernels, first remove the husk and any silky threads around the cob. Lay the cob flat on a cutting board. Using a sharp, serrated knife, start at the top and slice downward to remove several rows of kernels. Rotate the cob and repeat until all the kernels are removed; gather them up and add to the recipe.

SALTING PASTA WATER. Do this. Always. It adds wonderful flavor to whatever dish you are making. Adding about 1 Tbsp kosher salt per 4 qt/ 3.8 L of water ought to do it.

STORE-BOUGHT BROTH. My thoughts about buying (rather than making) broth to use in cooking and as the base for soup are the same as my thoughts on canned versus dried beans. If you like making your own vegetable, chicken, or beef stock, by all means do. But for the recipes in this book, store-bought broths are convenient and still add great flavor. Just steer clear of the super-processed broths or bouillons filled with MSG and preservatives. My favorite all-purpose broth is Imagine brand's Organic No-Chicken Broth. If you are on a low-salt diet, look for low-sodium versions.

STORING SPICES. Just like milk and eggs, spices have a shelf life. Old spices won't hurt you, but they won't make your food taste particularly good either. To maximize your spice cabinet's usefulness, start with fresh spices and store them in airtight containers in a cool, dark place. The top of your stove is not a great spot because the emanating heat dulls spices quickly. If possible, buy dried herbs and spices in the bulk section of the supermarket so you can get exactly the amount you need. And when it's time to toss and replace, just do it. Let your nose tell you when a spice has lost its punch, or follow these guidelines: Replace dried herbs like oregano and basil after one year, ground spices like paprika and cinnamon after two, and whole spices like peppercorns and cumin seeds after three years.

VEGETABLE OILS. Vegetable oil is a broad category of cooking oils used for baking, sautéing, and frying. Technically olive oil is a vegetable oil, but the category usually refers to milder-tasting oils (like corn, soybean, grapeseed, sunflower, safflower, and canola) and oil blends. I personally prefer the mild taste of sunflower and safflower oils, which have the benefit of also being polyunsaturated. I use organic versions of these oils in just about every recipe that calls for vegetable oil.

CHAPTER ONE

BREAKFAST

APPLE AND HONEY GRANOLA

Bring the flavors of Rosh Hashanah to the breakfast table with this honey-sweetened granola that brims with dried apples and nuts. It pairs deliciously with yogurt or milk, but I particularly like the way its sweet flavor and crisp texture taste on top of vanilla ice cream.

SERVES 6 TO 8

⅓ CUP/115 G HONEY

⅓ CUP/80 ML VEGETABLE OIL

2 TBSP LIGHT BROWN SUGAR

2 TSP GROUND CINNAMON

1 TSP GROUND GINGER

½ TSP KOSHER SALT

2½ CUPS/265 G OLD-FASHIONED ROLLED OATS

1 CUP/115 G WALNUTS, ROUGHLY CHOPPED

½ CUP/55 G ROASTED UNSALTED ALMONDS, ROUGHLY CHOPPED

1 CUP/60 G CHOPPED DRIED APPLE

½ CUP/85 G GOLDEN RAISINS

1. Preheat the oven to 375°F/190°C and line a large rimmed baking sheet with parchment paper.

2. Whisk together the honey, vegetable oil, brown sugar, cinnamon, ginger, and salt in a small bowl.

3. Combine the oats, walnuts, and almonds in a large bowl. Drizzle with the honey mixture and stir to completely coat.

4. Spread the granola on the prepared baking sheet. Bake, stirring occasion-ally, until deep golden brown and toasty smelling, 20 to 25 minutes. (The mixture will look wet; don't worry, it will crisp up as it cools.)

5. Remove the baking sheet from the oven, add the apple and raisins, and stir to combine. Set the baking sheet on a wire rack to cool completely. Store in an airtight container for up to 1 week.

BLACK PEPPER AND PISTACHIO GRANOLA

A word of caution about this granola: It is extremely addictive. It might be the combination of sweet golden raisins and dried cranberries, or the copious amounts of pistachios, almonds, and walnuts swimming amidst the oats. Or it could be the unexpected flinty heat and warm tingle coming from the mixture of black pepper and cayenne. Have plenty of yogurt or milk nearby—you're going to need it.

SERVES 6 TO 8

NOTE

Save money by shopping for the oats, nuts, and dried fruit for granola in bulk, and only buying as much as you need.

The flavor and texture of this granola develops dramatically as it cools, so do your best to hold off on snacking until it cools completely.

⅓ CUP/80 ML PURE MAPLE SYRUP

⅓ CUP/80 ML VEGETABLE OIL

2 TBSP LIGHT BROWN SUGAR

2 TSP COARSELY GROUND BLACK PEPPER

2 TSP GROUND CINNAMON

½ TSP GROUND GINGER

½ TSP KOSHER SALT

⅛ TSP CAYENNE PEPPER, OR MORE TO TASTE

2½ CUPS/265 G OLD-FASHIONED ROLLED OATS

⅔ CUP/80 G SHELLED UNSALTED PISTACHIOS

⅔ CUP/60 G SLICED ALMONDS

⅔ CUP/70 G WALNUTS, ROUGHLY CHOPPED

½ CUP/85 G GOLDEN RAISINS

½ CUP/85 G DRIED CRANBERRIES

1. Preheat the oven to 375°F/190°C and line a large rimmed baking sheet with parchment paper.

2. Whisk together the maple syrup, vegetable oil, brown sugar, pepper, cinnamon, ginger, salt, and cayenne in a small bowl.

3. Combine the oats, pistachios, almonds, and walnuts in a large bowl. Drizzle with the maple syrup mixture and stir to completely coat.

4. Spread the granola on the prepared baking sheet. Bake, stirring occasionally, until deep golden brown and toasty smelling, 20 to 25 minutes. (The mixture will look wet; don't worry, it will crisp up as it cools.)

5. Remove the baking sheet from the oven, add the raisins and cranberries, and stir to combine. Set the baking sheet on a wire rack to cool completely. Store in an airtight container for up to 1 week.

MATZO GRANOLA WITH WALNUTS AND COCONUT

Breakfast can be tough going during Passover (see page 330). With toast, bagels, cereal, waffles, muffins, oatmeal, and pretty much every other starchy breakfast staple off the menu, the options are seriously limited. Enter this granola. The crumbled matzo that replaces the typical rolled oats gets toasty and crisp in the oven, and is then tossed with chopped walnuts, shredded coconut, and raisins. I won't promise that it will become your new year-round breakfast. (Very little can compare with a perfect stack of pancakes.) But I can promise that it will make Passover infinitely sweeter.

SERVES 6

¼ CUP/60 ML VEGETABLE OIL

⅓ CUP/115 G HONEY

3 TBSP PURE MAPLE SYRUP

1 TBSP GROUND CINNAMON

½ TSP KOSHER SALT

5 SHEETS MATZO, CRUMBLED INTO
  ½-IN/12-MM PIECES

1 CUP/115 G WALNUTS, ROUGHLY
  CHOPPED

½ CUP/45 G COARSELY SHREDDED
  UNSWEETENED COCONUT

⅔ CUP/105 G BLACK RAISINS

1. Preheat the oven to 350°F/180°C and line a large rimmed baking sheet with parchment paper.

2. Whisk together the vegetable oil, honey, maple syrup, cinnamon, and salt in a large bowl. Add the matzo and stir to completely coat.

3. Spread the granola on the prepared baking sheet. Bake for 10 minutes. Add the walnuts and coconut and stir to combine. Bake, stirring once, until the matzo browns and the walnuts and coconut are toasted, 10 to 12 minutes more. (The mixture will look wet; don't worry, it will crisp up as it cools.)

4. Remove the baking sheet from the oven and immediately transfer the granola to a large heat-safe bowl. Stir in the raisins. Let cool completely, stirring occasionally to break up any large clumps. Store in an airtight container for up to 1 week.

LEMON AND ROSE WATER SCONES

These scones have none of the dense, dry, or bready texture issues that can plague other scone recipes. They are airy and delicate with a hint of buttery shortbread crispness around the edges. Brightened with citrus from a double dose of lemon zest and lemon extract and perfumed with a floral-scented rose water glaze, they bring Middle Eastern flavor to English teatime. I like to serve them when I have friends over for breakfast, and then eat the leftovers with tea or coffee as an afternoon (or late-night) snack.

MAKES 16 SCONES

NOTE

Rose water and lemon extract can be found in specialty and international food shops. Check page 343 for online sources.

If you don't like the taste of rose water, serve the scones unglazed, or substitute 2 tsp water for the rose water.

FOR THE SCONES

2 TO 2¼ CUPS/255 TO 285 G ALL-PURPOSE FLOUR

⅓ CUP/65 G GRANULATED SUGAR

2 TSP BAKING POWDER

½ TSP KOSHER SALT

½ CUP/115 G COLD UNSALTED BUTTER, CUT INTO SMALL PIECES

¾ CUP/180 ML HEAVY CREAM, PLUS MORE FOR BRUSHING

1 EGG

2 TSP LEMON ZEST

1½ TSP LEMON EXTRACT

FOR THE GLAZE

⅔ CUP/70 G CONFECTIONERS' SUGAR, PLUS MORE IF NEEDED

2 TBSP HEAVY CREAM

1 TO 2 TSP ROSE WATER

1. Make the scones: Preheat the oven to 400°F/200°C and line a large rimmed baking sheet with parchment paper.

2. Whisk together 2 cups/255 g of the flour, the granulated sugar, baking powder, and salt in a large bowl. Add the butter and, using your fingers or a pastry cutter, combine until the mixture is crumbly and the butter pieces are pea-size.

3. In a small bowl, whisk together the heavy cream, egg, lemon zest, and lemon extract. Make a well in the dry ingredients and pour in the cream mixture; stir until a dough begins to form. Transfer the dough to a lightly floured surface. With the heel of your hand, knead the dough a few times in the bowl, adding up to ¼ cup/30 g additional flour as needed, 1 Tbsp at a time, until you have a soft and moist (but not sticky) dough.

4. Divide the dough into two equal balls. Lay the balls on a lightly floured surface and pat each into a 6-in/15-cm circle that is about ½ in/12 mm thick. Slice each round into eight wedges and transfer to the prepared baking sheet, spacing them about 1 in/2.5 cm apart. Brush the tops with a little heavy cream. Bake until puffed and golden, 16 to 18 minutes. Transfer the scones to a wire rack to cool completely.

5. Meanwhile, make the glaze: Stir together the confectioners' sugar, heavy cream, and 1 tsp of the rose water in a small bowl. You want a thick but spreadable glaze. If it appears too thick, stir in up to 1 tsp more rose water, ½ tsp at a time, until you reach the right consistency. If the glaze is too watery and thin, stir in a little more confectioners' sugar until it thickens.

6. Generously brush the tops of the cooled scones with two coats of glaze. These scones are best eaten the day they are made, but can be stored in an airtight container for up to 3 days.

SPICY CHEDDAR BISCUITS

These fluffy, cheddar-laced biscuits give way to an unexpected and lovely bit of lip-tingling heat, thanks to the cayenne pepper in the dough. They are the best thing to happen to Sunday brunch since bagels, lox, and the Sunday *New York Times*. Increase or decrease the amount of cayenne to taste, and serve topped with butter and honey.

MAKES 12 BISCUITS

2¼ CUPS/285 G ALL-PURPOSE FLOUR

1 TBSP BAKING POWDER

1 TBSP SUGAR

½ TSP CAYENNE PEPPER

1 TSP SALT

½ CUP/115 G COLD UNSALTED BUTTER, CUT INTO SMALL PIECES

¾ CUP/85 G GRATED SHARP CHEDDAR

1 CUP/240 ML BUTTERMILK

1. Preheat the oven to 400°F/200°C. Stir together the flour, baking powder, sugar, cayenne, and salt in a large bowl. Add the butter and, using your fingers or a pastry cutter, combine until the mixture is crumbly and the butter pieces are pea-size. Stir in the cheddar.

2. Make a well in the center of your dry ingredients and pour in the buttermilk; stir until a dough begins to form. Transfer the dough to a lightly floured surface and knead well, about 1 minute. (The dough may appear shaggy at first, but will come together as you knead and the butter gets distributed throughout.)

3. Pat the dough into a 9-in/23-cm circle that is about ¾ in/2 cm thick. Using a 2½-in/6-cm round biscuit cutter, cut out eight biscuits and place on a large ungreased baking sheet, spacing them 1 in/2.5 cm apart. Gather the scraps, pat them into a 5-in/12-cm circle, and cut out four additional biscuits.

4. Bake the biscuits until golden, about 20 minutes. Transfer to a wire rack to cool slightly. Serve warm. Store leftovers in an airtight container for up to 3 days. Reheat briefly in a toaster oven before serving.

MY GREAT-GRANDMOTHER'S BREAKFAST

My great-grandmother Lillian Zweigbaum liked to read the newspaper with her breakfast. The only problem was, she could not read English. Lillian emigrated from Lithuania to Minneapolis with her husband and children in the early twentieth century, and her English vocabulary was limited to a few key phrases. Things like "*You vant a coo-kie hunny?*" which she would ask my mom with twinkling eyes while holding out a rugelach. And, so I'm told, every morning she sat at the breakfast table with a plate of something delicious, like coffee cake—its crumb moist and springy from the full-fat sour cream nobody thought to fear—and the daily broadsheet spread out before her. With a determined brow, she'd complete her morning ritual: wetting her thumb and nodding thoughtfully as she turned each page.

Some 65 years later and 1,200 miles away in Brooklyn, I try to channel my great-grandmother at breakfast time. Of course, my husband, Yoshie, and I are all too likely to eat our morning meal while scrolling down a newsfeed on a laptop or phone, or nibble a piece of toast held in a paper towel en route to the subway. But just like Lillian, I maintain a deep love for a good breakfast—particularly a Jewish breakfast. Whenever I can, I seek out the opportunity to pore over the morning paper with a slice of the Sour Cream Coffee Cake with Pecan Streusel (page 31) I developed with her in mind, and linger, even if just for a moment, at the breakfast table.

SOUR CREAM COFFEE CAKE WITH PECAN STREUSEL

Sometimes I wonder what happened to the coffee cake; the moist, streusel-topped pastry that once sat at the center of family breakfasts and served as the premise for countless afternoon get-togethers for another generation. You don't see it much anymore, and it likely has something to do with our society's long-standing fear of fat. Enriched with both butter and sour cream, coffee cake has plenty of it. Or maybe we are simply too busy these days to spend so much time chitchatting over a slice of something sweet? But I think this cake is worth finding time for. Simple to make and covered with a layer of toasty, caramelized pecan streusel that sinks into the tender crumb, this is the sour cream coffee cake your grandmother made. Or maybe she didn't. Either way, the cake's old-world flavor, and the conversations that come with it, are yours for the baking.

SERVES 12

FOR THE STREUSEL

- ⅔ CUP/130 G PACKED DARK BROWN SUGAR
- ½ CUP/60 G ALL-PURPOSE FLOUR
- 1 CUP/115 G PECANS, ROUGHLY CHOPPED
- 1 TBSP GROUND CINNAMON
- 1 TSP GROUND GINGER
- ¼ TSP KOSHER SALT
- 6 TBSP/85 G COLD UNSALTED BUTTER, CUT INTO SMALL PIECES

FOR THE CAKE

- 2½ CUPS/315 G ALL-PURPOSE FLOUR
- 2 TSP BAKING POWDER
- 1 TSP BAKING SODA
- 1 TSP KOSHER SALT
- ½ CUP/115 G UNSALTED BUTTER, AT ROOM TEMPERATURE
- 1 CUP/200 G GRANULATED SUGAR
- 3 EGGS
- 1 TSP VANILLA EXTRACT
- ¼ TSP LEMON ZEST (OPTIONAL)
- 1½ CUPS/360 ML SOUR CREAM

CONFECTIONERS' SUGAR, FOR DUSTING

1. Preheat the oven to 350°F/180°C and grease a 9-by-13-in/23-by-33-cm metal baking pan.

2. Make the streusel: In a medium bowl, stir together the brown sugar, flour, pecans, cinnamon, ginger, and salt. Add the butter and, using your fingers or a pastry cutter, combine until the mixture is crumbly and the butter pieces are pea-size.

CONTINUED

3. Make the cake: Sift together the flour, baking powder, baking soda, and salt into a medium bowl.

4. In a stand mixer fitted with the paddle attachment or using a handheld electric mixer and a large bowl, cream the butter and granulated sugar on medium speed until pale and fluffy, about 2 minutes. Add the eggs, one at a time, followed by the vanilla and lemon zest (if using), beating after each addition until fully incorporated. Add approximately half of the sour cream and beat on medium-low until incorporated, then add half of the flour mixture and beat until incorporated. Repeat with the remaining sour cream and flour mixture.

5. Pour the batter into the prepared pan and smooth with a rubber spatula. Top evenly with a thick layer of streusel. Bake until the cake is golden brown, springy to the touch, and a tester inserted into the center comes out clean, 35 to 45 minutes. Remove from the oven and set the pan on a wire rack to cool slightly. Dust with confectioners' sugar just before serving. Serve warm or at room temperature. Store in an airtight container for up to 3 days.

PUMPKIN–CHOCOLATE CHIP MUFFINS

As the temperature begins to drop in autumn, my urge to bake—or more precisely, to warm up my kitchen and eat fresh baked goods—kicks into high gear. Fortunately, these muffins satisfy on all fronts. They are flavored with pumpkin, which is a staple of Sephardi Jewish cuisine, and speckled with chocolate chips. Bake a batch to serve at Sunday brunch on a chilly morning, perfuming your house with the warming scents of pumpkin and cinnamon. Feel free to swap out some or all of the chocolate chips for finely chopped walnuts or crystallized ginger. Learn more about white whole-wheat flour on page 280.

MAKES 12 MUFFINS

1¼ CUPS/155 G ALL-PURPOSE FLOUR

½ CUP/60 G WHITE WHOLE-WHEAT FLOUR

½ CUP/100 G GRANULATED SUGAR

2 TSP BAKING POWDER

¼ TSP KOSHER SALT

1 TSP GROUND CINNAMON

½ TSP GROUND NUTMEG

1 CUP/245 G FRESH OR CANNED PUMPKIN PURÉE

¼ CUP/50 G PACKED LIGHT BROWN SUGAR

½ CUP/120 ML MILK OR ALMOND MILK

⅓ CUP/80 ML VEGETABLE OIL

1 EGG

1 CUP/180 G SEMISWEET CHOCOLATE CHIPS

1. Preheat the oven to 400°F/200°C and line a 12-cup muffin tin with paper liners.

2. Whisk together the all-purpose flour, whole-wheat flour, granulated sugar, baking powder, salt, cinnamon, and nutmeg in a medium bowl.

3. In a separate bowl, whisk together the pumpkin, brown sugar, milk, vegetable oil, and egg until smooth. Add to the flour mixture and stir to combine. Fold in the chocolate chips.

4. Divide the batter equally among the prepared muffin cups. Bake until the tops are springy and a tester inserted into the center of a muffin comes out clean, 20 to 22 minutes. Transfer the muffins to a wire rack to cool completely. Store in an airtight container for up to 5 days.

CINNAMON-SUGAR APPLE PANCAKES

If onions and garlic are the backbone of Jewish cooking, then cinnamon is the perfume. Hailing from the bark of the Ceylon and cassia trees, cinnamon spices up dishes across Ashkenazi, Sephardi, and Mizrahi cuisine, from Passover charoset to chewy rugelach and babka to flavorful Moroccan tagines. In that tradition, these tender buttermilk pancakes come topped with a compote of apples softened with butter and sugar and brightened with spicy-sweet cinnamon. They're perfect for a cozy Sunday brunch or as the centerpiece of my favorite under-the-radar meal: breakfast for dinner.

SERVES 2 TO 4

FOR THE APPLES

1 TBSP UNSALTED BUTTER

3 TBSP LIGHT BROWN SUGAR

1 TSP GROUND CINNAMON

1 LB/455 G CRISP, SWEET APPLES, PEELED, QUARTERED, CORED, AND FINELY CHOPPED

¼ CUP/40 G GOLDEN RAISINS

ZEST OF ½ LEMON

FOR THE PANCAKES

1½ CUPS/185 G ALL-PURPOSE FLOUR

2½ TSP BAKING POWDER

1 TBSP SUGAR

½ TSP KOSHER SALT

1½ CUPS/360 ML BUTTERMILK

2 TBSP VEGETABLE OIL, PLUS MORE FOR COOKING

1 EGG

1 TSP VANILLA EXTRACT

YOGURT AND MAPLE SYRUP FOR SERVING

1. Make the apples: Melt the butter until foaming in a large nonstick pan set over medium heat. Add the brown sugar and cinnamon, followed by the apples and raisins. Cook, stirring often, until the apples soften, about 10 minutes. Remove from the heat, stir in the zest, and set aside. If desired, mash with a potato masher to a chunky consistency.

2. Make the pancakes: Whisk together the flour, baking powder, sugar, and salt in a medium bowl.

3. In a separate medium bowl, whisk together the buttermilk, vegetable oil, egg, and vanilla. Make a well in the center of the dry ingredients and pour in the buttermilk mixture; stir until just combined (don't overstir; the batter should have some lumps). Let the batter rest for 5 minutes to allow the leavening to activate. The batter should appear very thick at this point.

4. Place a large rimmed baking sheet in the oven and preheat the oven to 200°F/95°C. Meanwhile, heat a large frying pan or griddle over medium heat. Once hot, add about 1 tsp oil and use a pastry brush to spread it evenly on the hot surface.

5. Working in batches, ladle ¼ cup/60 ml of the batter into the pan for each pancake and gently nudge the batter into circles. Cook until browned on the bottom and lightly puffed, 2 to 3 minutes. Flip and cook the other side until browned and cooked through, 1 to 2 minutes. Transfer the cooked pancakes to the baking sheet in the oven to keep warm. Continue cooking pancakes until the batter is used up, adding more oil as needed and adjusting the heat if the pancakes start to brown too quickly. Divide the pancakes among plates and serve warm, topped with the cooked apples, a dollop of yogurt, and a drizzle of maple syrup.

SAVORY FRENCH TOAST WITH SEARED TOMATOES AND ZA'ATAR BUTTER

Here's a secret: French toast does not always have to be sweet. (My head exploded a little when I realized that.) This decidedly savory take on French toast is fried in a fragrant compound butter packed with the Middle Eastern flavors of za'atar and lemon zest. And instead of maple syrup, it gets topped with seared tomatoes that melt into a delicious pool on top of the bread. Add a tangy punch to your breakfast by using thickly sliced sourdough, or go the decadent route and use challah. Make a double batch of the za'atar butter and use the extra to top veggies or sweet corn, or dress up pasta and baked fish.

SERVES 2 OR 3

FOR THE ZA'ATAR BUTTER

6 TBSP/85 G UNSALTED BUTTER, AT ROOM TEMPERATURE

½ TSP KOSHER SALT

½ TSP FRESHLY GROUND BLACK PEPPER

1 TBSP ZA'ATAR

ZEST OF 1 LEMON

6 EGGS

¾ CUP/180 ML MILK

½ TSP SALT, PLUS MORE FOR SPRINKLING

6 SLICES BREAD, EACH ABOUT 1 IN/ 2.5 CM THICK

2 RIPE MEDIUM TOMATOES, THINLY SLICED

1. Make the za'atar butter: Place the butter in a small bowl and mash with a fork. Add the salt, pepper, za'atar, and lemon zest and stir until fully combined. Transfer the za'atar butter to a ramekin or small bowl, cover with plastic wrap, and refrigerate for up to 1 day.

2. Preheat the oven to 250°F/120°C. Whisk together the eggs, milk, and salt in a shallow baking dish. Working in batches, lay the bread in the egg mixture and let stand, turning once, until soaked through, 2 to 3 minutes per side. Melt about 1 Tbsp of the za'atar butter until foaming in a large skillet set over medium heat. Fry half of the bread, turning once, until golden brown on both sides, 2 to 3 minutes per side. Transfer to a small baking sheet and place in the warm oven. Repeat with 1 Tbsp of the za'atar butter and the remaining bread slices.

3. Raise the heat to medium-high. Add the tomatoes to the skillet and cook, turning once, until softened and beginning to fall apart, 2 to 3 minutes total. Divide the French toast among plates, and top each serving with a couple of tomato slices, an additional pat of za'atar butter, and a sprinkle of salt to serve.

BAKED TOMATOES AND EGGS

Shakshuka—the North African dish of eggs poached in tomato sauce—is enjoying its moment. Already popular throughout Israel, it has more recently found its way to cafés and restaurants in the United States. I love shakshuka for breakfast or dinner, particularly served family style in a big cast-iron skillet alongside baskets of pita for mopping up wayward sauce and runny egg yolks. But sometimes I get a little grumpy about having to share and find myself elbowing toward that last poached egg a bit too aggressively. That's when I turn to baked tomatoes and eggs, a dish that takes all the major components of shakshuka—a thick spicy tomato sauce, creamy poached eggs, and a generous sprinkling of parsley and za'atar—and bakes them into individual ramekins. Served with warm pita, toast, or Spicy Cheddar Biscuits (page 28), they are beautiful, delicious, and all mine. If you prefer family-style shakshuka, see the variation that follows.

SERVES 4 TO 6

¼ CUP/60 ML EXTRA-VIRGIN OLIVE OIL, PLUS MORE FOR DRIZZLING

2 YELLOW ONIONS, FINELY CHOPPED

1 CARROT, PEELED AND FINELY CHOPPED

1 STALK CELERY, FINELY CHOPPED

1 JALAPEÑO, SEEDED AND FINELY CHOPPED

4 GARLIC CLOVES, FINELY CHOPPED

1 TSP DRIED OREGANO

1 TSP DRIED BASIL

1 TSP SWEET OR SMOKED PAPRIKA

KOSHER SALT AND FRESHLY GROUND BLACK PEPPER

ONE 28-OZ/800-G CAN DICED TOMATOES

1 TBSP TOMATO PASTE

6 EGGS

ZA'ATAR, CRUMBLED FETA, AND CHOPPED FRESH CILANTRO OR FLAT-LEAF PARSLEY FOR SERVING

1. Heat the olive oil in a large pan set over medium heat. Stir in the onions, carrot, celery, and jalapeño. Cover and cook, stirring occasionally, until the vegetables are softened, about 10 minutes. Uncover the pan, add the garlic, oregano, basil, paprika, 1 tsp salt, and ½ tsp pepper and cook, stirring, until fragrant, 1 to 2 minutes. Raise the heat to medium-high and stir in the diced tomatoes with their juice and the tomato paste. Bring to a simmer, then turn the heat to low and cook uncovered, stirring occasionally, until thickened and saucy, about 15 minutes. Taste and season with additional salt, if desired. Remove from the heat. (You can make the sauce 1 day ahead and store it, covered, in the refrigerator.)

2. Preheat the oven to 425°F/220°C. Grease six 4-oz/120-ml ramekins and set them on a large rimmed baking sheet. Divide the tomato sauce among the ramekins and make a shallow well in the center of each with the back of a soupspoon. Bake the sauce-filled ramekins until hot, 7 to 8 minutes. Remove the baking sheet from the oven and crack 1 egg into the center of each ramekin. Bake again until the sauce is bubbling and the egg whites have set, but the yolks are still soft, 10 to 12 minutes more.

3. Remove from the oven and top each egg with a little pepper, a drizzle of olive oil, and a sprinkle of za'atar, feta, and cilantro. Serve hot.

VARIATION

If you do not have ramekins or would rather make a more traditional shak-shuka, follow the recipe through step 1. Make six small indentations in the sauce with the back of a soupspoon. Break the eggs into small cups and slide them into the indentations. Cover the pan and cook until the egg whites are set but the yolks are still a bit runny, 4 to 5 minutes.

SHALLOT, LEEK, AND GINGER OMELET

Despite my best intentions, I occasionally fall into a bit of an omelet rut. I start out the morning with high hopes and a pile of fresh veggies at hand, and then somehow my omelet ends up tasting the same as it always does. Granted, even boring eggs are tasty, but they leave me wanting something more. That's where this dish comes in. The mixture of shallots and earthy leek is enough to elevate this omelet to special status, but it's the addition of freshly grated ginger that really sets it apart. Softened in the butter, the ginger caramelizes and turns sweet, resulting in a breakfast unlike any other.

SERVES 2 OR 3

3 TBSP UNSALTED BUTTER

1 SMALL LEEK, WHITE AND LIGHT GREEN PARTS, HALVED LENGTH-WISE AND THINLY SLICED

2 MEDIUM SHALLOTS, FINELY CHOPPED

KOSHER SALT

ONE 2-IN/5-CM PIECE FRESH GINGER, PEELED AND GRATED ON THE LARGE HOLES OF A BOX GRATER

4 GARLIC CLOVES, FINELY CHOPPED

¼ TSP RED PEPPER FLAKES (OPTIONAL)

6 EGGS

FRESHLY GROUND BLACK PEPPER

1. Melt 2 Tbsp of the butter until foaming in a large nonstick pan set over medium-low heat. Add the leek, shallots, and a sprinkle of salt and cook, stirring occasionally, until softened and lightly browned, 6 to 8 minutes. Add the ginger, garlic, and red pepper flakes (if using) and cook, stirring often, until fragrant, 1 to 2 minutes. Remove the pan from the heat and transfer the leek-shallot mixture to a bowl.

2. Meanwhile, whisk together the eggs and ½ tsp salt in a small bowl and season with pepper. Set the pan back over medium heat and add the remaining 1 Tbsp butter. When the butter is foaming, pour in the eggs and cook, undisturbed, for 30 seconds. Use a rubber spatula to push the cooked eggs from the sides of the pan in several places, allowing the uncooked eggs to spill toward the bottom. Cover and cook until the eggs are just set and no longer runny on top, 4 to 5 minutes.

3. Uncover the pan and spread the leek-shallot mixture down the center of the eggs. Use the spatula to gently fold one-third of the omelet over to the center, followed by the other side, tucking the filling inside. Slide out of the pan onto a serving platter and serve hot.

MOZZARELLA, TOMATO, AND BASIL FRITTATA

Inspired by a Caprese salad, this frittata is filled with the bright flavors of the Mediterranean. It makes a beautiful, stress-free brunch centerpiece, and doubles as a tasty dinner or a summery dish to bring to a Shabbat potluck or picnic. It is best made when tomatoes are in season and at their flavorful peak.

SERVES 4

2 TBSP EXTRA-VIRGIN OLIVE OIL, PLUS MORE FOR DRIZZLING

2 MEDIUM SHALLOTS, FINELY CHOPPED

3 RIPE PLUM TOMATOES; 2 CORED, SEEDED, AND CHOPPED, 1 THINLY SLICED

8 EGGS

2 TSP FINELY CHOPPED FRESH THYME

1 TSP KOSHER SALT

FRESHLY GROUND BLACK PEPPER

8 TO 10 FRESH BASIL LEAVES, CUT INTO THIN RIBBONS (SEE PAGE 18)

2½ OZ/70 G FRESH MOZZARELLA, CUT INTO BITE-SIZE PIECES

1. Preheat the oven to 400°F/200°C.

2. Heat the olive oil in a large ovenproof pan set over medium heat. Add the shallots and cook, stirring occasionally, until just softened, 3 to 5 minutes. Add the chopped tomatoes and cook, stirring occasionally, until they soften and the shallots turn golden brown, 3 to 4 minutes.

3. Meanwhile, whisk together the eggs, thyme, and salt in a medium bowl and season with pepper. Pour the egg mixture into the pan and stir gently. Arrange the sliced tomato and basil over the top of the eggs and place the pan in the oven. Bake until almost cooked through and slightly puffed, 10 to 12 minutes.

4. Layer the mozzarella on top of the frittata and continue baking until melted, 1 to 2 minutes more. Slice and then drizzle with olive oil and sprinkle with pepper. Serve warm or at room temperature.

THREE-IN-ONE MATZO BREI

Matzo brei, one of Passover's signature breakfasts, dates back to turn-of-the-twentieth-century America. The dish joined the mainstream several decades later when delicatessens and diners in New York and across the country added it to their menus. All of a sudden, the humble concoction of crumbled matzo soaked in egg and fried in butter became an available (and acceptable!) year-round breakfast option. This version tops the classic "Passover French toast" in one of three ways: with a traditional sprinkling of cinnamon and sugar, juicy roasted strawberries, or a savory mélange of leeks and mushrooms.

SERVES 4 TO 6

5 SHEETS MATZO, CRUMBLED INTO 2-IN/5-CM PIECES

1 CUP/240 ML ROOM-TEMPERATURE WATER

3 EGGS

½ TSP KOSHER SALT

4 TBSP/60 G UNSALTED BUTTER

GROUND CINNAMON AND SUGAR FOR SPRINKLING; ROASTED STRAWBERRIES (FACING PAGE); OR LEEKS AND MUSHROOMS (FACING PAGE)

1. Spread the matzo in an even layer in a large baking dish. Add the water and gently stir until the matzo is moistened. Let stand until the matzo softens, 1 to 2 minutes, then pour out any excess water.

2. Whisk together the eggs and salt in a medium bowl. Pour the egg mixture over the softened matzo and stir to combine.

3. Melt the butter until foaming in a large nonstick frying pan set over medium heat. Add the matzo-egg mixture and, using a spatula, press it into an even layer. Cook, undisturbed, until the bottom is golden brown and the mixture sets, 5 to 7 minutes. Flip the matzo brei and continue cooking until the second side is golden brown, about 5 minutes more.

4. Transfer the matzo brei to a serving platter or divide among plates. Sprinkle with cinnamon and sugar or top with the strawberries or leeks and mushrooms. Serve immediately.

ROASTED STRAWBERRIES

1 LB/455 G SLICED FRESH STRAWBERRIES

¼ CUP/50 G SUGAR

JUICE OF ½ LEMON

Preheat the oven to 400°F/200°C. Line a large rimmed baking sheet with aluminum foil. Stir together the strawberries, sugar, and lemon juice. Spread the mixture on the prepared baking sheet and roast, stirring occasionally, until soft and juicy, 20 to 25 minutes. Let cool slightly.

LEEKS AND MUSHROOMS

2 TBSP BUTTER

1 TBSP EXTRA-VIRGIN OLIVE OIL

2 LEEKS, WHITE AND LIGHT GREEN PARTS, THINLY SLICED

2 CUPS/225 G THINLY SLICED WHITE MUSHROOMS

2 GARLIC CLOVES, FINELY CHOPPED

KOSHER SALT AND FRESHLY GROUND BLACK PEPPER

CRUMBLED GOAT CHEESE FOR SPRINKLING (OPTIONAL)

Heat the butter and olive oil in a medium saucepan set over medium heat. Add the leeks, mushrooms, and garlic. Cook, stirring occasionally, until the leeks and mushrooms soften, 8 to 10 minutes. Season with salt and pepper. Sprinkle with goat cheese if desired.

SMOKED SALMON HASH WITH LEMON-MINT VINAIGRETTE

I love Passover (see page 330), but somewhere around day five of the weeklong holiday, I begin to tire of the same old "matzo plus ____" routine. (Although matzo plus smashed avocado and sea salt is pretty special.) This dish, which gives corned beef hash a Jewish makeover, solves the problem of Passover monotony. Studded with chunks of smoky salmon and drizzled with a lemony, herb-packed vinaigrette, it is delicious all Passover long. It also makes an impressive centerpiece for breakfast or brunch year-round. The lemon-mint vinaigrette tastes great served over eggs, fish, chicken, steak, or roasted vegetables such as Breaded Eggplant and Tomato Stacks (page 206).

SERVES 6 TO 8

FOR THE LEMON-MINT VINAIGRETTE

¼ CUP/10 G FINELY CHOPPED FRESH MINT

¼ CUP/60 ML EXTRA-VIRGIN OLIVE OIL

½ TSP LEMON ZEST

1 TBSP FRESH LEMON JUICE

1 SMALL GARLIC CLOVE, MINCED OR PUSHED THROUGH A PRESS

¼ TSP RED PEPPER FLAKES (OPTIONAL)

¼ TSP KOSHER SALT

FRESHLY GROUND BLACK PEPPER

FOR THE HASH

2 TBSP EXTRA-VIRGIN OLIVE OIL

1½ LB/680 G YUKON GOLD POTATOES, PEELED AND CUT INTO ½-IN/12-MM CUBES

1 TSP WATER

KOSHER SALT AND FRESHLY GROUND BLACK PEPPER

1 MEDIUM SWEET ONION, SUCH AS VIDALIA, FINELY CHOPPED

4 OZ/115 G SLICED SMOKED SALMON, CUT INTO BITE-SIZE PIECES

1. Make the vinaigrette: Stir together the mint, olive oil, lemon zest, lemon juice, garlic, red pepper flakes (if using), and salt in a small bowl. Season with black pepper. Set aside.

2. Make the hash: Heat the olive oil in a large frying pan set over medium heat. Add the potatoes and water, season generously with salt and pepper, and stir to coat. Cover and cook, stirring once, until the potatoes are just cooked through and brown in several places, 8 to 10 minutes.

3. Add the onion and stir to combine. Cook, uncovered, stirring occasionally, until the potatoes are a deep golden brown, 8 to 10 minutes more.

4. Remove from the heat and immediately stir in the salmon. Taste and season with more salt and pepper, if desired.

5. Divide among plates and serve warm topped with the vinaigrette.

HOME FRIES WITH SMOKED PAPRIKA

From crispy latkes to pillowy potato-filled knishes and blintzes, Jewish cuisine shares a long-standing love affair with the potato. These spiced-up home fries are not part of the traditional potato canon, but they should be. The potatoes are tender and browned, the onions silky and slightly sweet, and the smoked paprika deeply flavorful without adding a lot of heat. Serve them alongside the Mozzarella, Tomato, and Basil Frittata (page 41), or your favorite egg dish.

SERVES 4 TO 6

2 LB/910 G YUKON GOLD POTATOES, SCRUBBED AND CUT INTO ½-IN/12-MM CUBES

¼ CUP/60 ML VEGETABLE OIL

2 MEDIUM YELLOW ONIONS, HALVED AND THINLY SLICED

KOSHER SALT

1 MEDIUM GREEN BELL PEPPER, SEEDED AND CUT INTO ½-IN/12-MM PIECES

4 GARLIC CLOVES, FINELY CHOPPED

½ TSP SMOKED PAPRIKA

FRESHLY GROUND BLACK PEPPER

⅓ CUP/45 G CRUMBLED FRESH GOAT CHEESE (OPTIONAL)

1. Place the potatoes in a large saucepan and cover with cold water by 1 in/ 2.5 cm. Bring to a boil over high heat; immediately turn the heat to medium, and simmer, uncovered, until just tender, 6 to 10 minutes. Drain the potatoes well and return them to the pan. The residual heat from the pan will help any remaining moisture to evaporate. Set aside.

2. Meanwhile, heat the vegetable oil in a large nonstick pan set over medium-high heat. Add the onions and cook, stirring occasionally, until softened and beginning to brown, 6 to 8 minutes. Season with a generous pinch of salt, add the bell pepper, garlic, and the potatoes and cook, stirring occasionally, until browned, 10 to 15 minutes.

3. Turn off the heat and immediately stir in the paprika and season with salt and pepper. Serve warm, topped with the goat cheese, if desired.

ROASTED GARLIC–POTATO BLINTZES

Along with cheese and berries, potatoes are one of the most common blintz fillings. This version takes the mashed potato filling one typically finds inside a blintz and amps it up with softened shallots and roasted garlic. Served with grainy mustard, it offers a sophisticated take on classic Jewish comfort food.

SERVES 4

FOR THE BLINTZ BATTER

1 CUP/240 ML MILK OR ALMOND MILK

3 EGGS

2 TBSP SUGAR

1 CUP/125 G ALL-PURPOSE FLOUR

½ TSP KOSHER SALT

FOR THE FILLING

2 HEADS GARLIC, UNPEELED, TOPS TRIMMED TO EXPOSE CLOVES

2 TSP EXTRA-VIRGIN OLIVE OIL, PLUS 2 TBSP

1 LB/455 G RUSSET POTATOES, PEELED AND CUT INTO 1-IN/2.5-CM PIECES

3 MEDIUM SHALLOTS, FINELY CHOPPED

KOSHER SALT AND FRESHLY GROUND BLACK PEPPER

BUTTER FOR FRYING

SOUR CREAM AND WHOLE-GRAIN MUSTARD FOR TOPPING

1. Make the blintz batter: Combine the milk, eggs, sugar, flour, and salt in a blender and blend until smooth, scraping down the sides as necessary. Let the batter rest for at least 30 minutes to let the gluten relax, or cover and refrigerate overnight.

2. Meanwhile, make the filling: Preheat the oven to 400°F/200°C. Place each head of garlic on a square of aluminum foil, drizzle each with 1 tsp olive oil, wrap tightly, and place in a baking dish. Roast until the cloves are soft and browned, 35 to 40 minutes. Remove from the oven and let cool to the touch. Squeeze the cloves out of their skins into a bowl.

3. Bring a medium pot of water to a boil. Add the potatoes and cook, stirring occasionally, until very tender, 15 to 20 minutes. Drain well.

4. Heat the remaining 2 Tbsp olive oil in a small pan over medium heat. Add the shallots and cook, stirring occasionally, until softened, about 5 minutes. Remove from the heat and let cool slightly. Mash the potatoes with a potato masher and add the mashed potatoes and shallots to the roasted garlic. Season generously with salt and pepper.

5. Rip eight large squares of parchment paper and set aside. Melt 1 tsp butter until foaming in an 8-in/20-cm nonstick skillet set over medium heat. Once hot, pour a little less than ⅓ cup/80 ml of the batter into the pan; immediately pick up the pan and tilt it in all directions to coat the bottom evenly with a thin layer of batter. Cook until the bottom is golden and the center is just dry, about 1 minute. (Do not flip the blintz wrapper.) Remove the wrapper with a spatula and place it on a piece of parchment paper. Continue making the wrappers with the remaining batter, stacking them in between squares of parchment as you go.

6. Spoon about 2 Tbsp of the filling onto the lower third of a wrapper, leaving a 1-in/2.5-cm uncovered border at the bottom. Fold that uncovered border up over the filling, then fold in each side toward the center. Roll the blintz up and away from you, tucking the filling inside a neat package. Repeat with the remaining wrappers and filling, setting the blintzes on a plate as you go.

7. Melt about 1 Tbsp butter until foaming in a nonstick pan set over medium heat. Working in batches, place the blintzes, seam-side down, in the pan and cook, turning once, until golden on both sides, 1 to 2 minutes per side. Transfer to a platter and serve hot, topped with sour cream and mustard.

ORANGE-SCENTED CHEESE BLINTZES

Cheese blintzes are a special indulgence. It's not often that we have the opportunity to top a rich, fried, cheese-filled pastry with sour cream and feel like we are doing *exactly* the right thing. Traditionally served on Shavuot (see page 333), blintzes were also popular at the many dairy restaurants that once populated the Lower East Side. According to New York legend, cheese blintzes were the favorite food of infamous Jewish mobsters Bugsy Siegel and Meyer Lansky, who were both regulars at the now-closed kosher dairy restaurant Ratner's. This version adds fragrant orange zest to the sweet cheese filling, making it a standout favorite in my kitchen.

SERVES 4

FOR THE BLINTZ BATTER

1 CUP/240 ML MILK OR ALMOND MILK

3 EGGS

¼ CUP/50 G GRANULATED SUGAR

1 CUP/125 G ALL-PURPOSE FLOUR

1 TSP VANILLA EXTRACT

½ TSP KOSHER SALT

FOR THE FILLING

2 CUPS/455 G FULL-FAT OR LOW-FAT RICOTTA CHEESE

6 TBSP/45 G CONFECTIONERS' SUGAR

1 TSP ORANGE ZEST

BUTTER FOR FRYING

SOUR CREAM AND SLICED STRAW-BERRIES FOR TOPPING

1. Make the blintz batter: Combine the milk, eggs, granulated sugar, flour, vanilla, and salt in a blender and blend until smooth, scraping down the sides as necessary. Let the batter rest for at least 30 minutes to let the gluten relax, or cover and refrigerate overnight.

2. Meanwhile, make the filling: Stir together the ricotta, confectioners' sugar, and orange zest in a small bowl. Cover and refrigerate for up to 1 day.

3. Rip eight large squares of parchment paper and set aside. Melt 1 tsp butter until foaming in an 8-in/20-cm nonstick skillet set over medium heat. Once hot, pour a little less than ⅓ cup/80 ml of the batter into the pan; immediately pick up the pan and tilt it in all directions to coat the bottom evenly with a thin layer of batter. Cook until the bottom is golden and the center is just dry, about 1 minute. (Do not flip the blintz wrapper.) Remove the wrapper with a spatula and place it on a piece of parchment paper. Continue making the wrappers with the remaining batter, stacking them in between squares of parchment as you go.

CONTINUED

4. Spoon about 2 Tbsp of the filling onto the lower third of a wrapper, leaving a 1-in/2.5-cm uncovered border at the bottom. Fold that uncovered border up over the filling, then fold in each side toward the center. Roll the blintz up and away from you, tucking the filling inside a neat package. Repeat with the remaining wrappers and filling, setting the blintzes on a plate as you go.

5. Melt about 1 Tbsp butter until foaming in a nonstick pan set over medium heat. Working in batches, place the blintzes, seam-side down, in the pan and cook, turning once, until golden on both sides, 1 to 2 minutes per side. Transfer to a platter and serve hot, topped with sour cream and sliced strawberries.

APPLE-CRANBERRY CHREMSLACH

Chremslach do not have the same star power as matzo balls or matzo brei. But they are no less wonderful. Like many Passover foods (see page 330), they repurpose the holiday's unleavened bread into something far more interesting, in this case a rustic matzo fritter traditionally served with honey. Chremslach can be served for breakfast or dessert, and made simply or souped up by adding nuts, cottage cheese, or fruit to the batter. I like stirring in grated apple and dried cranberries—a combination that would be equally appropriate at Hanukkah (see page 340).

MAKES ABOUT 48 CHREMSLACH

2 SHEETS MATZO

1 APPLE, SUCH AS GALA OR FUJI, PEELED, GRATED ON THE LARGE HOLES OF A BOX GRATER, AND SQUEEZED DRY

⅓ CUP/55 G DRIED CRANBERRIES

2 EGGS, SEPARATED

⅓ CUP/35 G MATZO MEAL (SEE PAGE 18)

⅓ CUP/65 G SUGAR

1 TSP GROUND CINNAMON

ZEST OF 1 LEMON

1 TBSP FRESH LEMON JUICE

¼ TSP KOSHER SALT

VEGETABLE OIL FOR FRYING

HONEY FOR DRIZZLING

1. Soak the matzo in room-temperature water in a large baking dish for 10 minutes. Squeeze dry with your hands and transfer to a medium bowl. Add the apple, cranberries, egg yolks, matzo meal, sugar, cinnamon, lemon zest, lemon juice, and salt and mix well to combine.

2. In a stand mixer fitted with a whisk attachment or using a handheld electric mixer and a medium bowl, beat the egg whites at medium-high speed until they hold stiff peaks, about 2 minutes. Gently fold the egg whites into the matzo-apple mixture.

3. Line a baking sheet with two layers of paper towels. Heat ¼ in/6 mm of vegetable oil until shimmering in a wide saucepan set over medium heat. Working in batches, spoon the batter by the rounded tablespoonful into the oil, pressing down gently with the back of the spoon to flatten. Fry, turning once, until golden brown on both sides, 2 to 3 minutes total. Use a slotted spoon to transfer the chremslach to the prepared baking sheet to drain. Serve hot, warm, or at room temperature, drizzled with honey.

CHAPTER TWO

SALADS AND SPREADS

SPRING PEA SALAD WITH BROWNED BUTTER VINAIGRETTE

A few years ago, I ate a wonderful meal at a tapas restaurant called Cúrate in Asheville, North Carolina. Everything I tried was delicious—but the standout dish was a salad topped with browned butter vinaigrette. The salad itself was a simple mix of delicate lettuces and freshly shelled spring peas. But the vinaigrette was exceptional, thanks to the nutty flavor and velvety texture of the browned butter. I just may have licked the plate. My take on Cúrate's vinaigrette includes fresh dill, adding a hint of Eastern European flavor to my favorite springtime salad.

SERVES 4 TO 6

FOR THE VINAIGRETTE

3 TBSP UNSALTED BUTTER

2 TSP RED WINE VINEGAR

½ TSP APPLE CIDER VINEGAR

1 TBSP FINELY CHOPPED SHALLOT

2 TBSP FINELY CHOPPED FRESH DILL

KOSHER SALT AND FRESHLY GROUND BLACK PEPPER

¼ CUP/60 ML EXTRA-VIRGIN OLIVE OIL

1 SMALL HEAD BOSTON OR RED LEAF LETTUCE, TORN INTO BITE-SIZE PIECES

1 LB/455 G PEAS IN THE POD, SHELLED

6 RADISHES, THINLY SLICED

1 STALK CELERY, THINLY SLICED

1. Make the vinaigrette: Melt the butter until fragrant and browned in a small saucepan set over medium-low heat, swirling the pan often, about 3 minutes. (Watch carefully so it doesn't burn.) Immediately remove the pan from the heat and strain the butter through a fine-mesh sieve into a small bowl.

2. Combine the browned butter, the red wine vinegar, cider vinegar, shallot, dill, ½ tsp salt, and ⅛ tsp pepper in a blender and purée until well combined, scraping down the sides as necessary. Add the olive oil and blend until thickened. Taste and season with more salt and pepper, if desired.

3. Combine the lettuce, peas, radishes, and celery in a large bowl and gently toss to combine. Divide the salad among plates and drizzle with the warm vinaigrette. Serve immediately. (Store any leftover vinaigrette in an airtight container and refrigerate for up to 1 week. Warm the container in a hot water bath to melt the congealed butter before drizzling over the salad.)

SUGAR SNAP PEA, CORN, AND BASIL SALAD

In the height of summer, when it is too hot to even think about cooking, I basically live off of fresh salads. This is one of my favorites: a crunchy, sweet, and tangy mix of sugar snap peas, cherry tomatoes, hearts of palm, and fresh corn. Thinly sliced fresh basil and a hint of lemon zest add unexpected brightness. Serve it as a side salad when entertaining, or add canned tuna, hard-boiled eggs, or crumbled feta to transform it into a satisfying summer meal.

SERVES 6

1 LB/455 G SUGAR SNAP PEAS, ENDS TRIMMED, STRING REMOVED, AND HALVED

1½ CUPS/240 G HALVED CHERRY TOMATOES

KERNELS FROM 2 EARS SWEET CORN (SEE PAGE 18) OR 1¼ CUPS/205 G THAWED FROZEN CORN KERNELS

ONE 14-OZ/400-G CAN HEARTS OF PALM, DRAINED THOROUGHLY AND SLICED

10 FRESH BASIL LEAVES, CUT INTO THIN RIBBONS (SEE PAGE 18)

2 TSP RED WINE VINEGAR

2 TSP APPLE CIDER VINEGAR

¼ CUP/60 ML EXTRA-VIRGIN OLIVE OIL

ZEST OF ½ LEMON

1 LARGE GARLIC CLOVE, MINCED OR PUSHED THROUGH A PRESS

½ TSP KOSHER SALT

¼ TSP FRESHLY GROUND BLACK PEPPER

1. Combine the snap peas, tomatoes, corn, hearts of palm, and basil in a large bowl.

2. In a small bowl, whisk together the red wine vinegar, cider vinegar, olive oil, lemon zest, garlic, salt, and pepper. Drizzle the salad with the dressing and gently toss to combine. Divide the salad among plates and serve immediately.

TOMATO SALAD WITH FRIED CAPERS

A perfectly ripe tomato needs little embellishment beyond a sprinkle of salt. But in the summer, when the farmers' market is filled with juicy, flavorful tomatoes, I find myself dreaming up new ways to eat them. Here's one idea: Simmer balsamic vinegar until it turns thick and dark. Slice up a bunch of ripe tomatoes and top them with crispy fried capers. Drizzle the beautiful balsamic syrup luxuriously over the top. Eat and repeat until tomato season is over.

SERVES 4

NOTE

This recipe makes more balsamic reduction than you need for the salad. Here are some ideas for the delicious leftovers: Drizzle it over pasta, dip fresh strawberries in it, add it to Chopped Chicken Liver (page 76), spoon a little over vanilla ice cream, or serve it with cheese.

1 CUP/240 ML BALSAMIC VINEGAR

EXTRA-VIRGIN OLIVE OIL FOR FRYING
  AND DRIZZLING

¼ CUP/40 G BRINE-PACKED CAPERS,
  DRAINED AND PATTED DRY

1½ LB/680 G RIPE TOMATOES, CUT INTO
  ¼-IN/6-MM SLICES

FRESHLY SHAVED PARMESAN
  (OPTIONAL)

COARSE SALT AND FRESHLY GROUND
  BLACK PEPPER

1. In a small saucepan set over medium heat, bring the balsamic vinegar to a boil. Turn the heat to medium-low and simmer, stirring occasionally, until it thickens enough to coat a spoon, 15 to 20 minutes. Remove from the heat and cool completely.

2. Meanwhile, heat ¼ in/6 mm of olive oil in a small, heavy saucepan set over medium-high heat until shimmering. Add the capers and cook, stirring occasionally, until crisp, about 1 minute. Remove with a slotted spoon and transfer to paper towels to drain.

3. Arrange the tomato slices on a serving plate. Scatter with the fried capers and Parmesan (if using), and drizzle with olive oil and the balsamic reduction. Season with salt and pepper. Serve immediately.

WATERMELON ISRAELI SALAD

Chopped salads brimming with tomato, cucumber, and fresh herbs are popular across Middle Eastern cuisines, including in Israel. This version adds another summer staple to the traditional mix—crisp, sweet watermelon, which pairs beautifully with the juicy acidity of tomato. Toasted pepitas (another name for pumpkin seeds) add a bit of crunch, resulting in a salad that is gorgeous to look at and refreshing to eat. Enjoy this salad in midsummer when tomatoes and watermelon are at their flavorful peak.

SERVES 6 TO 8

⅓ CUP/45 G RAW PEPITAS

1½ LB/680 G TOMATOES, CORED, SEEDED, AND CUT INTO ½-IN/ 12-MM CHUNKS

2 KIRBY CUCUMBERS, PEELED, SEEDED, AND CUT INTO ½-IN/12-MM CHUNKS

3 CUPS/475 G CUBED SEEDLESS WATERMELON (ABOUT ½-IN/ 12-MM CUBES)

½ MEDIUM RED ONION, FINELY CHOPPED

⅓ CUP/15 G FINELY CHOPPED FRESH FLAT-LEAF PARSLEY

¼ CUP/10 G FINELY CHOPPED FRESH CILANTRO OR MINT

⅓ CUP/55 G CRUMBLED FETA (OPTIONAL)

ZEST AND JUICE OF 2 LEMONS

2 TBSP EXTRA-VIRGIN OLIVE OIL

1 TSP ZA'ATAR OR GROUND SUMAC

½ TSP KOSHER SALT

¼ TSP FRESHLY GROUND BLACK PEPPER

1. Place the pepitas in a small pan set over medium-low heat. Cook, stirring occasionally, until fragrant and lightly browned, 5 to 7 minutes. Transfer to a small bowl to cool completely.

2. Combine the tomatoes, cucumbers, watermelon, onion, parsley, cilantro, and feta (if using) in a large bowl.

3. In a small bowl, whisk together the lemon zest, lemon juice, olive oil, za'atar, salt, and pepper. Drizzle over the salad, top with the toasted pepitas, and gently toss to combine. Divide the salad among plates and serve immediately. (If not serving right away, keep the salad and dressing in separate containers; combine and toss just before serving.)

CARROT SALAD WITH MINT AND DATES

Moroccan carrot salads flavored with cumin and coriander have become a staple of the Jewish table. But to be honest, they're not really my thing. I offer this dish as an alternative. Grated carrots get paired with Mediterranean ingredients like dates, fresh mint, and hazelnuts for a sweet, crunchy, lemon-kissed salad that might just become your new favorite.

SERVES 4 TO 6

½ CUP/60 G RAW HAZELNUTS

2 TBSP FRESH LEMON JUICE, PLUS
  MORE AS NEEDED

2 TBSP FINELY CHOPPED SHALLOT

2 TBSP EXTRA-VIRGIN OLIVE OIL

KOSHER SALT AND FRESHLY GROUND
  BLACK PEPPER

1 LB/455 G CARROTS, PEELED

⅓ CUP/50 G FINELY CHOPPED PITTED
  DEGLET NOOR DATES

¼ CUP/10 G ROUGHLY CHOPPED FRESH
  MINT LEAVES

3 CUPS/75 G BABY ARUGULA

1. Place the hazelnuts in a small pan set over medium-low heat. Cook, stirring occasionally, until fragrant and lightly browned, 5 to 7 minutes. Remove from the heat and transfer to a small bowl to cool completely, then peel off the skins with your fingers and roughly chop.

2. Whisk together the lemon juice, shallot, and olive oil in a small bowl, and season with salt and pepper.

3. Grate the carrots on the large holes of a box grater or with a food processor fit with a shredding blade. Combine the grated carrots, toasted hazelnuts, dates, mint, and arugula in a large bowl. Drizzle with the dressing and gently toss to combine. Taste and add more lemon juice, if desired. Divide the salad among plates and serve immediately. (If not serving right away, keep the dressing and salad in separate containers; combine and toss just before serving.)

ROMAINE WEDGE SALAD WITH BUTTERMILK DRESSING

Buttermilk, the tangy, cultured liquid left behind after churning butter from cream, is an old-school ingredient. It's largely forgotten in modern cooking outside of the occasional buttermilk pancake or biscuit. But at the turn of the twentieth century, buttermilk was so popular that people drank it by the glass. Jewish cooks, meanwhile, stirred it into baked goods. Here, I have paired buttermilk with another vintage favorite: the wedge salad. Thick wedges of crunchy romaine get drizzled with a wonderfully tart buttermilk dressing. Eat it with a fork and knife, and prepare to take a culinary step back in time.

SERVES 6

FOR THE CROUTONS

2 THICK SLICES SOURDOUGH BREAD, CUT INTO ½-IN/12-MM CUBES

3 TBSP EXTRA-VIRGIN OLIVE OIL

KOSHER SALT

FOR THE DRESSING

⅓ CUP/80 ML BUTTERMILK

½ CUP/120 ML SOUR CREAM OR 2 PERCENT PLAIN GREEK YOGURT

1 TBSP RED WINE VINEGAR

2 TSP DIJON MUSTARD

1 SMALL GARLIC CLOVE, MINCED OR PUSHED THROUGH A PRESS

2 TSP DRIED DILL

KOSHER SALT AND FRESHLY GROUND BLACK PEPPER

3 ROMAINE HEARTS, HALVED LENGTHWISE

1 CUP/160 G HALVED CHERRY TOMATOES

2 KIRBY CUCUMBERS, PEELED, HALVED LENGTHWISE, SEEDED, AND THINLY SLICED

1. Make the croutons: Preheat the oven to 375°F/190°C. Place the bread cubes on a large rimmed baking sheet. Drizzle with the olive oil, sprinkle with a generous pinch of salt, and toss to coat. Bake, stirring occasionally, until golden brown and crispy, 7 to 10 minutes. Remove from the oven and set aside.

2. Make the dressing: Whisk together the buttermilk, sour cream, vinegar, mustard, garlic, and dill in a small bowl. Season with salt and pepper.

3. Divide the halved romaine hearts among six plates, cut-side up, and top each with some tomatoes, cucumbers, and croutons. Drizzle a little dressing over the top of each, and serve immediately. Pass the remaining dressing at the table.

AVOCADO–WHITE BEAN SALAD WITH BASIL-MINT PESTO

This summery salad-spread hybrid combines two of my favorite things: pesto and avocado. The dairy-free pesto, which is amped up with mint leaves and red pepper flakes, gets tossed with cubes of avocado, creamy white beans, and crunchy bits of celery. Serve it as a chunky dip along with pita chips, or get a little fancy and scoop it into leaves of Belgian endive.

SERVES 6

FOR THE PESTO

1 CUP/30 G LOOSELY PACKED
    FRESH BASIL

1 CUP/30 G LOOSELY PACKED
    FRESH MINT

¼ CUP/40 G PINE NUTS

1 GARLIC CLOVE, ROUGHLY CHOPPED

¼ TSP RED PEPPER FLAKES, OR MORE
    TO TASTE

KOSHER SALT AND FRESHLY GROUND
    BLACK PEPPER

1 TBSP FRESH LEMON JUICE, OR MORE
    TO TASTE

⅓ CUP/80 ML EXTRA-VIRGIN OLIVE OIL

2 RIPE AVOCADOS, PEELED, HALVED,
    AND CUT INTO CUBES

ONE 15-OZ/430-G CAN WHITE BEANS,
    SUCH AS CANNELLINI OR GREAT
    NORTHERN, RINSED AND DRAINED

1 STALK CELERY, FINELY CHOPPED

3 SCALLIONS, WHITE AND GREEN
    PARTS, THINLY SLICED

1. Make the pesto: Combine the basil, mint, pine nuts, garlic, red pepper flakes, and 1 tsp salt in a food processor. Season with pepper and process until a chunky paste forms. With the motor running, slowly drizzle in the lemon juice and olive oil until well combined. Taste and add more lemon juice, red pepper flakes, salt, and pepper, if desired. (Store in an airtight container in the refrigerator for up to 1 day.)

2. Place the avocados, white beans, celery, and scallions in a medium bowl. Add the pesto and gently toss to combine. Divide the salad among plates and serve immediately.

GRILLED PEAR, FENNEL, AND TOASTED WALNUT SALAD

Summer may be the year's official salad season, but there is no reason to pack up the salad tongs once cooler weather arrives. Instead, I welcome the way fall breaks up summer's tomato and cucumber marathon, ushering in hearty, seasonal ingredients like pears and crisp fennel. This autumnal salad is incredibly flavorful, thanks to the smoky and tender grilled pears, a sprinkle of toasted walnuts, and the brown sugar dressing topping things off.

SERVES 6

NOTE

The walnuts and pears can be prepared up to one day in advance and added to the salad just before serving. Store the cooled, toasted walnuts in an airtight container at room temperature and the pears, covered, in the refrigerator.

½ CUP/55 G WALNUTS

2 TBSP RED WINE VINEGAR

1 TBSP LIGHT BROWN SUGAR

2 TSP DIJON MUSTARD

KOSHER SALT AND FRESHLY GROUND BLACK PEPPER

¼ CUP/60 ML EXTRA-VIRGIN OLIVE OIL

2 RIPE MEDIUM PEARS, QUARTERED, CORED, AND CUT INTO ½-IN/12-MM WEDGES

2 MEDIUM FENNEL BULBS, HALVED, CORED, AND THINLY SLICED

3 CUPS/75 G BABY ARUGULA

1. Place the walnuts in a small pan set over medium heat. Cook, stirring occasionally, until fragrant and lightly browned, 5 to 7 minutes. Transfer to a small bowl to cool completely, then roughly chop.

2. Preheat a gas or charcoal grill, or set a grill pan over medium heat. While it heats, whisk together the vinegar, brown sugar, and mustard in a medium bowl. Season with salt and pepper. Slowly drizzle in the olive oil, whisking continuously until the dressing is combined and thickened.

3. Brush the grill or grill pan with oil. Grill the pears, turning once with tongs, until grill marks form and the pears are tender but not falling apart, 2 to 3 minutes per side.

4. Combine the fennel and arugula in a large shallow bowl. Drizzle with about two-thirds of the dressing and gently toss to coat. Arrange the pears on top and sprinkle with the walnuts. If desired, drizzle with the remaining dressing and sprinkle with pepper. Divide the salad among plates and serve immediately.

NEW ISRAELI CUISINE
GOES GLOBAL

For the last two centuries, Jewish cooking in America has been intimately, almost exclusively, linked to the foods of Central and Eastern Europe. Pockets of non-Ashkenazi Jewish communities, like Brooklyn's Syrian Jews or the Iranian Jews who live in Los Angeles, have added to the conversation over the years. But if pressed to name five Jewish foods, the majority of Americans would still likely say, "matzo ball soup, gefilte fish, chopped liver, pastrami, and bagels." Foods, in other words, that are undeniably Ashkenazi.

In recent decades, however, dishes that are popular in Israel and the Middle East—such as hummus (see page 73), tabbouleh (see page 71), bourekas (see pages 245 and 246), and shakshuka (see page 208)—have made their way into the Jewish American culinary lexicon. Meanwhile, rose water, the herbaceous spice mix za'atar, and tangy pomegranate molasses now take a seat next to schmaltz and poppy seeds as identifiably "Jewish" ingredients. Not *exclusively* Jewish—these ingredients are beloved by people throughout the Middle East—but certainly important parts of the Jewish food canon.

The introduction of these foods and flavors to the American Jewish diet began in the 1970s and 1980s as American tourists to Israel came back with bags of spices in their luggage and vivid memories of the exciting new flavors they had tasted. More recently, the trend has accelerated, thanks to Israel's most important culinary export: chefs. Whether working as sous chefs in larger kitchens or running their own critically acclaimed restaurants—like Einat Admony in New York (Taïm, Balaboosta, and Bar Bolonat) and Michael Solomonov in Philadelphia (Zahav and Dizengoff)—these Israeli-born chefs have contributed significantly to the mainstreaming of Middle Eastern food in the States.

Perhaps the most influential of these chefs is Yotam Ottolenghi, a native Israeli who lives and cooks in London. Along with his good friend and business partner, Sami Tamimi, who is Palestinian, Ottolenghi published the hugely popular cookbooks *Plenty* and *Jerusalem*. I like to think of these two as the Julia Child equivalents in Middle Eastern cooking. Just as Child successfully convinced American home cooks to attempt French classics like beef bourguignon, within months of *Jerusalem's* publication, American cooks, Jewish and otherwise, were burning eggplants on purpose, drizzling tahini over everything, and scouring specialty food shops for ingredients like the cracked green wheat called *freekeh*.

The land of Israel is ancient and storied, but the modern state of Israel, which was founded in 1948, is still quite young. For the first several decades of its current existence, Israeli residents focused on surviving and building. People ate, of course, but there wasn't excess time or resources to focus on cuisine. Things have changed. Today, there is a huge amount of creative energy around food and cooking as Israel's chefs increasingly embrace and explore not only the diverse produce and ingredients available, but the full range of cuisines—Iraqi, Moroccan, Tunisian, Iranian, Palestinian, Lebanese, Yemenite, Eastern European, and Ethiopian, among others—simmering in the country's melting pot. This emerging phenomenon, which is often referred to as "New Israeli cuisine," is evolving within the country and influencing food scenes abroad.

I have a feeling that, when it comes to the impact that New Israeli cuisine will have in the States, we are just at the beginning. And yet Ashkenazi food lovers needn't worry. Old-world classics like brisket, blintzes, kugel, and knishes are not going anywhere anytime soon. As Israel's melting pot bubbles over onto America's plates, the Jewish food buffet will simply get more exciting.

ROASTED BEET SALAD WITH PRESERVED LEMON

With all due respect to the classic pairing of beets and goat cheese, there are other ways to serve cooked beets! Take this salad, which tosses them with preserved lemon, fennel, basil, and capers. The lemon and capers act as a tangy counterpart to the sweet Mediterranean root, and the fresh fennel adds delicious crunch.

SERVES 6

2 LB/910 G MEDIUM BEETS, ENDS TRIMMED AND SCRUBBED

2 SMALL FENNEL BULBS, QUARTERED, CORED, AND THINLY SLICED

1 TBSP BRINE-PACKED CAPERS, DRAINED, PATTED DRY, AND ROUGHLY CHOPPED

10 LARGE BASIL LEAVES, CUT INTO THIN RIBBONS (SEE PAGE 18)

3 TBSP FINELY CHOPPED PRESERVED LEMON PEEL (SEE PAGE 320)

2 TBSP FINELY CHOPPED SHALLOT

2 TBSP FRESH LEMON JUICE

3 TBSP EXTRA-VIRGIN OLIVE OIL

½ TSP SALT

¼ TSP FRESHLY GROUND PEPPER

1. Preheat the oven to 400°F/200°C. Wrap each beet tightly in a piece of aluminum foil and place in a baking dish. Roast in the oven until a fork can be easily inserted into the center, 50 to 70 minutes. (Time will vary depending on the size of your beets, so start checking at 50 minutes and keep cooking if not soft.) Remove from the oven and let cool to the touch. Use a paper towel to rub off the skin, or peel with a vegetable peeler. Cut the beets into bite-size pieces. (Store, covered, in the refrigerator for up to 1 day.)

2. Combine the beets, fennel, capers, basil, and preserved lemon peel in a medium bowl. In a small bowl, whisk together the shallot, lemon juice, olive oil, salt, and pepper. Drizzle over the salad and gently toss to combine. Let stand for 15 minutes. Divide the salad among plates and serve.

ROASTED BELL PEPPER AND BLACK OLIVE SALAD

Have you ever tried homemade roasted bell peppers? If not, this salad is worth making just so you can experience the magical transformation peppers undergo after a slow roast in the oven. The jarred store-bought versions do not come close to the delicate specimens that emerge from this recipe. And they certainly do not permeate your house with an intoxicating perfume. So get roasting, then toss the peppers with olives, basil, capers, croutons, and crunchy romaine for a salad worthy of its starring ingredient.

SERVES 6

2 SMALL RED BELL PEPPERS

3 CUPS/100 G CUBED DAY-OLD RUSTIC BREAD

2 TBSP EXTRA-VIRGIN OLIVE OIL, PLUS ¼ CUP/60 ML

KOSHER SALT AND FRESHLY GROUND BLACK PEPPER

2 ROMAINE HEARTS, CHOPPED INTO BITE-SIZE PIECES

⅓ CUP/60 G BLACK OLIVES, PITTED AND ROUGHLY CHOPPED

2 TBSP BRINE-PACKED CAPERS, DRAINED, PATTED DRY, AND ROUGHLY CHOPPED

¼ CUP/10 G ROUGHLY CHOPPED FRESH FLAT-LEAF PARSLEY

10 BASIL LEAVES, CUT INTO THIN RIBBONS (SEE PAGE 18)

4 SCALLIONS, WHITE AND GREEN PARTS, THINLY SLICED

2 TBSP RED WINE VINEGAR

1 GARLIC CLOVE, MINCED OR PUSHED THROUGH A PRESS

1. Preheat the oven to 375°F/190°C and line a large rimmed baking sheet with aluminum foil. Place the bell peppers on the prepared baking sheet and roast, using tongs to rotate the peppers every 15 minutes, until the skin is puffed and blistered in several spots, 45 to 55 minutes. Remove from the oven and let cool to the touch. Cut the roasted peppers in half, remove the stem and seeds, and peel off the skin with your fingers. Slice the peppers into thin 1-in-/2.5-cm-long strips and set aside. (Store in an airtight container in the refrigerator for up to 1 day.)

2. Place the bread in a medium pan set over medium heat. Drizzle with the 2 Tbsp olive oil, season with salt and pepper, and cook, stirring occasionally, until toasted and golden, 6 to 8 minutes. Remove from the heat and let cool.

3. Combine the romaine, olives, capers, parsley, basil, scallions, and roasted peppers in a large bowl. In a small bowl, whisk together the remaining ¼ cup/ 60 ml oil, vinegar, and garlic. Season with salt and pepper. Drizzle over the salad and scatter the croutons on top; gently toss to combine. Divide the salad among plates and serve immediately.

RED CABBAGE AND BEET SLAW WITH CARAMELIZED WALNUTS

Borscht lovers, meet your new favorite salad. This gorgeous slaw pairs red cabbage, grated beets, and a sprinkling of sweet and crunchy caramelized walnuts tossed together in just the right amount of creamy, tangy dressing. It is the perfect dish to bring to a picnic or potluck.

SERVES 6

¼ CUP/50 G PACKED LIGHT BROWN SUGAR

1½ TSP BALSAMIC VINEGAR

¾ CUP/90 G RAW WALNUT HALVES

2 MEDIUM BEETS, PEELED

2 MEDIUM CARROTS, PEELED

1 SMALL HEAD RED CABBAGE, HALVED AND CORED

3 SCALLIONS, WHITE AND GREEN PARTS, THINLY SLICED

⅔ CUP/165 ML SOUR CREAM OR MAYONNAISE

2 TBSP APPLE CIDER VINEGAR

3 TBSP FINELY CHOPPED SHALLOT

1 TBSP DIJON MUSTARD

1 TBSP HONEY

KOSHER SALT AND FRESHLY GROUND BLACK PEPPER

1. Line a plate with parchment paper. Combine the brown sugar, balsamic vinegar, and walnuts in a small pan set over medium-low heat. Cook, stirring often, until the nuts are coated with sugar and smell toasty (be careful they do not burn), 3 to 5 minutes. Immediately transfer the nuts to the prepared plate and let cool completely, then roughly chop.

2. Grate the beets and carrots on the large holes of a box grater or with a food processor fit with a shredding blade. Shred the cabbage with a sharp knife. Combine the beets, carrots, cabbage, and scallions in a medium bowl.

3. In a small bowl, whisk together the sour cream, apple cider vinegar, shallot, mustard, and honey. Season with salt and pepper. Pour the dressing over the slaw and top with the caramelized walnuts; gently toss to combine. Divide the salad among plates and serve immediately. (If not serving right away, keep the nuts, dressing, and salad in separate containers; combine and toss just before serving.)

MATBUCHA

This saucy, savory North African salad made from cooked tomatoes, bell peppers, and sometimes eggplant is an integral part of Middle Eastern cuisine and has become very popular in Israel. It is typically served as part of the mezze course along with hummus, baba ghanoush, and other cold salads, but I think it has a much broader appeal. I serve it with challah or pita whenever I have people over for Shabbat dinner. Then I spread left-overs onto sandwiches (I particularly love it in a grilled cheese); pile it on top of steak, baked fish, or grilled vegetables; and occasionally spoon it right from the bowl.

SERVES 8

1 LARGE EGGPLANT

KOSHER SALT

8 TBSP/120 ML EXTRA-VIRGIN OLIVE OIL

1 YELLOW ONION, FINELY CHOPPED

1 TBSP SUGAR

3 MEDIUM RED BELL PEPPERS, SEEDED AND CUT INTO ½-IN/12-MM CHUNKS

1 JALAPEÑO, SEEDED AND FINELY CHOPPED

4 GARLIC CLOVES, FINELY CHOPPED

1 TBSP SWEET PAPRIKA

½ TSP RED PEPPER FLAKES

ONE 28-OZ/800-G CAN DICED TOMATOES

FRESHLY GROUND BLACK PEPPER

1. Peel the eggplant with a serrated knife. Starting at the top, gently saw downward, following the curve of the fruit. Cut the eggplant into bite-size cubes, place in a colander, sprinkle with 2 Tbsp salt, and mix with your hands to coat. Let stand for 45 minutes, then rinse well and thoroughly pat dry with paper towels.

2. Meanwhile, preheat the oven to 400°F/200°C.

3. Spread the eggplant cubes on a large rimmed baking sheet. Drizzle with 2 Tbsp of the olive oil and roast, stirring occasionally, until soft and browned in spots, 20 to 30 minutes.

4. Meanwhile, heat another 2 Tbsp olive oil in a large saucepan set over medium heat. Add the onion and sugar and sauté, stirring occasionally, until softened and lightly browned, 5 to 7 minutes. Add the bell peppers and jalapeño and continue cooking until the peppers soften, 8 to 10 minutes. Add the garlic, paprika, and red pepper flakes and cook, stirring often, until fragrant, 1 to 2 minutes.

5. Stir in the roasted eggplant and the tomatoes with their juice, and bring the mixture to a simmer. Turn the heat to low and cook, partially covered and stirring often, until the vegetables are very tender, about 20 minutes. Stir in the remaining 4 Tbsp/60 ml olive oil and use a potato masher to mash to a chunky consistency with some larger pieces. Continue cooking, partially covered, until the mixture thickens, 10 to 15 minutes more. Season with salt and pepper. Remove from the heat and let cool. Serve at room temperature.

HEIRLOOM TABBOULEH

Back in the 1980s, when I was a little kid, tabbouleh—the refreshing salad of chopped herbs, tomato, and bulgur—was still relatively unfamiliar to the American palate. And for many years, tabbouleh, along with hummus and falafel, seemed to be among the only Middle Eastern dishes to make their way into America's mainstream repertoire. Today, thanks to the work of cookbook authors like the inimitable Claudia Roden and Anissa Helou and chefs like the Israeli-born Yotam Ottolenghi and Michael Solomonov, Americans have discovered a whole world of dishes and flavors from the region. And yet tabbouleh remains one of my favorites. The dish's name comes from the Arabic word for "seasoning," and the best versions are the ones that interpret that literally—treating the herbs as the main event and the bulgur as more of a garnish.

SERVES 6

NOTE

Bulgur comes in four grades, labeled fine, medium, coarse, and very coarse, or 1, 2, 3, and 4. Use numbers 1 or 2 for this recipe.

To make this dish kosher for Passover (see page 330), replace the bulgur with 1¾ cups/245 g cooked quinoa. Technically a seed, not a grain, quinoa is there-fore widely considered kosher for Passover.

½ CUP/85 G FINE- OR MEDIUM-GRADE BULGUR, RINSED AND DRAINED

1 CUP/240 ML BOILING WATER

1½ LB/680 G RIPE HEIRLOOM TOMATOES, HALVED, SEEDS GENTLY SQUEEZED OUT, AND FINELY CHOPPED

2 CUPS/80 G FINELY CHOPPED FRESH FLAT-LEAF PARSLEY

1½ CUPS/60 G FINELY CHOPPED FRESH MINT

¼ CUP/10 G FINELY CHOPPED FRESH CILANTRO

½ CUP/40 G SCALLIONS, WHITE AND GREEN PARTS, THINLY SLICED

ZEST OF 1 LEMON, PLUS ¼ CUP/60 ML FRESH LEMON JUICE

¼ CUP/60 ML EXTRA-VIRGIN OLIVE OIL

1½ TSP KOSHER SALT

½ TSP FRESHLY GROUND BLACK PEPPER

1. Combine the bulgur and boiling water in a medium bowl. Cover and let stand until the bulgur is tender but still chewy, 15 to 20 minutes. Drain well and transfer to a large bowl along with the tomatoes, parsley, mint, cilantro, and scallions.

2. In a small bowl, whisk together the lemon zest, lemon juice, olive oil, salt, and pepper. Drizzle over the tabbouleh and gently toss to combine. Divide the salad among plates and serve immediately.

FATTOUSH

Nearly every cuisine has developed methods for using up leftover bread by repurposing it in tasty ways. In the Middle East, one solution to the stale bread conundrum is fattoush, a chopped vegetable salad that incorporates toasted pita into the ubiquitous mix of tomatoes, cucumbers, and onions. It is a close cousin of panzanella, Italy's bread salad. This version is topped with a tangy yogurt and sumac dressing and brightened by lots of fresh herbs.

SERVES 6

TWO 6-IN/15-CM WHITE OR WHOLE-WHEAT PITA ROUNDS

4 TBSP/60 ML EXTRA-VIRGIN OLIVE OIL

½ CUP/120 ML PLAIN FULL-FAT OR LOW-FAT YOGURT

2 TSP GROUND SUMAC OR ZA'ATAR, PLUS MORE FOR SPRINKLING

2 TBSP FRESH LEMON JUICE

1 LARGE GARLIC CLOVE, MINCED OR PUSHED THROUGH A PRESS

½ TSP KOSHER SALT

⅛ TSP FRESHLY GROUND PEPPER

2 RIPE MEDIUM TOMATOES, CORED, SEEDED, AND CHOPPED

3 KIRBY CUCUMBERS, PEELED, HALVED LENGTHWISE, SEEDED, AND CUT INTO HALF-MOONS

5 RADISHES, THINLY SLICED

½ SMALL RED ONION, FINELY CHOPPED

4 SCALLIONS, WHITE AND GREEN PARTS, THINLY SLICED

¼ CUP/10 G ROUGHLY CHOPPED FRESH FLAT-LEAF PARSLEY

¼ CUP/10 G ROUGHLY CHOPPED FRESH MINT

1. Preheat the oven to 400°F/200°C. Lay the pitas on a large rimmed baking sheet and bake until dry and crisp, about 15 minutes. Remove from the oven and let cool completely, then break into bite-size pieces. Transfer to a bowl, drizzle with 2 Tbsp of the olive oil, and stir to coat.

2. Whisk together the remaining 2 Tbsp olive oil, yogurt, sumac, lemon juice, garlic, salt, and pepper in a small bowl.

3. In a large bowl, stir together the tomatoes, cucumbers, radishes, red onion, scallions, parsley, and mint. Fold in the toasted pita pieces. Drizzle the dressing over the top and gently toss to combine. Divide the salad among plates, sprinkle with sumac, and serve immediately.

SUPREMELY CREAMY HUMMUS

As someone who grew up in the 1980s, I remember a time before hummus. The creamy chickpea and tahini spread had already become the dip of choice for health food fans, but it had hardly penetrated the mainstream. While hummus is not specifically Israeli in origin (it has been eaten throughout the Middle East for centuries), according to Gil Marks's book *The Encyclopedia of Jewish Food*, Jews returning from visits to Israel and wandering Israelis "initially helped popularize hummus in the West."

Today, hummus can be found in virtually every supermarket and even on pub menus. And just about everyone seems to have a recipe for hummus, ranging from thick, chunky spreads to smooth, fluffy dips.

My version is richly flavored and creamy in texture. Some recipes suggest peeling the chickpeas with your fingers, but I have never found the process to be worth it. My secret instead is to blend in some of the liquid from the can of chickpeas, and to press the hummus through a fine-mesh sieve to rid it of any bumpy bits of chickpea skin. It only takes an extra five minutes, and the resulting hummus is smooth as silk.

SERVES 8

½ CUP/120 ML TAHINI

⅓ CUP/80 ML EXTRA-VIRGIN OLIVE OIL, PLUS MORE FOR DRIZZLING

1 LARGE GARLIC CLOVE, ROUGHLY CHOPPED

3 TBSP FRESH LEMON JUICE

KOSHER SALT

TWO 15½-OZ/445-G CANS CHICKPEAS, DRAINED THROUGH A FINE-MESH SIEVE AND LIQUID RESERVED

ZA'ATAR FOR SPRINKLING

1. Combine the tahini, olive oil, garlic, lemon juice, and 2 tsp salt in a food processor and purée until slick and smooth.

2. Add the chickpeas and continue processing, using a spatula to scrape down the sides of the bowl as necessary, until a chunky paste forms, about 1 minute. With the motor running, slowly drizzle in ⅓ to ½ cup/80 to 120 ml of the reserved chickpea liquid to loosen the hummus. Continue processing until the hummus becomes whipped and very creamy, 2 to 3 minutes. Taste and add more lemon juice or salt, if desired.

3. Place a fine-mesh sieve over a large bowl. Working in batches, press the hummus through the sieve with a rubber spatula; discard the solids. Serve the hummus at room temperature drizzled with additional olive oil and sprinkled with za'atar. Cover and refrigerate for up to 1 week.

VARIATION

Add 1 cup/40 g roughly chopped fresh flat-leaf parsley to the food processor along with the tahini, oil, garlic, lemon juice, and salt, and blend until smooth. Continue as directed.

HUMMUS IM BASAR

There's nothing quite like really amazing hummus—unless, of course, that hummus is topped with warm spiced lamb and pine nuts. A lesser-known gem of Middle Eastern cuisine, Hummus im Basar, which literally means "hummus with meat" in Arabic, is practically a meal unto itself. Find a couple of friends to eat with, serve the hummus with plenty of warm pita and Watermelon Israeli Salad (page 57), and scoop your way to a blissful dinner.

SERVES 4 TO 6

8 OZ/225 G GROUND LAMB

2 GARLIC CLOVES, FINELY CHOPPED

1 TSP SWEET PAPRIKA

1 TSP GROUND CUMIN

½ TSP GROUND CORIANDER

½ TSP GROUND CINNAMON

¼ TSP CAYENNE PEPPER

½ TSP KOSHER SALT

¼ TSP FRESHLY GROUND BLACK PEPPER

2 TBSP EXTRA-VIRGIN OLIVE OIL, PLUS MORE FOR DRIZZLING

1 YELLOW ONION, FINELY CHOPPED

¼ CUP/40 G PINE NUTS

1 RECIPE SUPREMELY CREAMY HUMMUS (PAGE 73)

ZA'ATAR FOR SPRINKLING

1. Combine the lamb, garlic, paprika, cumin, coriander, cinnamon, cayenne, salt, and pepper in a large bowl and mix well with your hands. Cover and let rest for 15 minutes.

2. Meanwhile, heat the olive oil in a medium saucepan set over medium heat. Add the onion and pine nuts and cook, stirring occasionally, until the onion softens and turns light brown, 6 to 8 minutes. Add the lamb mixture and cook, breaking up the meat into small pieces with a wooden spoon, until just cooked through, 3 to 4 minutes.

3. Spoon the hummus onto a serving plate and make a wide, shallow well in it with the back of a soupspoon. Fill the well with the lamb mixture, then top with a generous sprinkle of za'atar and a drizzle of additional oil, if desired. Serve immediately.

CHOPPED CHICKEN LIVER

I first tried chopped chicken liver at a synagogue dinner my family attended. I was about nine years old and still a fairly picky eater, so I am not sure what compelled me to be so adventurous that evening. I remember thinking the earthy-tasting mixture spooned on my piece of challah was fine—not bad, but not something I cared to eat again soon. Sure enough, nearly two decades passed before I tried the Ashkenazi Jewish spread again. This time the liver was prepared by my friend Naf, a true meat connoisseur. His version was creamy, full flavored, and so much better than "just fine." This is my adaptation of his excellent recipe. The pomegranate molasses and cayenne pepper are decidedly not traditional, but add an extra hint of excitement.

SERVES 4 TO 6

NOTE

Pomegranate molasses is increasingly available at specialty stores. Find an online source for pomegranate molasses on page 342. If you prefer to use balsamic reduction, learn how to reduce balsamic vinegar into a sticky, concentrated syrup on page 56.

4 EGGS

1 LB/455 G CHICKEN LIVERS, RINSED AND PATTED DRY

KOSHER SALT

3 TBSP SCHMALTZ (SEE PAGE 318) OR VEGETABLE OIL, PLUS MORE IF NEEDED

2 MEDIUM YELLOW ONIONS, FINELY CHOPPED

1 TBSP POMEGRANATE MOLASSES OR BALSAMIC REDUCTION

¼ TSP CAYENNE PEPPER, OR MORE TO TASTE

FRESHLY GROUND BLACK PEPPER

1. Place the eggs in a small pot and cover with water by 1 in/2.5 cm. Bring to a boil; turn off the heat, cover, and let stand for 20 minutes. Drain the eggs and rinse well under cold water; peel, quarter, and set aside.

2. Preheat the broiler. Lightly sprinkle the livers with salt on both sides and place on a broiler pan. Broil, turning once, until light brown on both sides, 3 to 4 minutes per side. Remove from the broiler and rinse with cold water; pat dry and set aside.

3. Meanwhile, heat the schmaltz in a large pan set over medium heat. Add the onions and cook, stirring occasionally, until softened and browned, 20 to 25 minutes. Remove from the heat and let cool slightly.

4. Combine the eggs, livers, onions, pomegranate molasses, and cayenne in a medium bowl, and use a sturdy fork to mash to a chunky paste. Stir in 1 tsp salt, a generous amount of pepper, and a drizzle of additional schmaltz, if needed, to thin the mixture. Cover and refigerate for at least 3 hours, or up to 2 days. Serve chilled.

VEGETARIAN CHOPPED "LIVER"

Call it blasphemy if you want, but vegetarian chopped "liver" is a legitimate part of the Jewish food canon. Its heyday was the early and mid-twentieth century, when dairy restaurants (the meat-free cousins of delicatessens) were popular across the Lower East Side and other Jewish neighborhoods in New York. Along with cheese blintzes, sour cream–topped latkes, and noodles stirred with farmer cheese, "mock chopped liver" was considered a delicacy. And to be honest, I prefer it to the real thing. Dollop this hearty, creamy spread on challah, rye bread, or crackers, and enjoy it with great flourish and no shame! If you can, prepare this dish a day before you plan to serve it, as the flavors deepen in the refrigerator overnight.

SERVES 4 TO 6

NOTE

To make your hard-boiled eggs easier to peel, use slightly older eggs (new ones tend to cling to the shell) and put 2 to 3 tsp of baking soda in the water.

1 LB/455 G GREEN BEANS, TRIMMED AND HALVED

3 EGGS

3 TBSP VEGETABLE OIL

1 LARGE YELLOW ONION, CHOPPED

3 CUPS/225 G FINELY CHOPPED CREMINI MUSHROOMS

1 CUP/115 G WALNUTS

KOSHER SALT AND FRESHLY GROUND BLACK PEPPER

1. Bring a pot of salted water to a boil. Add the green beans and cook until completely tender, 10 to 12 minutes. Drain thoroughly and set aside to cool.

2. Meanwhile, place the eggs in a small pot and cover with water by 1 in/2.5 cm. Bring to a boil; turn off the heat, cover, and let stand for 20 minutes. Drain the eggs and rinse well under cold water; peel, quarter, and set aside.

3. Heat the vegetable oil in a large pan set over medium heat. Add the onion, cover, and let cook until softened and lightly browned, about 10 minutes. Uncover the pan, add the mushrooms, and continue to cook, stirring occasionally, until deeply browned, 7 to 10 minutes. Remove from the heat and let cool slightly.

4. Combine the green beans, eggs, onion-mushroom mixture, and the walnuts in a food processor and pulse until chunky, scraping down the sides of the bowl often. Generously season with salt and pepper and pulse until creamy. Transfer to a bowl, cover, and refrigerate for at least 2 hours, or up to overnight. Serve chilled or at room temperature.

CHAPTER THREE

SOUPS

20 CLOVES OF GARLIC BORSCHT

Yoshie and I have a bit of a borscht addiction. Our favorite version of the Eastern European beet soup is made at B&H Dairy, a hole-in-the-wall kosher restaurant that opened in New York's East Village in the 1940s, when the neighborhood was densely populated with Jewish delicatessens and Yiddish theaters. Times have changed, but B&H continues to serve up the best hot borscht I have ever eaten.

My tangy, ruby-colored version comes brimming with beets, carrots, cabbage, and potatoes. It is my ode to B&H, with a tasty twist. Following the advice of my sister-in-law, Temim Fruchter, I significantly amped up the garlic. The flavors meld together beautifully as they simmer, yielding a savory, fragrant soup.

SERVES 6 TO 8

NOTE

Peel a whole head of garlic in seconds—really! Get two metal bowls of the same size. Take a head of garlic and smash it against the counter to loosen the cloves. Place the head in one bowl and cover it with the second, inverted bowl. Shake the bowls like crazy. Uncover and your garlic will be peeled!

3 TBSP EXTRA-VIRGIN OLIVE OIL OR UNSALTED BUTTER

2 YELLOW ONIONS, HALVED THROUGH THE ROOT AND THINLY SLICED

2 LARGE CARROTS, PEELED AND THINLY SLICED

1½ LB/680 G BEETS, PEELED AND CUT INTO ½-IN/12-MM PIECES

KOSHER SALT

20 SMALL GARLIC CLOVES, FINELY CHOPPED

7 CUPS/1.7 L VEGETABLE BROTH

4 CUPS/280 G SHREDDED GREEN CABBAGE

2 MEDIUM YUKON GOLD POTATOES, PEELED AND CUT INTO ½-IN/12-MM CUBES

2 TBSP TOMATO PASTE

2 TBSP FRESH LEMON JUICE

1 TBSP RED WINE VINEGAR

1 TSP APPLE CIDER VINEGAR

½ TSP FRESHLY GROUND BLACK PEPPER

CHOPPED FRESH DILL AND SOUR CREAM FOR SERVING

1. Heat the olive oil in a large soup pot set over medium heat. Add the onions, carrots, beets, and a generous pinch of salt. Cook, stirring occasionally, until softened, 10 to 15 minutes. Add the garlic and cook, stirring often, until fragrant, about 2 minutes.

2. Add the broth, cabbage, potatoes, and tomato paste. Raise the heat to medium-high and bring to a boil, then turn the heat to medium-low, partially cover the pot, and simmer until the vegetables are tender, 20 to 30 minutes. Stir in the lemon juice, red wine vinegar, and cider vinegar. Season with 2½ tsp salt and the pepper. Divide the soup into bowls and top with dill and sour cream. Serve hot.

SOURDOUGH GAZPACHO

Spain's iconic cold tomato soup is perfectly refreshing in the summer. This version prepares it in the traditional way, using soaked bread and olive oil to thicken it. Crunchy sourdough croutons, meanwhile, lend a hint of delicatessen flavor. The result is cooling, creamy, and surprisingly elegant—the edible antidote to summer's heat.

SERVES 6

- 3 CUPS/100 G CUBED CRUSTLESS SOURDOUGH BREAD
- 2 LB/910 G RIPE TOMATOES
- ½ RED ONION, ROUGHLY CHOPPED
- 1 JALAPEÑO, SEEDED AND ROUGHLY CHOPPED
- 1 MEDIUM CUCUMBER, PEELED AND ROUGHLY CHOPPED
- 1 GARLIC CLOVE, ROUGHLY CHOPPED
- 1 TSP SWEET PAPRIKA
- 1 TBSP RED WINE VINEGAR
- ⅛ TSP CAYENNE PEPPER (OPTIONAL)
- KOSHER SALT AND FRESHLY GROUND BLACK PEPPER
- ⅓ CUP/80 ML EXTRA-VIRGIN OLIVE OIL, PLUS 1 TBSP

1. Place two-thirds of the bread in a medium bowl and cover with room-temperature water. Let stand for 15 minutes, then drain, squeeze out excess water, and place the moistened bread in a food processor.

2. Meanwhile, bring a medium pot of water to a boil. Make an ice bath by adding equal parts ice and cold water to a large bowl. Score a small *X* into the bottom of each tomato and drop into the boiling water, two or three at a time. Boil just until the skin begins to peel off, about 30 seconds, then transfer to the ice bath and let stand for 5 minutes. Peel off the skin with your fingers and discard; core and roughly chop the tomatoes.

3. Add the tomatoes (including seeds and pulp) to the food processor with the bread, along with the onion, jalapeño, cucumber, garlic, paprika, vinegar, cayenne (if using), 2½ tsp salt, and ½ tsp pepper and process until smooth. (If you can't fit all the vegetables in the processor at once, add as many as you can and purée until the mixture's volume goes down, then add the remaining vegetables.) With the motor running, drizzle in the ⅓ cup/80 ml olive oil and process until thickened. Transfer the gazpacho to a large bowl. Taste and season with more salt and pepper, if desired. Cover and refrigerate until chilled, at least 2 hours or up to 1 day.

4. Just before serving, heat the remaining 1 Tbsp olive oil in a small skillet set over medium heat. Add the remaining bread and cook, stirring occasionally, until toasted and browned, 7 to 8 minutes. Remove from the heat and sprinkle lightly with salt and pepper. Divide the chilled soup into bowls and top with the croutons. Serve cold.

TOMATO-CHICKPEA SOUP WITH SPINACH

Tomato soup is an iconic American dish immortalized—in a Campbell's can—by Andy Warhol and firmly fixed in the nation's collective childhood nostalgia. This version adds new dimension to the classic, spiking it with herbs and spices, and enriching it with chickpeas and fresh spinach. The result is smoky, spicy, and truly irresistible—equally delicious swirled with labneh, or served as a creamy companion to a grilled cheese sandwich. It also tastes great as is, so feel free to enjoy dairy-free.

SERVES 6

3 TBSP EXTRA-VIRGIN OLIVE OIL

1 LARGE YELLOW ONION, CHOPPED

2 STALKS CELERY, CHOPPED

2 CARROTS, PEELED AND CHOPPED

4 GARLIC CLOVES, CHOPPED

1½ TSP SMOKED PAPRIKA

1½ TSP GROUND CUMIN

½ TSP DRIED BASIL

½ TSP DRIED ROSEMARY

¼ TSP RED PEPPER FLAKES

TWO 15½-OZ/445-G CANS CHICKPEAS, DRAINED

ONE 14½-OZ/415-G CAN DICED TOMATOES

4 CUPS/960 ML VEGETABLE BROTH

1 TSP SUGAR

KOSHER SALT

½ TSP FRESHLY GROUND BLACK PEPPER

3 CUPS/75 G PACKED BABY SPINACH LEAVES

LABNEH OR YOGURT FOR SERVING

1. Heat the olive oil in a large pot set over medium-high heat. Add the onion, celery, and carrots and cook, stirring occasionally, until softened, 7 to 10 minutes. Add the garlic, paprika, cumin, basil, rosemary, and red pepper flakes and cook, stirring often, until fragrant, 1 to 2 minutes.

2. Add one can of chickpeas, the tomatoes with their juice, broth, and sugar. Bring to a boil, then turn the heat to medium-low and simmer, stirring occasionally, until the liquid is slightly reduced, about 20 minutes. Stir in 1 tsp salt and the pepper. Remove from the heat and let cool slightly.

3. Purée the soup until smooth using an immersion blender, or working in batches in a standard blender (see page 17.) Return the soup to the pot, set over low heat, and stir in the remaining one can of chickpeas and the spinach. Cook until the spinach wilts, about 2 minutes. Taste and season with more salt, if desired. Divide into bowls and dollop with labneh. Serve hot.

BUTTERNUT SQUASH AND PEAR SOUP

Butternut squash soup has become a staple of the Shabbat table in recent years. A thick, creamy soup that contains no actual cream or milk (and can therefore be served with either a meat or dairy meal in kosher households), it is both tasty and versatile. Dairy lovers, of course, can add a dollop of Greek yogurt or labneh to satisfy their cravings. My version combines the squash with pears and maple syrup, two autumn-friendly flavors that add a hint of sweetness.

SERVES 6

2 TBSP EXTRA-VIRGIN OLIVE OIL

4 MEDIUM SHALLOTS, THINLY SLICED

1 LB/455 G BUTTERNUT SQUASH, PEELED, SEEDED, AND CUT INTO ½-IN/12-MM PIECES

1 LB/455 G RIPE, FIRM-FLESHED PEARS, SUCH AS BARTLETT, PEELED, CORED, AND CUT INTO ½-IN/12-MM PIECES

2 TSP DRIED THYME

1 TBSP BALSAMIC VINEGAR

5 CUPS/1.2 L VEGETABLE BROTH

1 MEDIUM RUSSET POTATO, PEELED AND CUT INTO ½-IN/12-MM CHUNKS

KOSHER SALT AND FRESHLY GROUND BLACK PEPPER

GREEK YOGURT OR LABNEH FOR SERVING (OPTIONAL)

PURE MAPLE SYRUP FOR SERVING

1. Heat the olive oil in a large pot set over medium heat. Add the shallots and cook, stirring occasionally, until softened and lightly browned, about 5 minutes. Add the squash and pears and cook, stirring occasionally, until slightly softened and lightly browned, 7 to 8 minutes. Stir in the thyme and cook until fragrant, about 1 minute.

2. Add the vinegar, broth, and potato; raise the heat to medium-high; and bring to a simmer. Turn the heat to low and cook until the vegetables are very tender, about 15 minutes. Remove from the heat and let cool slightly.

3. Purée the soup until smooth using an immersion blender, or working in batches in a standard blender (see page 17). Taste and season with salt and pepper. Divide into bowls, dollop with yogurt (if desired), and drizzle with maple syrup. Serve hot.

JEWISH FARMING
IN AMERICA

I have never had much of a green thumb. With the exception of a tiny potted cactus that managed to survive my college years, I have a dismal track record with keeping plants alive. And yet, I harbor a not-so-secret obsession with farmers. They are the people, after all, who possess the magical ability to coax fruits and vegetables from the earth. And it is their labor that makes cooking and eating such a pleasure for the rest of us. Because of that, farmers are my rock stars.

For the first few years after college, when I worked for the Jewish environmental organization called Hazon, I had the privilege of getting to know a lot of local, sustainable farmers, including many Jewish ones. Some had grown up in farming families that stretched back generations. Others had left academia, office jobs, or other city pursuits to try their hand at tilling the soil.

I know, I know—the notion of a Jewish farmer might seem like the punch line to a bad joke. But historically speaking, Jews are an agricultural people. If you look at the canon of Jewish texts, you will find a multitude of laws, debates, and commentaries about the importance of letting one's land rest every seven years, when and how to celebrate a harvest festival, and the obligation to reserve the corners of one's field for less fortunate people to glean. These are guidelines aimed not at doctors or lawyers, but at people who grow food.

America has its own rich history of Jewish farming. In the years leading up to World War II, upstate New York and New Jersey were dotted with Jewish-owned dairy, egg, and vegetable farms. Out west in Petaluma, California, a community of chicken ranchers thrived from the 1920s to the 1960s. These communities, and others like them around the country, were beneficiaries of the Jewish Agricultural Society (yes, there was one!), an organization founded by German Jewish philanthropist Baron Maurice de Hirsch in 1900. For more than 50 years, the organization helped tens of thousands of Jewish families across America settle on homesteads and purchase seeds and equipment. It even published a magazine called *The Jewish Farmer*.

The Jewish Agricultural Society dwindled in the second half of the twentieth century and closed up shop by the 1970s. But today, Jewish involvement in farming continues on. The larger food movement, which has popularized the notions of eating locally, organically, and seasonally, has inspired many people, including many young Jews, to take up farming again. Programs like Adamah in Connecticut, Urban Adamah in Berkeley, Shoresh in Toronto, and the Jewish Farm School in Pennsylvania have taken up the charge and are reconnecting young Jews with their agricultural roots.

My own interaction with sustainable agriculture and food begins at the farmers' market, rather than in the field. So I have done my best to honor farmers by creating recipes that are fresh, seasonally driven, and do their work proud. I may not be able to grow my own vegetables, but I am endlessly appreciative of the people who do.

CREAMY SORREL SOUP WITH HARISSA

Eastern European Jews love sorrel—a green that resembles spinach but tastes sour like rhubarb—as the base for a summery soup called *schav*. Big pots of the summery green get simmered down with water and thickened with beaten egg yolk, then served chilled with sour cream, boiled potato, and chopped fresh radishes and scallions. I personally love *schav*, but have found that its distinctly old-world flavor is not everyone's cup of tea. This adaptation whirs the tangy greens and silky cooked potato into a creamy, full-flavored soup that can be served either warm or chilled. A drizzle of harissa (a North African hot chile sauce popular in Israel, see page 342 for an online source) adds a spicy, Middle Eastern counter note to this Ashkenazi-inspired dish.

SERVES 6

4 TBSP/55 G UNSALTED BUTTER

2 YELLOW ONIONS, FINELY CHOPPED

5 CUPS/1.2 L VEGETABLE BROTH

2 MEDIUM RUSSET POTATOES, PEELED AND CUT INTO 1-IN/2.5-CM CHUNKS

12 OZ/340 G SORREL, STEMMED AND ROUGHLY CHOPPED

1 CUP/240 ML HEAVY CREAM

KOSHER SALT AND FRESHLY GROUND BLACK PEPPER

SOUR CREAM OR LABNEH FOR SERVING

HARISSA FOR DRIZZLING

1. Melt the butter until foaming in a large saucepan set over medium heat. Add the onions and cook, stirring occasionally, until softened and lightly browned, 8 to 10 minutes. Add the broth, potatoes, and sorrel, stirring to help the sorrel begin to wilt. (It will seem like too much sorrel at first, but will cook down significantly). Raise the heat to medium-high and bring to a boil. Then turn the heat to low, cover, and simmer until the potatoes are tender, about 15 minutes. Remove from the heat and let cool slightly.

2. Purée the soup until smooth using an immersion blender, or working in batches in a standard blender (see page 17). Return the soup to the pan, set over low heat, and whisk in the heavy cream. Taste and season with salt and pepper.

3. To serve warm, divide into bowls, dollop with sour cream, and drizzle with harissa. To serve cold, let the soup cool slightly, then cover and refrigerate for at least 3 hours or up to 1 day. Divide into bowls, dollop with sour cream, and drizzle with harissa.

RUSTIC VEGETABLE SOUP WITH DILL DUMPLINGS

I really love this soup. It's got the golden, schmaltzy feel of chicken soup, minus the chicken, making it a lovely vegetarian option for Shabbat or holiday meals. It's loaded with vegetables, without crossing into stew territory. And best of all, the little dill dumplings have these rough, raggedy edges that closely resemble cauliflower, which means you never quite know if you are going to get a bite of cauliflower or a chewy dumpling. How many other soups can surprise you in such a delicious way? On Passover, swap out the dumplings for Parsley Matzo Balls (page 148).

SERVES 6

FOR THE DUMPLING BATTER

½ CUP/60 G ALL-PURPOSE FLOUR

1 TSP KOSHER SALT

½ TSP DRIED DILL

2 TBSP COLD UNSALTED BUTTER, CUT INTO SMALL PIECES

1 EGG, PLUS 1 EGG WHITE

FOR THE SOUP

¼ CUP/60 ML EXTRA-VIRGIN OLIVE OIL, PLUS 2 TBSP

1 LARGE YELLOW ONION, FINELY CHOPPED

1 LEEK, WHITE AND LIGHT GREEN PARTS, THINLY SLICED

2 STALKS CELERY, THINLY SLICED

4 GARLIC CLOVES, ROUGHLY CHOPPED

1 FENNEL BULB, QUARTERED, CORED, AND THINLY SLICED

2 MEDIUM ZUCCHINI, SEEDED AND CHOPPED

1 SMALL HEAD CAULIFLOWER, CORED AND CUT INTO ¾-IN/2-CM FLORETS

2 MEDIUM YUKON GOLD POTATOES, PEELED AND CUT INTO ½-IN/12-MM CUBES

8 CUPS/2 L VEGETABLE BROTH

1 TSP KOSHER SALT

½ TSP FRESHLY GROUND BLACK PEPPER

ROUGHLY CHOPPED FRESH FLAT-LEAF PARSLEY FOR SERVING

1. Make the dumpling batter: Stir together the flour, salt, and dill in a small bowl. Add the butter and, using your fingers or a pastry cutter, combine until the mixture is crumbly and the butter pieces are pea-size. Stir in the egg and egg white until a moist batter forms. Cover and refrigerate until ready to use.

2. Make the soup: Heat the ¼ cup/60 ml olive oil in a large pot set over medium heat. Add the onion, leek, and celery and cook, stirring occasionally, until softened, about 5 minutes. Add the garlic, fennel, and zucchini and cook, stirring occasionally, until slightly softened, about 5 minutes. Add the cauliflower, potatoes, and broth; raise the heat to high; and bring to a boil. Turn the heat to low, cover, and simmer until the vegetables soften, 10 to 15 minutes. Stir in the salt, pepper, and remaining 2 Tbsp olive oil.

3. Drop the dumpling batter, ½ tsp at a time, into the gently simmering soup and cook, stirring occasionally, until the dumplings are slightly puffed and cooked through, 3 to 5 minutes. Divide the soup and dumplings into bowls and sprinkle with chopped parsley. Serve hot. (To make the dumplings ahead, simmer them in a separate pot of water set over medium heat. Remove with a slotted spoon and let cool. Store in an airtight container in the refrigerator for up to 1 day. Rewarm the dumplings in the soup just before serving.)

WILD MUSHROOM AND BARLEY SOUP

When it comes to soup, taste is far more important than beauty. Take mushroom barley soup. Its porridge-like texture is hardly elegant, but its taste—rich and divinely savory—more than makes up for its humble appearance. Prized by Eastern European Jews for being filling and inexpensive, mushroom barley soup later became a staple of the Jewish delicatessen. This version gets a little bit fancy, while retaining the soup's original comfort-food feel. It swaps out regular white mushrooms for a mix of more exotic varieties, and adds dried morels for a boost of flavor. (Just be sure to rinse those rehydrated morels very well. Nothing ruins a tasty soup like a mouthful of gritty sediment!) Unexpected splashes of soy sauce and balsamic vinegar add extra depth.

SERVES 6

½ OZ/15 G DRIED MORELS

3 TBSP EXTRA-VIRGIN OLIVE OIL

1 LARGE YELLOW ONION, FINELY CHOPPED

1 LARGE CARROT, PEELED AND FINELY CHOPPED

2 STALKS CELERY, FINELY CHOPPED

6 GARLIC CLOVES, FINELY CHOPPED

1 LB/455 G ASSORTED FRESH MUSHROOMS (SUCH AS OYSTER, SHIITAKE, OR CHANTERELLES), STEMMED AND THINLY SLICED

2 TSP DRIED THYME, CRUSHED WITH A MORTAR AND PESTLE

1 TBSP BALSAMIC VINEGAR

2 TBSP SOY SAUCE OR TAMARI

2 TBSP TOMATO PASTE

6 CUPS/1.4 L VEGETABLE BROTH

⅓ CUP/70 G PEARL BARLEY

KOSHER SALT AND FRESHLY GROUND BLACK PEPPER

ROUGHLY CHOPPED FRESH FLAT-LEAF PARSLEY FOR SERVING

1. Bring 1 cup/240 ml water to a boil. Place the morels in a small bowl and cover with the boiling water. Let stand until tender, about 30 minutes. Remove the morels with a slotted spoon and rinse well. Drain and roughly chop. Strain the soaking liquid through a fine-mesh sieve into a small bowl, reserving the liquid and discarding any sediment.

2. Meanwhile, heat the olive oil in a large pot set over medium heat. Add the onion, carrot, celery, and garlic and cook, stirring occasionally, until softened, 6 to 8 minutes. Add the softened morels and the fresh mushrooms and cook, stirring occasionally, until soft and lightly browned, 7 to 10 minutes.

3. Add the thyme, balsamic vinegar, soy sauce, tomato paste, reserved soaking liquid, broth, and barley. Raise the heat to medium-high and bring to a boil, then turn the heat to medium-low. Simmer, partially covered, stirring occasionally, until the barley is tender, about 30 minutes. Taste and season with salt, if desired (the soup will already be salty from the soy sauce and broth), and pepper. Divide into bowls and top with chopped parsley. Serve hot.

CHORIZO, TOMATO, AND CABBAGE SOUP

The day my friends Naf and Anna Hanau launched their sustainable kosher meat company, Grow and Behold, in 2010 was the day I officially said good-bye to my decade-long run of being a vegetarian. I still prefer to eat a primarily meat-free diet, but I can't think of a better way to indulge than with this hearty soup, which I make with Grow and Behold's spicy chorizo. Brimming with diced tomatoes, shredded cabbage, and creamy potatoes, it is the perfect way to welcome autumn's chilly temperatures. It is also a great make-ahead soup—it tastes even better the second day, when the flavors have had a chance to meld and intensify. Find an online source for Grow and Behold's mild or spicy chorizo, and other kosher chorizo sources, on page 343. Vegetarians can substitute meat-free chorizo or another kind of firm, vegetarian sausage.

SERVES 8

2 TBSP EXTRA-VIRGIN OLIVE OIL, PLUS MORE FOR DRIZZLING

1 LARGE YELLOW ONION, FINELY CHOPPED

8 OZ/225 G MILD OR SPICY CHORIZO LINKS, CUT INTO ¼-IN/6-MM SLICES

6 GARLIC CLOVES, FINELY CHOPPED

¼ TSP RED PEPPER FLAKES

7 CUPS/1.7 L WATER

ONE 28-OZ/800-G CAN DICED TOMATOES

1 BAY LEAF

1½ LB/680 G YUKON GOLD POTATOES, PEELED AND CUT INTO ½-IN/ 12-MM CHUNKS

5 CUPS/455 G SHREDDED GREEN CABBAGE

2 TBSP KOSHER SALT

FRESHLY GROUND BLACK PEPPER

1. Heat the olive oil in a large pot set over medium-low heat. Add the onion and chorizo and cook, stirring occasionally, until the onion softens, about 8 minutes. Add the garlic and red pepper flakes and cook until fragrant, 1 to 2 minutes.

2. Add the water, tomatoes with their juice, bay leaf, and potatoes; raise the heat to high; and bring to a boil. Turn the heat to medium-low and simmer until the potatoes are tender, about 15 minutes.

3. Add the cabbage and simmer until it softens, 15 to 20 minutes. Remove from the heat, discard the bay leaf, and add the salt. Season with pepper. Divide into bowls and drizzle with olive oil. Serve hot.

CLASSIC CHICKEN SOUP

A million odes have been sung to a pot of chicken soup over the centuries. Here's mine: "Oh chicken soup, you gorgeous golden broth, there is nothing quite like you that can make my home smell so profoundly and immediately Jewish." With its tender hunks of meat, meltingly soft vegetables, and a broth that could cure the toughest cold (there's a reason why it's known as "Jewish penicillin"), chicken soup simmered with garlic, parsley, and onions is the epitome of Jewish comfort food. Serve this simple, classic version with egg noodles, rice, Matzo Balls (pages 148 and 149), or Beef Kreplach with Ginger and Cilantro (page 145).

SERVES 6 TO 8

3-TO 3½-LB/1.4-TO 1.6-KG WHOLE CHICKEN

3 LARGE CARROTS, PEELED AND HALVED CROSSWISE

3 STALKS CELERY, WITH LEAVES, HALVED CROSSWISE

2 YELLOW ONIONS, HALVED THROUGH THE ROOT

1 MEDIUM FENNEL BULB, QUARTERED AND CORED

1 BAY LEAF

6 GARLIC CLOVES, SMASHED

¼ CUP/10 G LOOSELY PACKED FRESH PARSLEY, WITH STEMS, PLUS ROUGHLY CHOPPED PARSLEY FOR SERVING

KOSHER SALT AND FRESHLY GROUND BLACK PEPPER

LEMON WEDGES FOR SERVING (OPTIONAL)

1. Place the chicken, carrots, celery, onions, fennel, bay leaf, garlic, and parsley stems in a large soup pot and cover with cold water by 1 in/2.5 cm. Bring to a boil over high heat, then turn the heat to low. Gently simmer, partially covered, skimming off any foam that accumulates, until the chicken is very tender and falling off the bone, 1 to 1½ hours. You want the soup to roll along at the gentlest simmer. If it starts to bubble too vigorously, nudge the heat down a little.

2. Remove the chicken and vegetables from the pot and transfer to a cutting board. Strain the broth through a fine-mesh sieve into a large bowl. Return the strained broth to the pot; discard the parsley stems and bay leaf. Using your fingers, remove the meat from the bones and roughly chop. Slice the vegetables into bite-size pieces and return them to the pot along with the chicken meat. Season with salt and pepper.

3. Divide into bowls and top with chopped parsley. Serve hot with lemon wedges for squeezing, if desired.

SPICY ETHIOPIAN CHICKEN STEW

On Friday nights, Ethiopian Jews' Shabbat dinner menu features a savory chicken and hard-boiled-egg stew flavored with ginger, garlic, and the Ethiopian spice blend berbere. I learned how to make this dish, called *doro wat*, from Beejhy Barhany, the founder of the Beta Israel of North America Cultural Foundation, an organization that fosters Ethiopian Jewish culture in America. I spent an afternoon at Barhany's apartment in Manhattan, chopping onions, and listening to her remarkable story of walking an unimaginable trek from Ethiopia to Sudan at the age of four, before being relocated to Israel. Today she is 1 of 1,000 Ethiopian Jews living in America (compared with 120,000 in Israel).

Barhany keeps a jar of her mother's homemade berbere in her refrigerator. For those of us who do not have a berbere source in the family, the version made by the Teeny Tiny Spice Co. of Vermont (see page 342) makes a tasty substitute.

SERVES 4 TO 6

6 EGGS

¼ CUP/60 ML VEGETABLE OIL

2 MEDIUM RED ONIONS, FINELY CHOPPED

6 GARLIC CLOVES, MINCED OR PUSHED THROUGH A PRESS

ONE 2-IN/5-CM PIECE FRESH GINGER, PEELED AND GRATED ON THE FINE HOLES OF A BOX GRATER

ONE 6-OZ/170-G CAN TOMATO PASTE

1 TSP TURMERIC

1 TSP GROUND CUMIN

1 TSP BERBERE, OR MORE TO TASTE

4 LB/1.8 KG SKIN-ON CHICKEN LEGS OR THIGHS (OR A COMBINATION)

KOSHER SALT AND FRESHLY GROUND BLACK PEPPER

STEAMED RICE OR INJERA, FOR SERVING (OPTIONAL)

1. Place the eggs in a medium saucepan and cover with water by 1 in/2.5 cm. Bring to a boil over high heat; turn off the heat, cover, and let stand for 20 minutes. Drain the eggs and rinse well under cold water; peel and set aside.

2. Meanwhile, heat the vegetable oil in a Dutch oven or large saucepan set over medium-low heat. Add the onions, garlic, and ginger and cook until just beginning to soften, about 5 minutes. Add about ¼ cup/60 ml water, cover, and cook until the onions are very soft, 5 to 6 minutes.

3. Stir in the tomato paste, turmeric, cumin, and berbere. Add the chicken and 2 cups/480 ml water, and season generously with salt and pepper. Raise the heat to medium and bring to a simmer. Re-cover and cook, stirring occasionally, until the sauce begins to thicken, 30 to 35 minutes. If the mixture begins to look dry while cooking, add a little more water.

4. Add the peeled eggs to the pot, re-cover, and cook until the chicken is cooked through, 10 to 15 minutes more. Taste and season with more salt, pepper, or berbere. Serve hot over rice, if desired.

GOULASH

Hungarian goulash is the mother of all beef stews—the perfect, warming dish to make on a chilly winter night. According to Gil Marks's *The World of Jewish Cooking*, in authentic Hungarian goulash, the meat is not browned before being simmered and the dish is never thickened with flour. This recipe breaks with tradition and does both. It may be a more contemporary interpretation, but the resulting dish still has a wonderfully nourishing old-world flavor and will make your kitchen smell intoxicating while it cooks. If you'd like, serve the goulash in bowls over egg noodles or rice, or with crusty bread for mopping up all the fragrant, saucy stew.

SERVES 4 TO 6

2 TBSP ALL-PURPOSE FLOUR

2 LB/910 G BEEF CHUCK, TRIMMED OF EXCESS FAT AND CUT INTO 1-IN/ 2.5-CM CUBES

3 TBSP VEGETABLE OIL, PLUS MORE IF NEEDED

2 MEDIUM YELLOW ONIONS, FINELY CHOPPED

2 MEDIUM CARROTS, PEELED AND FINELY CHOPPED

2 STALKS CELERY, FINELY CHOPPED

4 GARLIC CLOVES, THINLY SLICED

1 TBSP APPLE CIDER VINEGAR

4 CUPS/960 ML CHICKEN BROTH

1 CUP/240 ML TOMATO SAUCE

2 TBSP SWEET PAPRIKA, PREFERABLY HUNGARIAN

¼ TSP CAYENNE PEPPER, OR MORE TO TASTE

2 BAY LEAVES

1 LB/455 G YUKON GOLD POTATOES, PEELED AND CUT INTO 1-IN/ 2.5-CM PIECES

KOSHER SALT AND FRESHLY GROUND BLACK PEPPER

1. Place the flour in a shallow baking dish. Working in batches, add the beef and roll the pieces around until coated.

2. Heat the vegetable oil in a Dutch oven or large pot set over medium-high heat. Working in batches, add the beef and cook, stirring occasionally, until browned, about 5 minutes per batch. If the pot looks dry, drizzle in more oil. Transfer the browned meat to a plate.

3. Turn the heat to medium and add the onions, carrots, and celery to the pot. Cook, stirring occasionally and scraping up any browned bits on the bottom of the pot, until softened and lightly browned, 8 to 10 minutes. Add the garlic and vinegar and cook, stirring often, until fragrant, 1 to 2 minutes.

4. Return the beef to the pot along with the broth, tomato sauce, paprika, cayenne, and bay leaves. Partially cover the pot and bring to a boil. Turn the heat to low, cover completely, and simmer until the meat is very tender, about 1¾ hours. Add the potatoes and cook, partially covered, until the potatoes soften and the stew thickens, 20 to 30 minutes. Season with salt and pepper, and remove and discard the bay leaves. Divide into bowls and serve hot.

BLACK BEAN– SWEET POTATO CHILI

During the ten years I was a vegetarian, meat-free chili was one of my staples. Even now that I occasionally eat meat again, I still love vegetarian chili, especially when it's packed with black beans and sweet potato. This version is layered with complex flavor, thanks to three unusual additions: brown sugar, cocoa powder, and balsamic vinegar. Combined, they bring out the earthy sweetness of the sweet potato and add richness and depth to the beans. I like to serve this flavor-packed chili for Shabbat lunch during the winter, and eat the leftovers for dinner throughout the week.

SERVES 6

¼ CUP/60 ML EXTRA-VIRGIN OLIVE OIL

1 LARGE YELLOW ONION, FINELY CHOPPED

1 MEDIUM CARROT, PEELED AND FINELY CHOPPED

1 LARGE SWEET POTATO, PEELED AND CUT INTO ½-IN/12-MM CHUNKS

1 TBSP LIGHT BROWN SUGAR

8 GARLIC CLOVES, FINELY CHOPPED

1 TBSP PLUS 1½ TSP CHILI POWDER

1½ TSP GROUND CUMIN

1 TBSP COCOA POWDER

¼ TSP CAYENNE PEPPER

ONE 14½-OZ/415-G CAN PEELED WHOLE TOMATOES

2 TBSP BALSAMIC VINEGAR

TWO 15½-OZ/445-G CANS BLACK BEANS, DRAINED AND LIQUID RESERVED

½ CUP/120 ML WATER

2 TSP SALT

SOUR CREAM, GRATED CHEDDAR, CHOPPED SCALLIONS, CHOPPED FRESH CILANTRO, AND DICED AVOCADO FOR TOPPING (OPTIONAL)

1. Heat the olive oil in a Dutch oven or large pot set over medium heat. Add the onion, carrot, sweet potato, and brown sugar and cook, stirring occasionally, until the vegetables soften slightly, 8 to 12 minutes. Add the garlic, chili powder, cumin, cocoa powder and cayenne and cook, stirring often, until fragrant, 1 to 2 minutes.

2. Pour the tomatoes with their juice into a large bowl and gently squeeze with your hands until they burst. Stir the tomatoes and their juice into the pot along with the vinegar, black beans, ½ cup/120 ml of the reserved bean liquid, and the water. Bring to a boil, then turn the heat to low, partially cover, and simmer, stirring occasionally, until the mixture thickens, 15 to 25 minutes. Stir in the salt. Divide into bowls. Serve hot, topped as desired.

CHAPTER FOUR

VEGETABLES

GARLIC-MARINATED ZUCCHINI

This dish, *concia*, is an ancient Roman Jewish dish that marinates olive oil-fried vegetables—typically zucchini or eggplant—to the edge of disintegration in a mix of vinegar, chopped garlic, and fresh herbs. According to Edda Servi Machlin, the cookbook author who helped introduce Italian Jewish cuisine to America more than three decades ago, the dish is not widely known outside of the Jewish ghetto neighborhood in Rome, where it originated. It should be. Like many Italian recipes, concia marries simple ingredients and straightforward technique into something much larger than the sum of its parts. During the summer, when zucchini is at its most abundant, I tend to make this dish weekly. When it's really hot out, I grab a hunk of cheese and some crusty bread for mopping up the juices, and call it dinner.

SERVES 4

2 LB/910 G ZUCCHINI, CUT INTO ¼-IN/6-MM SLICES

KOSHER SALT

2 TBSP FINELY CHOPPED FRESH BASIL

¼ CUP/10 G FINELY CHOPPED FRESH FLAT-LEAF PARSLEY

3 GARLIC CLOVES, FINELY CHOPPED

⅓ CUP/80 ML EXTRA-VIRGIN OLIVE OIL

¼ CUP/60 ML RED WINE VINEGAR

FRESHLY GROUND BLACK PEPPER

1. Place the zucchini in a colander, sprinkle with about 2 Tbsp salt, and toss with your hands to coat. Let stand for 30 minutes, then rinse well and thoroughly pat dry with paper towels. Stir together the basil, parsley, and garlic in a small bowl and set aside.

2. Heat the olive oil in a large frying pan set over medium heat. Working in batches, fry the zucchini, turning once, until softened and lightly browned on both sides, about 6 minutes total. Transfer half of the zucchini to a shallow ceramic, glass, or Pyrex (not metal) baking dish and top with half of the herb mixture and half of the vinegar. Taste and season lightly with salt, if desired (zucchini should already be salty), and pepper. Repeat with the remaining zucchini, herbs, and vinegar.

3. Let stand at room temperature, basting occasionally with the juices in the baking dish, for at least 30 minutes, or up to 2 hours, before serving. Serve at room temperature. Store leftovers, covered, in the refrigerator.

GRILLED ZUCCHINI WITH BALSAMIC DRESSING

The grill does wonderful things to zucchini. A few minutes over a hot flame renders it unbelievably tender with a hint of smoke and char that I find irresistible. Make this recipe in the summer, when grilling season is at its peak and zucchini is abundant. Topped with a balsamic dressing sweetened with maple syrup and flavored with chopped fresh basil, zucchini tastes equally delicious warm or at room temperature, making it perfect for Shabbat lunch or a summer barbecue.

SERVES 6

1 TBSP BALSAMIC VINEGAR

3 TBSP EXTRA-VIRGIN OLIVE OIL

2 TBSP FINELY CHOPPED FRESH BASIL LEAVES

2 TSP PURE MAPLE SYRUP

2 TSP DIJON MUSTARD

1 LARGE GARLIC CLOVE, MINCED OR PUSHED THROUGH A PRESS

½ TSP SALT

¼ TSP FRESHLY GROUND BLACK PEPPER

6 MEDIUM ZUCCHINI, QUARTERED LENGTHWISE

1. Preheat a gas or charcoal grill, or set a grill pan over medium heat. Whisk together the vinegar, olive oil, basil, maple syrup, mustard, garlic, salt, and pepper in a small bowl.

2. Lightly oil the grill or pan. Working in batches, grill the zucchini, turning three times to grill all sides, until tender and grill marks form, 9 to 12 minutes total. Arrange the zucchini on a platter and drizzle with the balsamic dressing. Serve warm or at room temperature.

SAUTÉED GREEN BEANS WITH LABNEH AND SLICED ALMONDS

I often find myself wanting to like green beans more than I do. They are healthful (high in vitamins and iron), easy to find, and affordable. But sometimes, I just can't muster much enthusiasm about a bunch of beans—unless I'm making this dish. Dolloped with soft pillows of labneh (the tangy Middle Eastern yogurt) and flavored with lemon zest, fiery red pepper flakes, and toasted almonds, this is the type of green bean dish a person can get excited about.

SERVES 4 TO 6

⅓ CUP/30 G SLICED ALMONDS

2 LB/910 G GREEN BEANS, TRIMMED

2 TBSP EXTRA-VIRGIN OLIVE OIL, PLUS MORE FOR DRIZZLING

4 MEDIUM SHALLOTS, HALVED LENGTHWISE AND THINLY SLICED

3 GARLIC CLOVES, THINLY SLICED

½ TSP RED PEPPER FLAKES

½ TSP LEMON ZEST

1 TSP FRESH LEMON JUICE, OR MORE TO TASTE

KOSHER SALT AND FRESHLY GROUND BLACK PEPPER

LABNEH AND ZA'ATAR FOR SERVING

1. Place the almonds in a small pan set over medium-low heat. Cook, stirring occasionally, until fragrant and golden brown, about 5 minutes. Remove from the heat and let cool in the pan.

2. Meanwhile, bring a medium pot of generously salted water to a boil. Make an ice bath by adding equal parts ice and cold water to a large bowl. Place the green beans in the boiling water and cook until crisp-tender, about 5 minutes. Drain and immediately place in the ice bath to cool, then drain again.

3. Heat the olive oil in a large pan set over medium heat. Add the shallots and cook, stirring occasionally, until softened, about 5 minutes. Add the green beans, garlic, red pepper flakes, lemon zest, and lemon juice. Season with salt and pepper and cook, tossing occasionally with tongs, until the beans are warmed through, about 4 minutes. Taste and add more lemon juice, if desired. Transfer the mixture to a serving platter or bowl.

4. Top the beans with dollops of labneh, drizzle with olive oil, and sprinkle with the toasted almonds and za'atar. Serve warm.

SHABBAT DINNER IN ROME

A year after we got married, Yoshie and I spent two weeks traveling in Rome and Naples. We were on a tight budget, so we filled our time getting lost down the winding streets, gaping at fountains and cathedrals, and spending any extra Euros we found in our pockets on espresso and gelato. And yet, despite our limited funds, we managed to stumble into one of the best and most lavish meals of our lives.

While in Rome, I was on assignment researching a couple of stories about the ancient city's rich Jewish history and food culture. (Yoshie, meanwhile, had just finished playing a tour in France with his band. Alas, freelancers are always working, even on a belated honeymoon.) Despite Rome being the capital of a Catholic country, the city's Jewish community dates back to the second century B.C.E. Jews have lived there ever since, sometimes in relative peace; but for several centuries, forced inside a cramped and inhospitable ghetto.

Throughout the years, they developed a unique and delicious cuisine, filled with humble delicacies like fried artichokes, salt cod simmered in tomato sauce, baked endive and anchovies, a delicious zucchini and garlic dish called Conchia (page 100), and a sweet fruit- and nut-studded cookie called pizza Ebraica (or "Jewish pizza"). Today, the city's Jewish population numbers around 16,000 people, and the old ghetto neighborhood flourishes with kosher restaurants, bakeries, and a nearby Jewish community center.

But back to that meal. In search of Shabbat dinner plans, we reached out to Micaela Pavoncello, a guide who had led us on a walking tour of the former ghetto. (Note to travelers: Next time you are in Rome, look up Pavoncello's company Jewish Roma Walking Tours—she's the best.) A quick phone call later and Micaela hooked us up with her friend Giovanni Terracina, who owns a kosher catering company in Rome called Le Bon Ton.

With a bottle of wine in hand, we showed up at Giovanni's apartment to find his Shabbat table decadently covered with different meat dishes. A small plate of polenta sat perched to one side, like an afterthought. I was still a vegetarian at the time, but quickly decided to make an exception for the exceptional meal before us. Everything Giovanni made was impeccable. But the standout dish was his stracotto, a brisket-like dish that Roman Jews traditionally cook in tomato sauce and about half a bottle of red wine until it is falling-apart tender (I've given my interpretation of this dish in my recipe for Red Wine and Honey Brisket on page 197). Perfumed with garlic, bay leaves, and herbs, it was irresistible. Fortunately, Giovanni did not seem to notice or mind when I spooned a third helping onto my plate. Toasting our host and our incredible good fortune, we ate and drank for hours. We walked home singing—tipsy on wine, stracotto, and the unexpected gifts that only a Shabbat dinner in Italy can offer.

PURÉED CARROTS WITH ORANGE AND GINGER

When I was growing up, puréed carrots were a pretty common part of my family's Jewish holiday repertoire. But on a trip my husband and I took to Berlin a couple of years back, I tried a puréed carrot dish at a restaurant called Tim Raue that was nothing short of a revelation. Three ultrathin steamed carrots sat in a sultry pool of browned butter. Alongside it, Chef Raue had painted the plate with a few swipes of carrot purée spiked with fresh ginger and sprinkled the plate with crisp, floral-scented passion fruit seeds. If I could have a multi-Michelin-starred chef in my kitchen every day, I would. Until then I will console myself with these Raue-inspired puréed carrots with their sunset color, kick of ginger, buttery undertones, and hint of citrusy sweetness.

SERVES 4 TO 6

2 LB/910 G CARROTS, PEELED AND CUT INTO ½-IN/12-MM SLICES

2 CUPS/480 ML VEGETABLE BROTH

1 TBSP SUGAR

KOSHER SALT

4 TBSP/55 G UNSALTED BUTTER OR ¼ CUP/60 ML EXTRA-VIRGIN OLIVE OIL

1 TBSP FINELY GRATED PEELED FRESH GINGER

2 SMALL GARLIC CLOVES, MINCED OR GRATED

⅓ CUP/80 ML FRESH ORANGE JUICE

FRESHLY GROUND BLACK PEPPER

1. Place the carrots, vegetable broth, sugar, and ½ tsp salt in a medium saucepan set over medium heat; stir gently to combine. Bring to a simmer, cover, and cook until the carrots are very tender, 12 to 15 minutes. Drain the carrots, reserving the cooking liquid.

2. Meanwhile, melt the butter in a small saucepan set over medium-low heat. Add the ginger and garlic and gently cook, stirring frequently, until softened and fragrant, 1 to 2 minutes. Remove from the heat.

3. Combine the carrots, ginger-garlic mixture, and orange juice in a food processor and purée until smooth and creamy, scraping down the sides of the bowl as necessary. Adjust the consistency by adding the reserved cooking liquid, 1 tsp at a time, until the desired whipped texture is reached. Discard the remaining liquid. Season with salt and pepper. Serve warm.

LEMON-CAPER SMASHED POTATOES

One of my favorite Yiddish folk songs (don't get too impressed, I know about five in total) is "Bulbes"—a song that jokingly laments the monotony of the shtetl peasant diet. The lyrics go: "Sunday potatoes, Monday potatoes / Tuesday and Wednesday potatoes / Thursday and Friday potatoes / Shabbat for novelty a kugel with potatoes / Sunday, once again potatoes." Well, if you have to eat potatoes every day of the week, this is how to do it. Boiled until tender then lightly flattened, panfried, and drizzled with a lemony dressing spiked with capers and thyme, these potatoes are anything but boring. You can use either red- or yellow-skinned new potatoes (or a mix of both) for this dish; just make sure they are all about the same size so they cook evenly.

SERVES 4

1½ LB/680 G RED OR YELLOW NEW POTATOES, UNPEELED

⅓ CUP/80 ML EXTRA-VIRGIN OLIVE OIL, PLUS 3 TBSP

ZEST AND JUICE OF 1 LEMON

2 TBSP BRINE-PACKED CAPERS, DRAINED, PATTED DRY, AND ROUGHLY CHOPPED

1 TBSP FINELY CHOPPED SHALLOT

2 TSP FINELY CHOPPED FRESH THYME

1 TSP SWEET PAPRIKA

KOSHER SALT AND FRESHLY GROUND BLACK PEPPER

1. Place the potatoes in a medium pot and cover with cold water by 1 in/ 2.5 cm. Set over high heat, bring to a boil, and cook, partially covered, until tender but not falling apart, 10 to 20 minutes, depending on the size of the potatoes. Drain well and let cool to the touch, then transfer the potatoes to a flat surface and gently crush them with the heel of your hand. (The potatoes should be flattened but generally intact.)

2. Heat the ⅓ cup/80 ml olive oil in a large pan set over medium heat until shimmering. Lay the potatoes in a single layer in the pan and cook, turning once, until golden brown on both sides, 10 to 15 minutes total. (If they do not all fit in the pan at once, cook them in two batches.) With a slotted spoon, transfer the potatoes to a serving bowl.

3. In a medium bowl, stir together the remaining 3 Tbsp oil, the lemon zest and juice, capers, shallot, thyme, and paprika. Season with salt (if needed, the capers will make it salty) and pepper. Drizzle the potatoes with the lemon-caper sauce and gently stir to combine. Serve warm.

PAN-ROASTED TURNIPS

I used to dread getting turnips in our CSA share. Not because I don't like them, I just never knew what to do with them besides slicing them into salads. But on a visit Yoshie and I took to Ten Apple Farm—the homestead owned by our friends Karl Schatz and Margaret Hathaway in Maine—I got turned on to turnips pan-roasted with butter. Karl picked a bunch of the fat white roots from their huge garden, and set to sautéing them with a chunk of butter. A few minutes, some lemon juice, and a showering of salt later, and he proclaimed them done. I was admittedly skeptical, but then delighted to find that the turnips had softened and soaked up the butter's fresh, grassy flavor. Sometimes, the best dishes are the simplest ones.

SERVES 4 TO 6

4 TBSP/55 G UNSALTED BUTTER, CUT INTO SMALL PIECES

2 LB/910 G WHITE TURNIPS, TRIMMED, PEELED, AND CUT INTO BITE-SIZE PIECES

JUICE OF ½ LEMON

KOSHER SALT AND FRESHLY GROUND BLACK PEPPER

ROUGHLY CHOPPED FRESH FLAT-LEAF PARSLEY FOR SERVING

1. Melt the butter in a large pan set over medium-high heat until foaming. Add the turnips and cook, stirring occasionally, until tender and lightly browned, 8 to 10 minutes.

2. Stir in the lemon juice and cook, stirring often, until the liquid evaporates, about 1 minute. Season generously with salt and pepper. Remove from the heat and top with chopped parsley. Serve warm.

ROASTED DELICATA SQUASH WITH THYME BREAD CRUMBS

When I was a kid, winter squash came in three varieties: acorn, butternut, and spaghetti. These days, the farmers' market overflows with a seemingly endless assortment of bumpy and beautiful edible gourds. My favorite is the delicata, an oblong yellow- and green-striped squash with sweet, creamy flesh and a tender edible skin you do not have to peel off. (Do give them a good scrub, and trim off any blemishes.) As soon as the first chill hits the air in autumn, I stock up on these lovely squash, roast them until tender, and shower them with a crunchy layer of thyme-scented panko bread crumbs.

SERVES 4

2 LARGE DELICATA SQUASH, HALVED LENGTHWISE, SEEDED, AND CUT INTO ¼-IN/6-MM HALF-MOONS

3 TBSP EXTRA-VIRGIN OLIVE OIL

KOSHER SALT AND FRESHLY GROUND BLACK PEPPER

½ CUP/40 G PANKO BREAD CRUMBS

⅛ TSP RED PEPPER FLAKES

1 TBSP CHOPPED FRESH THYME

1. Preheat the oven to 400°F/200°C and line a large rimmed baking sheet with aluminum foil.

2. Place the squash on the prepared baking sheet, drizzle with 2 Tbsp of the olive oil, and season generously with salt and pepper. Toss the squash with your hands to coat. Roast, stirring occasionally, until tender when pricked with a fork, 20 to 30 minutes.

3. Meanwhile, stir together the bread crumbs, red pepper flakes, remaining 1 Tbsp olive oil, ⅛ tsp salt, and a pinch of pepper in a medium skillet set over medium heat. Cook, stirring often, until toasted and golden, 6 to 8 minutes. Stir in the thyme and remove from the heat.

4. Transfer the squash to a serving platter and sprinkle with the bread crumb mixture. Serve hot.

MISO–ROASTED ASPARAGUS

Roasted asparagus spears are a small miracle all their own—caramelized, tender, and undeniably springlike. But topped with a tangy miso sauce, they are a revelation. Use white miso, which is mellow and slightly sweet, making it the perfect complement to fragrant sesame oil and tangy rice vinegar. If the asparagus you are using are very thick at the bottom, use a vegetable peeler to shave them down.

SERVES 4 TO 6

2 LB/910 G ASPARAGUS, TRIMMED

4 TBSP/60 ML EXTRA-VIRGIN
  OLIVE OIL

KOSHER SALT AND FRESHLY GROUND
  BLACK PEPPER

2 TBSP WHITE MISO

4 TSP RICE VINEGAR

2 TSP TOASTED SESAME OIL

2 TSP HONEY

1. Preheat the oven to 450°F/230°C. Arrange the asparagus in a single layer on two large rimmed baking sheets. Drizzle with 2 Tbsp of the olive oil, season with salt and pepper, and toss to coat. Roast, stirring occasionally, until tender, 12 to 15 minutes.

2. Meanwhile, in a small bowl, whisk together the remaining 2 Tbsp olive oil, the miso, vinegar, sesame oil, and honey.

3. Transfer the asparagus to a serving platter and drizzle with the miso sauce. Serve warm.

ROASTED EGGPLANT AND TAHINI CROSTINI

I love crostini. Or, rather, I love toast piled with delicious ingredients, and crostini is simply the Italian name for that. The thing is, when you serve someone toast with toppings, they say thank you. But when you serve them "crostini," they suddenly get all kinds of impressed—as if you put in a bunch more work beyond crisping up some bits of bread and rounding up tasty things to put on it. Here, crostini gets the Middle Eastern treatment, with a mix of tender roasted eggplant and sultry red onions flavored with whole cumin seeds and drizzled with tahini and honey. If you have silan (a Middle Eastern, molasses-colored syrup made from dates, also called date honey; see page 342 for an online source) on hand, try using it in place of the honey.

SERVES 6

1 LARGE EGGPLANT

KOSHER SALT

4 TBSP/60 ML EXTRA-VIRGIN OLIVE OIL, PLUS MORE FOR BRUSHING

FRESHLY GROUND BLACK PEPPER

2 RED ONIONS, QUARTERED AND THINLY SLICED

1½ TSP CUMIN SEEDS

2 GARLIC CLOVES, FINELY CHOPPED

1 MEDIUM CIABATTA OR OTHER RUSTIC BREAD, CUT DIAGONALLY INTO ½-IN/12-MM SLICES

FULL-FAT OR 2 PERCENT PLAIN GREEK YOGURT, TAHINI, HONEY, AND FINELY CHOPPED FRESH PARSLEY FOR TOPPING

1. Peel the eggplant with a serrated knife. Starting at the top, gently saw downward, following the curve of the fruit. Cut the eggplant into bite-size cubes, place in a colander, sprinkle with 2 Tbsp salt, and mix with your hands to coat. Let stand for 45 minutes, then rinse well and thoroughly pat dry with paper towels. Don't skimp on the drying, or your eggplant will get mushy.

2. Meanwhile, preheat the oven to 400°F/200°C.

3. Spread the eggplant cubes on a large rimmed baking sheet; drizzle with 2 Tbsp of the olive oil and season with pepper. Roast, stirring occasionally, until soft and browned in spots, 20 to 30 minutes.

4. Meanwhile, heat the remaining 2 Tbsp olive oil in a medium pan set over medium-low heat. Add the onions and a pinch of salt and cook, stirring occasionally, until softened and lightly browned, 10 to 15 minutes. Add the cumin seeds and garlic and cook, stirring often, until fragrant, 1 to 2 minutes. Remove from the heat, add the eggplant cubes, and stir to combine. Taste and season with more salt and pepper, if desired. Let the mixture cool to room temperature.

CONTINUED

5. Meanwhile, brush one side of the bread slices with a little olive oil and place on a large baking sheet. Bake, turning once, until crisp and golden, 8 to 10 minutes total. Remove from the oven and let cool slightly.

6. Spread each bread slice with 1 to 2 tsp yogurt, and top with a layer of the eggplant-onion mixture. Drizzle with tahini and honey and sprinkle with parsley. Serve immediately. (If not serving right away, you can prepare the various components of this dish up to 8 hours ahead of time and assemble the crostini just before serving. Store the eggplant-onion mixture in the refrigerator, but let them come to room temperature before topping the crostini.)

BALSAMIC-ROASTED MUSHROOMS AND CORN

Balsamic vinegar and cremini mushrooms complement each other so well, they might just be the new peas and carrots. Once, when I brought these to a Shabbat potluck dinner, a friend grabbed me by the arm and asked, "What did you *do* to those mushrooms?" For a quick second I feared I had done something horribly wrong, but then I noticed her scooping a second helping onto her plate. Earthy and deeply flavored, with a hint of sweetness from the honey and roasted red onions, this dish makes a great side for steak, chicken, or tofu. Wrapped in a warm tortilla and topped with a little grated cheese, fresh baby spinach, and sliced avocado, it also doubles as a simple and filling vegetarian main.

SERVES 4 TO 6

⅓ CUP/80 ML BALSAMIC VINEGAR

⅓ CUP/80 ML SOY SAUCE OR TAMARI

⅓ CUP/80 ML EXTRA-VIRGIN OLIVE OIL

2 TBSP HONEY

4 GARLIC CLOVES, MINCED OR PUSHED THROUGH A PRESS

¼ TSP CAYENNE PEPPER

1½ LB/680 G CREMINI MUSHROOMS, STEMMED AND HALVED OR QUARTERED (IF LARGE)

2 SMALL RED ONIONS, HALVED THROUGH THE ROOT AND CUT INTO ¼-IN/6-MM SLICES

2 EARS SWEET CORN, KERNELS REMOVED, OR 1¼ CUPS/205 G THAWED FROZEN CORN KERNELS

FRESHLY GROUND BLACK PEPPER

2 TBSP ROUGHLY CHOPPED FRESH MINT OR FLAT-LEAF PARSLEY

1. Preheat the oven to 400°F/200°C and line two large rimmed baking sheets with aluminum foil.

2. In a medium bowl, whisk together the vinegar, soy sauce, olive oil, honey, garlic, and cayenne.

3. Divide the mushrooms, onions, and corn evenly between the prepared baking sheets. Drizzle each vegetable mixture with half of the vinegar mixture and gently toss with tongs to coat. Season with pepper. Roast, stirring once, until soft and tender, 15 to 20 minutes. Using tongs, transfer the vegetables to a serving platter or bowl; pour over 1 to 2 Tbsp of the cooking liquid and discard the rest. While still warm, toss with the mint and serve.

ROASTED BROCCOLI WITH SHALLOTS AND LEMON

Often when I am hosting Shabbat dinner, I have this last-minute, late-Friday-afternoon freak-out that there won't be enough food. (Maybe you are familiar with this feeling?) That is when I turn to this dish. It takes roasted broccoli, which is wonderful all on its own, and adds a mix of sweet cooked shallots and tart lemon. It's an easy, high-impact combination that complements nearly everything.

SERVES 6

2 LB/910 G BROCCOLI, CUT INTO 1-IN/ 2.5-CM FLORETS

6 TBSP/90 ML EXTRA-VIRGIN OLIVE OIL

KOSHER SALT

4 LARGE SHALLOTS, FINELY CHOPPED

1 TSP SUGAR

ZEST OF 1 LEMON

1 TBSP FRESH LEMON JUICE

FRESHLY GROUND BLACK PEPPER

1. Preheat the oven to 425°F/220°C and line a large rimmed baking sheet with aluminum foil. Spread the broccoli on the prepared baking sheet in a single layer and drizzle with 4 Tbsp/60 ml of the olive oil. Sprinkle with a little salt and toss to coat. Roast, stirring occasionally, until tender and browned in spots, 20 to 25 minutes. Remove from the oven and let cool slightly. Transfer to a serving bowl.

2. Meanwhile, heat the remaining 2 Tbsp olive oil in a medium pan set over medium heat. Add the shallots and sugar and cook, stirring every few minutes, until softened and well browned, 15 to 20 minutes. Add the shallots, lemon zest, and lemon juice to the broccoli. Season with salt and pepper and toss to combine. Taste and add more lemon juice, if desired. Serve warm.

ROASTED CAULIFLOWER AND RED ONION

Oven roasting brings out the best in most cold-weather vegetables, concentrating their flavors and leaving them singed and softened. But of all the vegetables that benefit from the high-heat treatment, I love cauliflower most. The crisp florets grow sweet and gloriously tender without losing their "little tree" shape. Paired with slices of red onion and whole cloves of earthy garlic, this might be your new winter favorite.

SERVES 4

2 LB/910 G CAULIFLOWER, CORED AND CUT INTO 1-IN/2.5-CM FLORETS

1 MEDIUM RED ONION, HALVED THROUGH THE ROOT AND CUT INTO ½-IN/12-MM SLICES

12 GARLIC CLOVES, PEELED

4 SPRIGS FRESH THYME

¼ CUP/60 ML EXTRA-VIRGIN OLIVE OIL

KOSHER SALT OR COARSE SEA SALT AND FRESHLY GROUND BLACK PEPPER

1. Preheat the oven to 425°F/220°C. Place the cauliflower, onion, garlic, and thyme in a large bowl. Drizzle with the olive oil, sprinkle generously with salt and pepper, and toss to coat.

2. Transfer the vegetables to a large rimmed baking sheet and spread into a single layer. Roast, stirring occasionally, until tender and browned in spots, 25 to 35 minutes. Taste and season with more salt and pepper, if desired. Serve hot.

FRIED CAULIFLOWER WITH CREAMY CILANTRO SAUCE

Fried cauliflower is a popular side dish in Sephardi cuisine. This version breaks from the custom of serving it simply sprinkled with salt and squeezed with a little lemon juice. Instead, the crispy florets come paired with a creamy, spicy, and entirely addictive cilantro sauce. Think of it as the Jewish answer to the jalapeño popper.

SERVES 4 TO 6

FOR THE SAUCE

2 CUPS/80 G ROUGHLY CHOPPED FRESH CILANTRO

1 JALAPEÑO, SEEDED AND ROUGHLY CHOPPED

½ TSP LEMON ZEST

2 TBSP FRESH LEMON JUICE

1 SMALL GARLIC CLOVE

1 TBSP EXTRA-VIRGIN OLIVE OIL

¼ TSP SALT

FRESHLY GROUND BLACK PEPPER

1 CUP/240 ML FULL-FAT OR LOW-FAT PLAIN YOGURT

¼ CUP/60 G MAYONNAISE

FOR THE CAULIFLOWER

2 LB/910 G CAULIFLOWER, CORED AND CUT INTO 1-IN/2.5-CM FLORETS

VEGETABLE OIL FOR FRYING

1½ CUPS/185 G ALL-PURPOSE FLOUR

1 TSP TURMERIC

SALT

½ TSP FRESHLY GROUND BLACK PEPPER

5 EGGS

1. Make the sauce: Combine the cilantro, jalapeño, lemon zest, lemon juice, garlic, olive oil, and salt in a food processor. Season with pepper and process until combined and the mixture resembles a wet pesto, scraping down the sides of the bowl as necessary. Add the yogurt and mayonnaise and process until smooth. Transfer to a bowl, cover, and refrigerate for up to 1 day.

2. Make the cauliflower: Bring a large pot of water to a boil over high heat. Meanwhile, make an ice bath by adding equal parts ice and water to a separate large bowl. Add the cauliflower to the boiling water and cook until just tender, about 5 minutes. Drain and immediately transfer to the ice bath; drain again and dry thoroughly with paper towels. Don't skimp on the drying, or the cauliflower won't crisp properly when you fry it.

3. Heat ½ in/12 mm of vegetable oil in a large saucepan set over medium heat until shimmering, and line a baking sheet with two layers of paper towels. Meanwhile, stir together the flour, turmeric, ½ tsp salt, and the pepper in a shallow baking dish. Whisk the eggs in a separate bowl.

4. Working in batches, dip the cauliflower in the flour mixture, shaking off excess. Dip in the egg, then again in the flour. Fry, flipping once, until golden and crisp, 2 to 3 minutes total. (If the cauliflower is browning too quickly, lower the heat slightly.) Use a slotted spoon to transfer to the paper towel–lined baking sheet to drain, and sprinkle lightly with a little more salt. Serve hot with the cilantro sauce on the side for dipping.

SEPHARDI LEEK PATTIES

Sephardi Jewish cuisine is filled with all kinds of fritters and fried goodies. These crispy leek patties, keftes de prasa, which are traditionally served on Hanukkah and Passover (bound together with matzo meal instead of bread crumbs), are among my favorites. They have the salty, oil-kissed flavor found in any great fritter, with a gentle fiery kick from the leeks that sets them apart.

SERVES 4 TO 6

3 MEDIUM LEEKS, WHITE AND LIGHT GREEN PARTS, THINLY SLICED

2 TSP SALT

3 EGGS, LIGHTLY BEATEN

½ CUP/55 G PLAIN BREAD CRUMBS

¼ CUP/10 G ROUGHLY CHOPPED FRESH CILANTRO

¼ CUP/10 G ROUGHLY CHOPPED MINT LEAVES

¼ TSP RED PEPPER FLAKES

½ TSP GROUND CINNAMON

½ TSP GROUND CORIANDER

½ TSP FRESHLY GROUND BLACK PEPPER

VEGETABLE OIL FOR FRYING

LEMON WEDGES FOR SERVING

1. Bring a medium pot of water to a boil. Add the leeks and 1 tsp of the salt, turn the heat to medium, and simmer until tender, 6 to 8 minutes. Drain, rinse with cool water, and drain again, then wrap the leeks in a dish towel and squeeze out any excess water.

2. Combine the leeks, the remaining 1 tsp salt, eggs, bread crumbs, cilantro, mint, red pepper flakes, cinnamon, coriander, and pepper in a large bowl and mix well.

3. Heat ¼ in/6 mm of vegetable oil in a large pan set over medium heat until shimmering, and line a baking sheet with two layers of paper towels. Working in batches, drop the batter by the heaping tablespoonful into the pan and gently press with a spatula to flatten. Fry, turning once, until golden brown on both sides, 3 to 4 minutes total. Use a slotted spoon to transfer the patties to the paper towel–lined baking sheet to drain.

4. Serve hot with lemon wedges for squeezing. (The leek patties can also be cooked in advance, allowed to cool, and stored in the refrigerator or freezer. When ready to serve, place them on a baking sheet and warm them in a 400°F/200°C oven until crisp.)

POTATO LATKES WITH APPLE-DATE CHUTNEY AND CINNAMON SOUR CREAM

Latkes are, without question, my favorite Jewish food. The fried potato pancakes, which are traditionally served by Ashkenazi Jews on Hanukkah (see page 340), are both incredibly delicious and also have serious nostalgic appeal. My mom made them nearly every year, and hers always seemed to strike that elusive balance of crisp, lacy edges and a tender, savory center. My brother and I would eat them in a frenzy, burning hot from the pan and crowned with a dollop of cool sour cream and a spoonful of her homemade applesauce.

Now that I am the primary latke-fryer in my house, I have tried to stay true to my mom's basic latke-making methodologies. Why mess with perfection? But when it comes to toppings, I believe there is room for experimentation. My apple-date chutney and cinnamon sour cream both take a playful approach to tradition, while bridging the sweet-savory divide. If you haven't made latkes before, or want a refresher, check out the deep and shallow frying tips on page 122.

SERVES 4

FOR THE CHUTNEY

1 LB/455 G CRISP, TART APPLES, PEELED, QUARTERED, CORED, AND CUT INTO ½-IN/12-MM CHUNKS

⅓ CUP/50 G FINELY CHOPPED DATES

⅓ CUP/50 G FINELY CHOPPED YELLOW ONION

ONE 2-IN/5-CM PIECE FRESH GINGER, PEELED AND FINELY CHOPPED

¼ CUP/60 ML RED WINE VINEGAR

2 TBSP APPLE CIDER VINEGAR

½ CUP/100 G PACKED LIGHT BROWN SUGAR

2 TBSP HONEY

ZEST OF 1 LEMON

½ TSP GROUND ALLSPICE

FOR THE CINNAMON SOUR CREAM

½ CUP/120 ML SOUR CREAM

½ TSP GROUND CINNAMON

1 TSP PURE MAPLE SYRUP

FOR THE LATKES

2 LB/910 G RUSSET POTATOES, SCRUBBED AND UNPEELED

1 MEDIUM YELLOW ONION

2 EGGS, LIGHTLY BEATEN

⅓ CUP/40 G ALL-PURPOSE FLOUR

1½ TSP SALT

½ TSP FRESHLY GROUND BLACK PEPPER

VEGETABLE OIL FOR FRYING

CONTINUED

1. Make the chutney: Stir together the apples, dates, onion, ginger, red wine vinegar, cider vinegar, brown sugar, honey, lemon zest, and allspice in a medium saucepan set over medium-high heat. Bring to a boil, then turn the heat to low, cover, and simmer, stirring occasionally, until the apples are very tender, about 30 minutes. Uncover, raise the heat to medium, and simmer, stirring often, until the liquid reduces to a syrup, 10 to 15 minutes. Remove from the heat and let cool completely. (Store for up to 1 day, covered, in the refrigerator, but let come to room temperature before topping the latkes.)

2. Make the cinnamon sour cream: Stir together the sour cream, cinnamon, and maple syrup in a small bowl. (Cover and refrigerate for up to 1 day.)

3. Make the latkes: Grate the potatoes and onion on the large holes of a box grater, or cut them into quarters and shred in a food processor fitted with the shredding blade. Working in batches, wrap the grated potatoes and onion in a dish towel or several layers of paper towels and squeeze as much water as you can out of them. Don't skimp; really get your squeeze on here.

4. Place the shredded, squeezed potatoes and onion in a large bowl. Add the eggs, flour, salt, and pepper and mix with a wooden spoon until the ingredients are fully incorporated.

5. Heat ¼ in/6 mm of vegetable oil in a large pan set over medium-high heat until shimmering but not smoking, and line a large rimmed baking sheet with two layers of paper towels. Working in batches of three or four, drop the batter by the ¼-cup into the pan and gently press with a spatula to flatten. Fry, turning once, until browned on both sides and cooked through, 8 to 10 minutes total. Continue frying latkes with the remaining batter, adding additional oil to the pan if necessary and adjusting the heat if the latkes are browning too quickly or not quickly enough. With a slotted spoon, transfer the latkes to the paper towel–lined baking sheet to drain.

6. Serve hot, topped with apple-date chutney and cinnamon sour cream. Or, let the latkes cool and store in the refrigerator or freezer. When ready to serve, arrange in a single layer on a baking sheet and reheat in a 400°F/200°C oven (see page 123).

WISE FRY: DEEP-FRYING LIKE A PRO

Hanukkah is often called the Festival of Lights, but it could just as easily be called the festival of fried foods. Oil, after all, plays an important role in the Hanukkah story. As the legend goes, after the Maccabees recaptured the Temple in Jerusalem from the Syrian Greeks, they found just enough oil to light the Grand Menorah for one day. And yet miraculously, the oil managed to last for eight days. That's why people celebrate Hanukkah by lighting a menorah in their homes and eating an impressive variety of fried, oily foods. For more on the Hanukkah story, see page 340.

Fresh, crackly edged latkes, fluffy sufganiyot (doughnuts), and other Hanukkah fritters are entirely worth the time, effort, and oil required to make them. But if you have never tried deep-frying, or only attempt it once a year, all that hot oil can be intimidating. Before you crank up the heat, read through these tips to ensure your Hanukkah fry fest is a delicious success.

DEEP-FRYING VS. SHALLOW FRYING

High-temperature frying includes deep-frying, where foods are completely submerged in oil, and shallow frying, when foods are only partially submerged and get flipped during the cooking process. Both methods require a heavy-bottomed pot, which helps ensure the oil heats up evenly. But, true to the name, the vessel used for deep-frying should have deep sides that can hold lots of oil without threatening to spill over when you add the food.

TEMPERATURE

The primary factor determining whether your fried food ends up light and crispy or soggy and leaden is the heat level of the oil. Hot oil helps sear a protective layer around the food, preventing oil from penetrating its surface while it cooks. But if things get too hot, your food can burn before the inside cooks completely. Use a deep-fry thermometer to keep track of your oil's temperature (325°F to 375°F/165°C to 190°C is typically a good range) and adjust the flame as necessary.

CHOOSE YOUR OIL WISELY

Refined, mild-tasting cooking oils, including peanut, sunflower, and safflower, are known for their high smoke points (the temperature at which oil starts to break down and emit harsh fumes). That means they can handle the temperatures necessary to get foods sizzling, making them ideal for both shallow and deep-frying. Unrefined extra-virgin olive oil and butter are delicious, but are better suited for flavoring dishes or salad dressings than for frying.

DON'T CROWD THE PAN

Frying takes time and patience, and it can be tempting to fill your pan with food to be fried in order to lessen the number of batches you need to fry. But adding food lowers the oil's temperature—add too much at once, and the temperature can dip into the greasy zone. Work in batches of three or four at a time and you will end up with crispier, tastier results.

KEEP THINGS DRY

Water and oil famously don't mix. This adage is especially true when it comes to high-heat frying. Adding watery foods to a frying pan or pot risks dangerous splattering and sputtering. Before frying, remove as much water from food as possible. Squeeze grated potatoes and onions dry in a dish towel or a double thickness of paper towels before adding them to latke batter, and pat foods dry before slipping them (carefully!) in the oil.

REHEATING

Shallow- and deep-fried foods taste best just out of the pan. But some fried foods, particularly potato latkes and other fritters, reheat and recrisp quite well, making them an ideal make-ahead food. Let the cooked latkes or fritters cool, wrap them well in plastic wrap, and store in an airtight container in the refrigerator for up to 2 days or in the freezer for up to 2 weeks. To reheat, preheat the oven to 400°F/200°C. Arrange the latkes or fritters in a single layer on a large rimmed baking sheet and cook until they are crisp and warmed through, 15 to 20 minutes. Stay away from reheating in the microwave, which promotes steam, resulting in soggy fritters.

DISPOSE OF OIL SAFELY

Never dispose of used cooking oil by pouring it down the kitchen sink or in the toilet, where it can cause serious backups in your home's plumbing system and even clog sewer systems. Instead, let the oil cool, then transfer it to a sturdy container with a lid (like the bottle it came in, a coffee can, or a large yogurt container), and throw it in the garbage. Better yet, find out if your city collects and recycles used cooking oil.

BEET LATKES WITH CHIVE GOAT CHEESE

During the past decade or so, home cooks have gotten very creative with their Hanukkah latkes. Today it is nearly as common to find the oil-crisped pancakes made from sweet potato, carrot, parsnip, apple, or zucchini as from the traditional potato. And it is not unusual to find latkes flavored with curry, cumin, cayenne, and other spices. I personally love making beet latkes. The deep-red root vegetable adds glorious color and sweet, earthy flavor to the fried Hanukkah dish. Topped with a mix of goat cheese and sour cream stirred with chives, they are a classy rendition of the holiday favorite.

SERVES 6

FOR THE CHIVE GOAT CHEESE

4 OZ/115 G FRESH GOAT CHEESE, AT ROOM TEMPERATURE

⅓ CUP/75 ML SOUR CREAM

¼ CUP/10 G SNIPPED FRESH CHIVES

FOR THE LATKES

1 LARGE BEET, PEELED

3 MEDIUM CARROTS, PEELED

½ YELLOW ONION, QUARTERED

1 GARLIC CLOVE, MINCED OR PUSHED THROUGH A PRESS

¼ CUP/30 G ALL-PURPOSE FLOUR

½ TSP BAKING POWDER

1 EGG, LIGHTLY BEATEN

1 TSP SALT

½ TSP FRESHLY GROUND BLACK PEPPER

VEGETABLE OIL FOR FRYING

SNIPPED FRESH CHIVES, FOR SERVING

1. Make the chive goat cheese: Stir together the goat cheese, sour cream, and chives in a medium bowl until fully combined. Set aside at room temperature until ready to serve.

2. Make the latkes: Using a food processor fitted with the shredding disk, shred the beet, carrots, and onion. Working in batches, wrap the grated vegetables in a dish towel or several layers of paper towels and squeeze as much water as you can out of them. Don't skimp; really get your squeeze on here.

3. Place the shredded, squeezed vegetables in a large bowl. Add the garlic, flour, baking powder, egg, salt, and pepper and mix with a wooden spoon until the ingredients are fully incorporated.

4. Heat ¼ in/6 mm of vegetable oil in a large pan set over medium heat until shimmering but not smoking, and line a large rimmed baking sheet with two layers of paper towels. Working in batches of four or five, drop heaping tablespoons of batter into the pan and gently press with a spatula to flatten. Fry, turning once, until crisp on both sides and cooked through, 4 to 5 minutes total. Continue frying latkes with the remaining batter, adding additional oil to the pan if necessary and adjusting the heat if the latkes are browning too quickly or not quickly enough. With a slotted spoon, transfer the latkes to the paper towel–lined baking sheet to drain.

5. Serve hot, topped with the goat cheese mixture and a sprinkle of chives. Or, let the latkes cool and store in the refrigerator or freezer. When ready to serve, arrange in a single layer on a baking sheet and reheat in a 400°F/200°C oven (see page 123).

FRIED GREEN OLIVES

This crunchy, briny snack is inspired by the highly addictive fried-olive appetizer served at Balaboosta, Israeli-born chef Einat Admony's popular New York City restaurant. Serve them alone or like Admony does—on top of a thick pool of labneh (the tangy Middle Eastern yogurt) and sprinkled with spicy harissa. With so few ingredients in the mix, each one counts, so use the best-quality olives you can find.

SERVES 6 AS AN APPETIZER

¼ CUP/30 G ALL-PURPOSE FLOUR

1 TSP SMOKED OR SWEET PAPRIKA

1 EGG, LIGHTLY BEATEN

¾ CUP/60 G PANKO BREAD CRUMBS

40 PITTED GREEN OLIVES, DRAINED AND PATTED DRY

VEGETABLE OIL FOR FRYING

1. Stir together the flour and paprika in a small bowl. Place the egg in a second small bowl and the bread crumbs in a third small bowl. Dredge the olives in the flour, shake off the excess and dip in the egg wash, then dredge in the bread crumbs, turning to coat.

2. Heat ¼ in/6 mm of vegetable oil in a medium saucepan set over medium heat until shimmering, and line a large plate with two layers of paper towels. Working in batches, fry the olives, turning once, until crisp and golden brown, 2 to 3 minutes total. Use a slotted spoon to transfer the olives to the paper towel–lined plate to drain. Serve hot.

POTATO-LEEK KUGEL

My husband, Yoshie, is a potato kugel fiend. As a musician, he gets his fill of the savory potato and onion squares by performing at Jewish weddings. But while he will never turn down a piece of his favorite Eastern European Jewish food, he admits that the catered versions tend to be excessively greasy and dense. This version delivers the crisp edges and soft, rich center he loves without being overly heavy. The browned leeks and chopped fresh thyme give the kugel a touch of potato-leek soup flavor.

SERVES 6

6 TBSP/90 ML VEGETABLE OIL OR SCHMALTZ (PAGE 318)

3 MEDIUM LEEKS, WHITE AND LIGHT GREEN PARTS, THINLY SLICED

KOSHER SALT

2 LB/910 G RUSSET POTATOES, PEELED

1 SMALL YELLOW ONION

3 EGGS, LIGHTLY BEATEN

1 TBSP CHOPPED FRESH THYME

1 TSP GARLIC POWDER

¼ TSP FRESHLY GROUND BLACK PEPPER

1. Preheat the oven to 375°F/190°C and grease the bottom and sides of an 8-in/20-cm square baking pan with 2 Tbsp of the vegetable oil.

2. Heat 2 Tbsp vegetable oil in a medium pan set over medium heat until shimmering. Add the leeks and a pinch of salt and cook, stirring occasionally, until softened and browned, about 10 minutes. Remove from the heat and let cool slightly in the pan.

3. Meanwhile, cut 2 of the potatoes into 1-in/2.5-cm chunks and place in a medium saucepan. Cover with cold water by 1 in/2.5 cm and set the pan over medium-high heat. Bring to a boil and cook until the potatoes are tender, 12 to 15 minutes. Drain well, transfer to a large bowl, and mash with a potato masher.

4. Cut the remaining 2 potatoes and the onion into quarters and grate on the large holes of a box grater or with a food processor fitted with the shredding blade. Working in batches, wrap the grated potatoes and onion in a dish towel or several layers of paper towels and squeeze as much water as you can out of them. Don't skimp, really get your squeeze on here. Add to the mashed potatoes, along with the cooked leeks, the remaining 2 Tbsp oil, the eggs, thyme, garlic powder, 2 tsp salt, and the pepper; mix until thoroughly combined.

5. Put the prepared baking pan in the oven and preheat for 10 minutes. Carefully remove from the oven, transfer the potato mixture to the pan (it should sizzle when it hits the hot pan), and smooth the top with a spatula. Bake until golden brown and cooked through, 60 to 75 minutes. Serve hot.

BUTTERNUT SQUASH KUGEL WITH CRISPY SHALLOTS

Kugels are the Jewish equivalent of soul food—warm, nourishing, and homey. The Ashkenazi baked puddings originated more than 800 years ago in southern Germany. Over time, they evolved from a basic steamed dumpling cooked inside a Shabbat stew (the word *kugel* means "ball") to a stand-alone side dish that can be made from potatoes, noodles, farfel, or practically any other starch. They are typically served at home on Shabbat or the holidays, but can also be found at some delicatessens and other Jewish eateries. This take on kugel tops puréed butternut squash flavored with orange zest and ginger with crispy fried shallots for a dish that beautifully straddles both the sweet and savory, as well as the creamy and crunchy divide.

SERVES 6

1 MEDIUM BUTTERNUT SQUASH, HALVED LENGTHWISE AND SEEDED

VEGETABLE OIL, FOR BRUSHING AND FRYING

2 TBSP MELTED UNSALTED BUTTER OR COCONUT OIL

⅓ CUP/65 G PACKED LIGHT BROWN SUGAR

2 EGGS, LIGHTLY BEATEN

½ CUP/60 G ALL-PURPOSE FLOUR

ZEST OF 1 ORANGE

½ TSP GROUND GINGER

KOSHER SALT AND FRESHLY GROUND BLACK PEPPER

6 SMALL SHALLOTS, THINLY SLICED AND RINGS SEPARATED

1. Preheat the oven to 400°F/200°C and line a large rimmed baking sheet with aluminum foil. Place the squash halves, cut-side up, on the prepared baking sheet, and brush the tops with about 1 Tbsp vegetable oil. Roast until the flesh is very tender and can be easily pierced with a knife, 50 to 70 minutes. Remove from the oven and let cool to the touch. Scoop the cooked squash into a large bowl, discarding the skin, and mash well with a potato masher. (Store the mashed squash, covered, in the refrigerator for up to 1 day.)

2. Turn the oven to 350°F/180°C and oil a 9-in/23-cm round baking pan. Combine the squash, melted butter, brown sugar, eggs, flour, orange zest, ginger, 1 tsp salt, and ½ tsp pepper in a bowl. Transfer the mixture to the prepared baking pan and smooth with a spatula. Bake, uncovered, until the kugel sets and lightly browns around the edges, 30 to 40 minutes.

3. Meanwhile, fill a medium pan with about ¼ in/6 mm of vegetable oil. Line a plate with paper towels. Add the shallots to the cold pan and set over medium-high heat. Cook, stirring occasionally, until the shallots are browned and crispy, 6 to 8 minutes. (Watch carefully so they don't burn.) Scoop the shallots from the pan with a slotted spoon, place on the paper towel–lined plate and let drain, then sprinkle lightly with salt. When ready to serve, scatter the crispy shallots on top of the kugel and scoop onto plates. Serve warm.

FENNEL GRATIN

File this under the "who knew?" category: Jews helped to usher in many of Italy's most iconic vegetables, including eggplants, artichokes, and fennel. Originally introduced by Arab traders traveling from the Near East and North Africa in the sixteenth century, these vegetables were largely ignored by the general public. Jewish Italian cooks, however, took to them quickly—partly out of necessity, since they tended to have fewer means—and created intriguing dishes with them. Within a few generations, they began to catch on in the mainstream and have since become an indispensable part of what we think of as Italian cuisine. This dish takes one of those vegetables, fennel, and braises it until it turns velvety, savory, and entirely irresistible.

SERVES 4 TO 6

4 MEDIUM FENNEL BULBS, QUARTERED AND CORED

2 TBSP UNSALTED BUTTER, CUT INTO SMALL PIECES

6 GARLIC CLOVES, THINLY SLICED

½ TSP DRIED THYME

KOSHER SALT AND FRESHLY GROUND BLACK PEPPER

1½ CUPS/360 ML VEGETABLE BROTH

3 TBSP HALF-AND-HALF

⅛ TSP GROUND NUTMEG

¼ CUP/20 G GRATED PARMESAN

1. Preheat the oven to 375°F/190°C. Arrange the fennel quarters in a Dutch oven or baking dish, and scatter the butter, garlic, and thyme on top. Season generously with salt and pepper. Add the broth, cover (with a lid for the Dutch oven and aluminum foil for the baking dish), and bake until just tender, about 45 minutes. Uncover and continue baking until very tender, about 30 minutes. Remove from the oven and drain off or spoon out most of the cooking liquid, leaving about ¼ cup/60 ml.

2. Preheat the broiler. Whisk together the half-and-half and nutmeg in a small bowl and pour over the fennel. Sprinkle with the Parmesan. Broil until the cheese is bubbling, 2 to 3 minutes. (Watch carefully so it does not burn.) Serve hot.

MANGO-GINGER TZIMMES

Tzimmes, the Ashkenazi root vegetable and dried fruit stew that is traditionally served on Rosh Hashanah (see page 334) and Sukkot (see page 338), is a very polarizing dish. Its critics tend to shun it wholeheartedly, turned off by the unusual combination of fruit and vegetables and the thick, syrupy texture. I happen to love tzimmes for exactly these reasons, but understand that it is not everyone's cup of tea. If you are a tzimmes fan or an open-minded first-timer, I think you will be delighted by this version, which amps up the traditional dish with mango and three different kinds of ginger: fresh, ground, and crystallized. If not, then no hard feelings—the tzimmes lovers in your midst will be thrilled to eat your share!

SERVES 6 TO 8

8 OZ/225 G CARROTS, PEELED AND CUT INTO 1-IN/2.5-CM PIECES

2 LB/910 G SWEET POTATOES, PEELED AND CUT INTO 1½-IN/4-CM PIECES

⅓ CUP/80 ML MANGO JUICE

ZEST OF 1 LIME

2 TBSP FRESH LIME JUICE

¼ CUP/95 G HONEY

1 TBSP LIGHT BROWN SUGAR

½ TSP GROUND CINNAMON

½ TSP GROUND GINGER

2 TSP FINELY GRATED FRESH GINGER

3 TBSP FINELY CHOPPED CRYSTALLIZED GINGER

½ TSP KOSHER SALT

2 RIPE MANGOES, PEELED AND CUT INTO 1-IN/2.5-CM PIECES

1 CUP/225 G PITTED PRUNES OR DRIED APRICOTS (OR HALF OF EACH)

1. Preheat the oven to 350°F/180°C. Bring a large saucepan of water to a boil over high heat. Add the carrots and sweet potatoes and cook until tender, but not completely soft, 12 to 15 minutes. Drain, rinse with cool water, and drain again.

2. Meanwhile, in a large bowl, whisk together the mango juice, lime zest, lime juice, honey, brown sugar, cinnamon, ground ginger, grated ginger, crystallized ginger, and salt. Add the cooked carrots and sweet potatoes along with the mangoes and prunes, and gently toss to coat.

3. Transfer the mixture to a 9-by-13-in/23-by-33-cm baking dish. Cover with aluminum foil and bake until tender and juicy, 25 to 30 minutes. Remove the foil, gently stir, and continue baking, uncovered, until the juices reduce slightly, 10 to 15 minutes. Remove from the oven and transfer to a bowl. Just before serving, gently stir to coat the tzimmes with the pan juices. Serve warm.

CARAWAY CABBAGE STRUDEL

In 2005, journalist, screenwriter, director, and unabashed food lover Nora Ephron wrote an ode in the *New York Times* to a fading old-world food: cabbage strudel. "It has a buttery, flaky, crispy strudel crust," she wrote, "with a moist filling of sautéed cabbage that's simultaneously sweet, savory, and completely unexpected, like all good things." At that point, my own experience with strudel was limited to the jam-filled Pillsbury Toaster Strudel pastries I squeezed packaged frosting on as a kid. And most of the Hungarian strudels I had heard about—which are traditionally served on Sukkot when stuffed foods dominate the table—came filled with cherries, apples, apricot, or other decidedly sweet things. But reading Ephron's words, I immediately yearned to try this beguiling version.

Traditionally, strudel dough is homemade and stretched into a large, impossibly thin sheet (often overtaking an entire tabletop!) before being filled. Today, readily available phyllo dough eliminates that arduous step. Despite the shortcut, I think this caraway-scented take on cabbage strudel would have delighted Ephron as much as it does me. The filling also makes a delicious side dish on its own, without the pastry and extra butter. Just follow the recipe through step 1 and serve warm alongside baked fish or tofu.

SERVES 4

10 TBSP/140 G UNSALTED BUTTER

1 LARGE YELLOW ONION, FINELY CHOPPED

½ SMALL HEAD GREEN CABBAGE, CORED AND SHREDDED

1¼ TSP KOSHER SALT

½ TSP FRESHLY GROUND BLACK PEPPER

1 TSP SUGAR

½ TSP CARAWAY SEEDS

7 SHEETS THAWED FROZEN PHYLLO DOUGH

1. Melt 2 Tbsp of the butter in a large pan set over medium heat until foaming. Add the onion and cook until softened, 6 to 8 minutes. Add the cabbage, cover, and cook, stirring occasionally, until just tender, about 10 minutes. Stir in the salt, pepper, sugar, and caraway seeds and cook, uncovered, until very tender, 5 to 7 minutes. Remove from the heat and let cool slightly. Drain off any excess liquid.

2. Preheat the oven to 400°F/200°C and line a large rimmed baking sheet with parchment paper.

3. Melt the remaining 8 Tbsp/115 g butter in a small pan set over low heat (or in the microwave); set aside. Lay a piece of parchment paper on a flat surface and place one sheet of phyllo on top. (Keep the other phyllo sheets covered with a damp dish towel.) Brush the phyllo with melted butter. Top with another sheet of phyllo and brush with melted butter. Repeat until all 7 phyllo sheets are used.

CONTINUED

4. Spoon the cabbage mixture in a 2-in/5-cm line along one of the short ends of the phyllo, leaving about ½ in/12 mm of the phyllo uncovered along the edge. Using the parchment paper to help, roll the dough around the cabbage, tucking the filling inside, until it's a long, stuffed cylinder. Brush the top and sides with more melted butter.

5. Use a sturdy spatula to carefully transfer the strudel to the prepared baking sheet and bake until golden, 20 to 30 minutes. Use a serrated knife to cut into slices. Serve warm or at room temperature.

CHAPTER FIVE

NOODLES, MATZO, GRAINS, AND BEANS

CREAMY NOODLES WITH LEMON, MINT, AND CHIVES

Egg noodles stirred with cottage cheese and sour cream was a favorite dish among the Jews of Eastern Europe. Simple, filling, and nourishing, it kept families happy on a budget. The picky six-year-old in me—the one who for years insisted on eating nothing but plain buttered pasta—is completely smitten. But my adult palate cries out for more flavor. That's why I dressed up this hearty dish of noodles and cottage cheese with sautéed shallots, lemon zest, chopped fresh herbs, and a hit of red pepper flakes. Served with a green salad and a glass of wine, it is one of my go-to weeknight dinners.

SERVES 6

12 OZ/340 G DRIED WIDE EGG NOODLES

2 TBSP UNSALTED BUTTER

3 MEDIUM SHALLOTS, FINELY CHOPPED

1 TSP SALT

½ TSP RED PEPPER FLAKES

2 SMALL GARLIC CLOVES, MINCED OR PUSHED THROUGH A PRESS

1¼ CUPS/310 G FULL-FAT OR LOW-FAT COTTAGE CHEESE

½ CUP/120 ML FULL-FAT OR LOW-FAT SOUR CREAM OR GREEK YOGURT

½ TSP LEMON ZEST

2 TBSP FINELY CHOPPED FRESH MINT

¼ CUP/10 G FINELY CHOPPED FRESH CHIVES, PLUS MORE FOR SERVING

FRESHLY GROUND BLACK PEPPER

1. Bring a large pot of generously salted water to a boil. Add the noodles and cook, stirring occasionally, until al dente, about 8 minutes (or follow the timing instructions on the package). Drain well and let cool slightly.

2. Meanwhile, melt the butter until foaming in a medium saucepan set over medium heat. Add the shallots and ½ tsp of the salt and cook, stirring occasionally, until softened, 5 to 7 minutes. Add the red pepper flakes and garlic and cook, stirring often, until fragrant, about 1 minute. Remove from the heat and transfer the mixture to a large bowl.

3. Add the cottage cheese, sour cream, lemon zest, mint, chives, remaining ½ tsp salt, and a generous pinch of pepper to the bowl and stir well to combine. Add the drained noodles and toss with tongs to fully coat. Sprinkle with chives. Serve hot.

SWEET NOODLE KUGEL WITH DRIED CHERRIES AND FIGS

Noodle kugel is just the best. The Ashkenazi baked pudding made from egg noodles (called *lokshen* in Yiddish) is a study in gorgeous excess. The dish comes enriched with sour cream, butter, eggs, and cottage cheese or pot cheese, and is sweetened with cinnamon and sugar, resulting in a rustic and decadent treat. Many people serve noodle kugel as a side dish at lunch or dinner on Shabbat and the holidays, but I have always found it too sweet to accompany savory foods. Instead, I prefer to serve it as a substantial brunch dish, or as part of a Yom Kippur break fast meal (see page 336).

My take on noodle kugel includes dried cherries and figs—two tart and jammy fruits that offset the pudding's richness. It gets topped off with a dusting of bittersweet chocolate shavings, which are optional but so good. You can certainly substitute low-fat cottage cheese and sour cream in this kugel if you like, but I would not recommend it. What I do recommend is using the best-quality full-fat ingredients you can find, inviting friends over to help you eat, savoring every glorious bite, and then giving yourself several months to recover before making it again.

SERVES 8 TO 10

12 OZ/340 G DRIED WIDE
EGG NOODLES

½ CUP/85 G DRIED CHERRIES

4 TBSP/55 G UNSALTED BUTTER,
MELTED

2 CUPS/435 G COTTAGE CHEESE

2 CUPS/435 G SOUR CREAM

5 EGGS

¾ CUP/150 G SUGAR

¼ TSP KOSHER SALT

1 TSP VANILLA EXTRACT

½ CUP/70 G FINELY CHOPPED DRIED
BLACK MISSION FIGS

GROUND CINNAMON FOR TOPPING

1 OZ/30 G BITTERSWEET BAKING
CHOCOLATE (OPTIONAL)

1. Preheat the oven to 350°F/180°C and lightly grease a 9-by-13-in/23-by-33-cm baking dish.

2. Bring a medium pot of water to a boil. Add the noodles and cook until just short of al dente, 5 to 7 minutes. Drain, reserving about 1 cup/240 ml of the cooking liquid. Place the cherries in a small bowl and pour the reserved pasta cooking liquid over them. Let stand until plumped, about 5 minutes. Drain the cherries and set aside.

3. In a stand mixer or using a handheld electric mixer and a large bowl, beat together the melted butter, cottage cheese, sour cream, eggs, sugar, salt, and vanilla on low speed until combined and smooth. Stir in the cooked noodles, cherries, and figs. Pour the mixture into the prepared baking dish.

CONTINUED

4. Bake until the kugel is set and the top is golden with some darker brown noodle tips, 50 to 60 minutes. (If an air bubble appears in the kugel while baking, deflate it with a small, sharp paring knife.) Remove from the oven and transfer to a wire rack to cool for 20 to 30 minutes.

5. Just before serving, sprinkle the kugel with cinnamon. If desired, use a vegetable peeler to shave the baking chocolate into curls and sprinkle over the warm kugel. (Do not top the kugel with chocolate when it is just-out-of-the-oven hot or it will melt.) Slice and serve warm or at room temperature.

KASHA VARNISHKES

Here are three tips for all the aspiring old Jewish men out there: (1) cultivate an enormous repertoire of jokes (preferably dirty ones), (2) pull your pants up above your waist and attach them to suspenders, and (3) eat kasha varnishkes. All kidding aside, despite its old-school appeal, kasha varnishkes is a remarkable side dish, with three distinct parts (chewy bow tie noodles, fluffy toasted buckwheat groats, and heaps of caramelized onions) that together make something sublime.

Some critics dismiss kasha varnishkes as a dry and tasteless dish, but that simply means they have not had it made properly. And by properly, I mean made with a delightfully obscene amount of fat. You can add a little chopped fresh parsley for color if you'd like. But like many Ashkenazi foods, the dish is perfect served as is: plain and shimmering with a gorgeous slick of oil or schmaltz.

SERVES 8

NOTE

Kasha, also known as toasted buckwheat, has a distinctly nutty smell and a reddish-brown color. Raw buckwheat is lighter in color with no strong aroma, and is not suitable for this dish.

1 LB/455 G FARFALLE (BOW-TIE NOODLES)

VEGETABLE OIL FOR DRIZZLING, PLUS ½ CUP/120 ML OIL OR SCHMALTZ (PAGE 318)

3 LARGE YELLOW ONIONS, FINELY CHOPPED

KOSHER SALT

2 CUPS/480 ML CHICKEN OR VEGETABLE BROTH

1 CUP/180 G KASHA

FRESHLY GROUND BLACK PEPPER

ROUGHLY CHOPPED FRESH PARSLEY FOR SERVING (OPTIONAL)

1. Bring a large pot of generously salted water to a boil. Add the farfalle and cook, stirring occasionally, until al dente, about 11 minutes (or follow the timing instructions on the package). Drain well, transfer the farfalle to a large bowl, drizzle with vegetable oil, toss to coat, and set aside.

2. Meanwhile, heat the ½ cup/120 ml vegetable oil and the onions in a large pan set over medium heat. Cover and cook, stirring occasionally, until the onions are soft, about 10 minutes. Uncover, season with salt, and continue cooking until the onions take on a deep golden hue, 10 to 15 minutes more.

3. Bring the broth to a boil in a medium saucepan. Stir in the kasha, turn the heat to low, cover, and simmer until the kasha is soft, 12 to 15 minutes. Remove the pan from the heat and let stand, covered, for about 5 minutes, then transfer to the bowl with the farfalle along with the cooked onions. Season with salt and pepper, and top with parsley, if desired. Serve warm or at room temperature.

BEEF KREPLACH WITH GINGER AND CILANTRO

Hiding a tasty filling inside a pocket of dough is a delicious technique found across many cultures and cuisines (think ravioli, wontons, empanadas). Kreplach are the Eastern European Jewish answer to this category. The dough is essentially a fresh pasta dough that can be filled with any number of things, from ground meat to potato to cheese, before being boiled or fried. The boiled version is often eaten on Shabbat as soup dumplings in Classic Chicken Soup. They are also served on Purim and during the festive meal eaten before Yom Kippur. Just like a dumpling, the Purim story's heroine, Queen Esther, hid her inner identity, though in her case it was in order to save the Jewish people from destruction. These kreplach spice up the traditional ground beef with a fragrant mixture of fresh ginger, sesame oil, and chopped fresh cilantro.

SERVES 6 TO 8

2 CUPS/255 G ALL-PURPOSE FLOUR

KOSHER SALT

3 EGGS

5 TBSP/80 ML WATER

½ SMALL YELLOW ONION, FINELY CHOPPED

1 TBSP TOASTED SESAME OIL

2 TSP FINELY GRATED FRESH GINGER

3 GARLIC CLOVES, FINELY CHOPPED

8 OZ/225 G GROUND BEEF

½ CUP/20 G FINELY CHOPPED FRESH CILANTRO

FRESHLY GROUND BLACK PEPPER

CLASSIC CHICKEN SOUP (PAGE 93) FOR SERVING OR VEGETABLE OIL FOR FRYING

CHUTNEY, SWEET AND SOUR SAUCE, OR HOT SAUCE FOR SERVING (OPTIONAL)

1. Combine the flour, ¼ tsp salt, 2 of the eggs, and the water in a food processor and process until the dough begins to come together in a ball, 30 seconds to 1 minute. Transfer the dough to a lightly floured surface and knead until soft and supple, 2 to 3 minutes. Wrap the dough loosely in plastic wrap and let rest at room temperature for 30 minutes.

2. Meanwhile, heat a pan over medium heat, add the onion, and cook, stirring occasionally, until softened, 3 to 4 minutes. Add the sesame oil, ginger, and garlic and cook, stirring often, until fragrant, 1 to 2 minutes. Remove from the heat and let cool slightly.

3. In a large bowl, combine the beef, the cooked onion mixture, cilantro, remaining 1 egg, ½ tsp salt, and ½ tsp pepper. Mix with your hands until well combined. Cover and refrigerate while you roll out the dough.

CONTINUED

4. Use a rolling pin to roll out the dough on a lightly floured surface until it is less than ⅛ in/4 mm thick. (You want it as thin as possible without tearing.) If the dough feels tough and difficult to roll out after resting, cover with a cloth and let stand for 5 to 10 minutes more to allow the gluten in the flour to relax. Use a 3-in/7.5-cm round cookie cutter or glass to cut out as many circles as possible.

5. Place a rounded 1 tsp of the beef mixture in the center of each circle. Wet your finger and run it around the edges, then fold the circle in half, enclosing the filling inside. (You should end up with a half-moon shape). Press the edges firmly to seal, and repeat with the remaining dough circles and filling. Cook the kreplach using one of the following two methods.

    Boiling: While rolling and filling the kreplach, bring a pot of generously salted water to a boil. Add the kreplach and cook, stirring occasionally, until tender, 15 to 20 minutes. Drain and serve them in chicken soup.

    Frying: Heat ⅛ in/4 mm of vegetable oil in a large skillet set over medium heat until shimmering. Working in batches, add the kreplach to the pan and fry, turning once, until golden brown and cooked through, about 3 minutes per side. Drain on a paper towel–lined plate before serving topped with chutney, sweet and sour sauce, or hot sauce, if desired.

SAVORY MATZO FARFEL

Farfel is a tiny, barley-shaped egg noodle prevalent in Eastern European Jewish cooking. Since regular pasta is not allowed during the holiday, Jewish cooks substitute matzo broken up into very small pieces. In this savory side dish, the matzo farfel is toasted and then tossed with a simple mixture of onions, carrot, celery, and thyme. It makes a quick and homey dish for the seder table or anytime during Passover, served alongside Roast Chicken with Fennel and Orange (page 188).

SERVES 4 TO 6

4 TBSP/60 ML VEGETABLE OIL OR SCHMALTZ (PAGE 318)

2 MEDIUM YELLOW ONIONS, FINELY CHOPPED

1 LARGE CARROT, PEELED AND FINELY CHOPPED

2 STALKS CELERY, FINELY CHOPPED

1 TSP SUGAR

KOSHER SALT

1½ TSP DRIED THYME

8 SHEETS MATZO, CRUMBLED INTO ½-IN/12-MM PIECES

2 CUPS/480 ML WATER

1½ TSP ONION POWDER

½ TSP GARLIC POWDER

FRESHLY GROUND BLACK PEPPER

FINELY CHOPPED FRESH DILL OR FLAT-LEAF PARSLEY FOR SERVING

1. Heat 3 Tbsp of the vegetable oil in a large pan set over medium heat. Add the onions, carrot, celery, sugar, and a generous sprinkle of salt and cook, stirring occasionally, until the vegetables soften, about 15 minutes. Add the thyme and cook, stirring often, until fragrant, about 1 minute.

2. Meanwhile, heat the remaining 1 Tbsp oil in a large saucepan set over medium-high heat. Add the crumbled matzo and cook, stirring occasionally, until toasty smelling, 4 to 5 minutes. Add the water, onion powder, garlic powder, and 1½ tsp salt, and season with pepper. Bring to a boil (it should boil pretty quickly), then turn the heat to low, cover, and cook until the matzo is softened and the water is absorbed, 7 to 10 minutes.

3. Combine the matzo and cooked vegetables in a serving bowl and stir to combine. Taste and season with more salt, if desired. Sprinkle with dill and serve warm.

PARSLEY MATZO BALLS

I have never met a matzo ball I didn't like. Floater, sinker, big, small, delicate, or dense—I will happily eat them all. These traditional beauties skew on the tender and fluffy side, thanks to the glug of seltzer lightening up the batter. A little chopped parsley adds color and a hint of freshness. Don't have matzo meal on hand? Save an extra trip to the grocery store by making your own. Break up a few matzo sheets and pulse them in the food processor until they take on a bread crumb–like consistency.

SERVES 6 TO 8

4 EGGS, LIGHTLY BEATEN

¼ CUP/60 ML VEGETABLE OIL OR
SCHMALTZ (PAGE 318)

1 TSP SALT

1 CUP/105 G MATZO MEAL

2 TBSP FINELY CHOPPED FRESH
FLAT-LEAF PARSLEY

3 TBSP SELTZER WATER

CLASSIC CHICKEN SOUP (PAGE 93)

1. Stir together the eggs, vegetable oil, salt, matzo meal, parsley, and seltzer in a large bowl. Cover and refrigerate for 30 minutes.

2. Meanwhile, bring a large pot of generously salted water to a boil. Turn the heat to medium-low and keep at a simmer while you form the matzo balls.

3. Moisten your hands with water. Scoop out a rounded 1 Tbsp of matzo ball batter and roll it into a 1-in/2.5-cm ball. Drop into the simmering water, and repeat with the remaining batter. You should end up with about 15 matzo balls. Cover the pot and simmer until the matzo balls are tender and puffed, 30 to 35 minutes. (If you cut one in half, it should be pale in color throughout.)

4. Remove the matzo balls from the pot with a slotted spoon, divide between bowls, and ladle soup over the top. (Matzo balls can be cooled to room temperature, then stored, covered, in the refrigerator for up to 1 day. Rewarm them in your soup before serving.)

JALAPEÑO-SHALLOT MATZO BALLS

People tend to get a little overprotective about Passover food. The rest of the year may be filled with exciting food adventures, but when it comes to the seder, time-tested dishes often rule the table. These matzo balls strike a happy medium between old school and new. From the outside, they look comfortingly familiar. But inside, the softened shallots, colorful specks of jalapeño, and the hint of heat they impart is a surprising but totally welcome addition to any pot of chicken soup.

SERVES 6 TO 8

NOTE

When working with jalapeños, and particularly if you have any cuts or scrapes, wear a pair of latex kitchen gloves to keep the fiery oils off your hands.

¼ CUP/60 ML VEGETABLE OIL OR SCHMALTZ (PAGE 318)

2 SHALLOTS, FINELY CHOPPED

1 SMALL JALAPEÑO, FINELY CHOPPED (REMOVE SEEDS FOR A LESS SPICY MATZO BALL)

4 EGGS, LIGHTLY BEATEN

1 TSP SALT

1 CUP/105 G MATZO MEAL (SEE PAGE 18)

3 TBSP SELTZER WATER

CLASSIC CHICKEN SOUP (PAGE 93)

1. Heat the vegetable oil in a medium pan set over medium heat. Add the shallots and jalapeño and cook, stirring occasionally, until softened, about 5 minutes. Remove the pan from the heat and transfer the jalapeño mixture, including the oil, to a large bowl (to speed up the cooling process). Let cool to the touch.

2. Once cooled, combine the eggs, salt, matzo meal, and seltzer in the bowl with the jalapeño mixture. Cover and refrigerate for 30 minutes.

3. Meanwhile, bring a large pot of generously salted water to a boil. Turn the heat to medium-low and keep at a simmer while you form the matzo balls.

4. Moisten your hands with water. Scoop out a rounded 1 Tbsp of matzo ball batter and roll it into a 1-in/2.5-cm ball. Drop into the simmering water, and repeat with the remaining batter. You should end up with about 18 matzo balls. Cover the pot and simmer until the matzo balls are tender and puffed, 30 to 35 minutes. (If you cut one in half, it should be pale in color throughout.)

5. Remove the matzo balls from the pot with a slotted spoon, divide between bowls, and ladle soup over the top. (Matzo balls can be cooled to room temperature, then stored, covered, in the refrigerator for up to 1 day. Rewarm them in your soup before serving.)

DOLMADES

Imagine you are a winemaker living in antiquity. The season has been kind and your baskets are overflowing with bunches of grapes. But one question lingers: What do you do with all of those grape leaves? Thankfully, some curious ancient cook with exactly this conundrum took a chance and stuffed them with spiced rice. To this day, stuffed grape leaves remain a Middle Eastern delicacy, particularly popular in Turkey and Greece. For the Jews in this region, they became a fixture of the Shabbat table and an edible symbol of abundance during the harvest holiday of Sukkot.

Premade stuffed grape leaves are easy to find in many grocery stores, and for most of my life, it never even occurred to me that you could make your own. They just came in a can, end of story. Then several years ago, a friend served some really stellar stuffed grape leaves at a Shabbat dinner. I asked her what brand they were and she told me she had made them. She was nonchalant and said, "What, these old things?" But my mind was blown—the store-bought version paled in comparison. I silently vowed that I would learn to make them. Don't be intimidated by the number of steps involved in rolling and steaming your own dolmades. If you have ever made blintzes, you can make stuffed grape leaves—the filling and rolling process is virtually identical. (And if you've never made blintzes, see page 46!) Serve them alongside olives and with lemon wedges for squeezing.

SERVES 6

⅓ CUP/50 G PINE NUTS

3 TBSP EXTRA-VIRGIN OLIVE OIL, PLUS ¼ CUP/60 ML

1 MEDIUM YELLOW ONION, FINELY CHOPPED

1 CUP/185 G LONG-GRAIN WHITE RICE

1⅔ CUPS/405 ML VEGETABLE BROTH

¼ CUP/10 G FINELY CHOPPED FRESH DILL

¼ CUP/10 G FINELY CHOPPED FRESH FLAT-LEAF PARSLEY

½ TSP GROUND CINNAMON

ZEST AND JUICE OF 1 LEMON

KOSHER SALT AND FRESHLY GROUND BLACK PEPPER

ONE 8-OZ/225-G BOTTLE GRAPE LEAVES (SEE PAGE 342), RINSED AND DRAINED

1. Place the pine nuts in a small pan set over medium-low heat. Cook, stirring occasionally, until lightly browned, 5 to 7 minutes. Remove from the heat and let cool.

2. Heat the 3 Tbsp of olive oil in a medium saucepan set over medium heat. Add the onion and cook, stirring occasionally, until softened, 5 to 7 minutes. Add the rice and cook, stirring often, until toasty smelling, about 1 minute. Add ⅔ cup/165 ml of the broth, turn the heat to low, and cook, uncovered, until the liquid is absorbed, about 5 minutes. (The rice should not be fully cooked at this point.) Remove the pan from the heat and stir in the toasted pine nuts, the dill, parsley, cinnamon, and lemon zest. Season with salt and pepper and let the mixture cool to the touch.

3. Bring a large pot of water to a boil. Add the grape leaves and boil until softened, about 5 minutes. Drain the leaves, rinse with cold water, and drain again. Pat dry with paper towels and trim off the nubby stem before filling.

4. Place 1 leaf, vein-side up, on a flat surface. Place a slightly rounded 1 Tbsp of filling at the base of the leaf. Fold the bottom of the leaf over the filling, then fold each side in to the center. Starting at the bottom, roll the leaf upward, tucking the filling inside, and squeeze gently to seal. Do not roll the grape leave packages too tightly, because the rice will continue to expand as they simmer. Continue with the remaining leaves and filling.

5. Place the stuffed grape leaves, seam-side down, in a single layer in a large Dutch oven or wide-bottomed saucepan. Pour the remaining 1 cup/240 ml broth, remaining ¼ cup/60 ml oil, and the lemon juice over the stuffed grape leaves. (If the liquid does not reach at least halfway up the sides of the grape leaves, add a little more water or broth.) Bring the mixture to a simmer over medium heat. Turn the heat to low and place an inverted heat-safe plate that fits inside the pot on top of the rolls to keep them in place. Cover the pan with a lid and simmer until the grape leaves are tender when pierced with a fork, 30 to 40 minutes. Serve warm or at room temperature.

DILLED RICE WITH LIMA BEANS

Sephardi and Mizrahi cooks hold the secret to truly delicious rice dishes. They have to. Rice, after all, is at the center of their cuisine, so there is pressure to keep things varied and interesting. As cookbook author Claudia Roden writes in *The Book of Jewish Food*, "Certain embellishments were developed to give [rice] a festive air, like coloring it yellow with saffron or turmeric, or sprinkling it with almonds and pistachios . . . or baking it in a piecrust." This quick and flavorful side is my riff on baghali polo, a Persian rice dish speckled with fresh dill and fava beans (I use lima beans, which are easier to find) that is traditionally served on Passover. People who do not eat kitniyot (see page 330) on Passover should enjoy this dish after the holiday.

SERVES 4 TO 6

- 2 CUPS/370 G LONG-GRAIN WHITE RICE
- 3 CUPS/720 ML CHICKEN OR VEGETABLE BROTH
- 2 TBSP EXTRA-VIRGIN OLIVE OIL, PLUS MORE FOR DRIZZLING
- 1 LARGE YELLOW ONION, FINELY CHOPPED
- 2 CUPS/220 G THAWED FROZEN LIMA BEANS
- 1 CUP/40 G FINELY CHOPPED FRESH DILL
- KOSHER SALT AND FRESHLY GROUND BLACK PEPPER

1. Put the rice in a bowl, cover with water, and swish the grains around with your hands until the water becomes cloudy. Drain in a colander, rinsing again with water as you drain. Heat the broth in a medium saucepan set over high heat. Bring to a boil, stir in the rice, turn the heat to low, cover and cook until the rice is tender, 18 to 20 minutes. Remove from the heat and let stand, covered, for 10 minutes. Fluff the rice with a fork and set aside.

2. Meanwhile, heat the olive oil in a medium pan set over medium heat. Add the onion and cook until softened and lightly browned, 6 to 8 minutes. Add the lima beans and cook until just tender, 4 to 5 minutes. Remove from the heat and add to the rice along with the dill. Season with salt and pepper and drizzle with olive oil, if desired. Stir to combine and serve warm.

SAFFRON RICE PILAF

Of all the spices, saffron—with its distinct buttery flavor and vibrant golden hue—is among the most prized in both Sephardi and Mizrahi Jewish cooking, and also in Arabic cuisine. Rice flavored with costly saffron threads is traditionally served for special occasions like Shabbat dinner and holiday meals. Since yellow is considered a color of happiness, saffron rice is also common at Sephardi and Mizrahi wedding celebrations. Always buy high-quality saffron threads. If you see a deal offering a large quantity of saffron for a small price, it likely is poor quality and will not impart good flavor. Buy it a little at a time, as needed, and splurge for the good stuff.

SERVES 6

1 PINCH SAFFRON THREADS, CRUSHED WITH A MORTAR AND PESTLE

1 TBSP BOILING WATER

1½ CUPS/285 G BASMATI RICE

¼ CUP/60 ML EXTRA-VIRGIN OLIVE OIL

½ CUP/60 G SLIVERED ALMONDS

1 YELLOW ONION, FINELY CHOPPED

2¾ CUPS/660 ML VEGETABLE OR CHICKEN BROTH

¾ TSP SALT

1. Combine the saffron and boiling water in a small bowl; set aside.

2. Put the rice in a bowl, cover with water, and swish the grains around with your hands until the water becomes cloudy. Drain in a colander, rinsing again with water as you drain, and set aside.

3. Line a plate with paper towels. Heat the olive oil in a large saucepan set over medium heat until shimmering. Add the almonds and cook, stirring often, until lightly browned, about 3 minutes. (Watch carefully so they don't burn.) Use a slotted spoon to transfer the almonds to the paper towels to drain.

4. Add the onion to the pan and cook, stirring occasionally, until softened, 6 to 7 minutes. Add the rice and cook, stirring often, until fragrant, 1 to 2 minutes. Stir in the broth, salt, and saffron mixture. Raise the heat to medium-high and bring to a boil, then turn the heat to low, cover, and cook until the water is fully absorbed, 16 to 18 minutes.

5. Remove the pan from the heat and let stand, covered, for 5 minutes. Fluff the rice with a fork and stir in the almonds. Serve warm.

BUKHARIAN BEEF AND CARROT RICE PILAF

The Bukharian Jews of Central Asia have a wonderfully complex cuisine. Like virtually all Jewish food, Bukharian food came together using ingredients and inspiration from neighboring cultures. Settled along the Silk Road, Bukharian Jews created a stunning mixture of Persian, Chinese, Indian, Uzbek, and Russian cooking.

Today, Queens, New York, is home to nearly 35,000 Bukharian Jews, and Yoshie and I regularly visit the restaurants there to enjoy an unfamiliar (to us, anyway) Jewish culture. We savor the hand-pulled noodle soups, glistening lamb kebabs, pickled vegetables, meat and vegetable dumplings, chewy flatbreads, and flavorful rice dishes. One of my favorites is plov, a Persian-inspired pilaf studded with beef and grated carrots. I almost always order it when we go out and, more recently, I have started making it at home. Many plov recipes call for barberries—tiny, tart berries that add little bursts of flavor. If you cannot find them, currants make a fine substitute. This recipe yields an ample amount and keeps well for several days, making it a great dish to prepare on Sunday and enjoy throughout the week.

SERVES 6 TO 8

⅓ CUP/80 ML VEGETABLE OIL

2 MEDIUM YELLOW ONIONS, FINELY CHOPPED

2½ LB/1.2 KG BEEF CHUCK, TRIMMED OF EXCESS FAT AND CUT INTO ¾-IN/2-CM CHUNKS

5 MEDIUM CARROTS, PEELED AND GRATED ON THE LARGE HOLES OF A BOX GRATER

KOSHER SALT AND FRESHLY GROUND BLACK PEPPER

1 TSP SWEET PAPRIKA

2 TSP GROUND CUMIN

½ TSP TURMERIC

1 TSP GROUND CORIANDER

5 GARLIC CLOVES, FINELY CHOPPED

2 BAY LEAVES

5 CUPS/1.2 L WATER

2½ CUPS/460 G LONG-GRAIN WHITE RICE

¼ CUP/40 G BARBERRIES OR CURRANTS

1. Heat the vegetable oil in a Dutch oven or large heavy-bottomed pot set over medium-high heat. Add the onions and cook, stirring occasionally, until softened and lightly browned, 6 to 8 minutes. Add the beef and cook, stirring occasionally, until browned, 7 to 10 minutes. Add the carrots and cook, stirring occasionally, until just softened, 3 to 5 minutes. Add 1½ tsp salt, ½ tsp pepper, the paprika, cumin, turmeric, coriander, garlic, and bay leaves and cook, stirring constantly, until fragrant, 1 to 2 minutes.

2. Stir in 2 cups/480 ml of the water and bring to a simmer. Turn the heat to low, cover, and cook until the meat is tender, 40 to 45 minutes.

3. Meanwhile, put the rice in a bowl, cover with water, and swish the grains around with your hands until the water becomes cloudy. Drain in a colander, rinsing again with water as you drain. Sprinkle the rice and 1 tsp salt over the beef mixture (do not stir—it can lead to mushiness). Pour the remaining 3 cups/720 ml water over the top (do not stir), raise the heat to high, and bring to a boil. Turn the heat to medium and simmer, uncovered, until the rice begins to swell and most of the water is absorbed (the surface should appear dry), 10 to 12 minutes.

4. Poke several deep holes into the mixture with the back of a wooden spoon to help the water continue evaporating. Sprinkle the barberries over the top, turn the heat to low, cover, and cook until the rice is tender and the water is fully absorbed, 15 to 20 minutes. Remove from the heat, discard the bay leaves, and gently stir to combine. Taste and season with more salt, if desired. Serve hot.

MAMALIGA

Mamaliga is a hearty Romanian cornmeal porridge. You have probably eaten it before, when it was Italian and called polenta. (The two dishes are virtually identical.) The difference is, Romanians eat mamaliga for breakfast, lunch, dinner, and dessert. They top it with sour cream and sharp cheese. They slice and panfry it, and eat it with stews or fried onions. They drizzle it with honey and smear it with jam. Mamaliga's ubiquity is captured in the famous 1920s Yiddish song, "Roumania, Roumania," by Aaron Lebedeff: "To live there is a pleasure / what your heart desires / you can get a mamaliga, a pastrami, a karnatzl [sausage] / and a glass of wine, aha!" This basic recipe tastes equally delicious served traditionally or any way you can dream up.

SERVES 4

1½ CUPS/360 ML MILK

1½ CUPS/360 ML WATER

2 TBSP UNSALTED BUTTER

1 TSP SALT

1 CUP/150 G MEDIUM-GRIND YELLOW CORNMEAL

1. Combine the milk, water, butter, and salt in a medium saucepan set over medium heat. Bring to a boil, then add the cornmeal in a slow stream, stirring constantly.

2. Turn the heat to low, cover the pan, and cook, stirring often, until the liquid is absorbed and the cornmeal thickens, 5 to 15 minutes. Serve immediately as a porridge, or spoon it into a lightly greased shallow bowl, like a round baking dish, and let stand until it sets, 10 to 15 minutes. Carefully invert the mamaliga onto a cutting board and slice into wedges. Serve warm or at room temperature.

SERVING MAMALIGA

The traditional Romanian way to serve mamaliga is topped with a decadent spoonful of sour cream. Some people also stir in crumbled feta cheese or dollop the top with jam.

Once fully cooled, mamaliga can be sliced and panfried in a little butter or oil. Serve it alongside eggs for breakfast.

My friend Julie, who grew up in Texas but lived in Romania for many years, tops her mamaliga with sautéed onion and black beans, slices of avocado, salsa, and cheddar cheese. Similarly, it would taste great under a pile of sautéed mushrooms and cherry tomatoes, or anything saucy and savory.

Mamaliga would pair wonderfully with several of the main dishes in this book, including Tilapia in Spicy Tomato Sauce (page 174), Ful Medames with Poached Eggs (page 165), and Cinnamon-Roasted Seitan and Onions (page 223).

PINE NUT AND SCALLION COUSCOUS

Inspired by the fruit and nut pilafs found in Mizrahi cuisine, this couscous-based side dish comes together in well under 20 minutes, while delivering a beautifully balanced mix of sweet golden raisins, spicy scallions, and fragrant toasted pine nuts. I make it regularly for Shabbat dinner, and have found that it complements just about any dish.

SERVES 6

2 CUPS/480 ML CHICKEN OR VEGETABLE BROTH

1½ CUPS/250 G COUSCOUS

2 TBSP EXTRA-VIRGIN OLIVE OIL, PLUS MORE FOR DRIZZLING

1 BUNCH SCALLIONS, WHITE AND GREEN PARTS, THINLY SLICED

½ CUP/80 G PINE NUTS

1 CUP/170 G GOLDEN RAISINS

KOSHER SALT AND FRESHLY GROUND BLACK PEPPER

1. In a medium saucepan, bring the broth to a boil. Once boiling, turn off the heat and immediately stir in the couscous. Cover the pan and let stand until the liquid is absorbed, 5 to 10 minutes.

2. Meanwhile, heat the olive oil in a medium pan set over medium heat. Add the scallions and pine nuts and cook, stirring occasionally, until the scallions soften and the pine nuts grow fragrant, 5 to 7 minutes.

3. Uncover the couscous and fluff with a fork. Transfer the couscous to a large serving bowl and stir in the scallions, pine nuts, and raisins. Drizzle with a little more oil, if desired, and season with salt and pepper. Serve warm.

COUSCOUS WITH WINTER SQUASH AND CHICKPEAS

In Morocco, Jews customarily serve couscous topped with a stew of seven vegetables on Rosh Hashanah—the number seven representing that the holiday falls on the seventh month of the Jewish calendar. In addition to adding flavor to the final dish, each vegetable holds some symbolic significance. This riff on the traditional couscous dish is brightly colored with butternut squash and tomatoes, sweetened with golden raisins, enriched with chickpeas, and perfumed with a heady mixture of garlic and spices. Measure all of the spices before you start cooking, so you can add them all at once.

SERVES 6 TO 8

¼ CUP/60 ML EXTRA-VIRGIN OLIVE OIL

2 YELLOW ONIONS, HALVED THROUGH THE ROOT AND THINLY SLICED

4 RIPE PLUM TOMATOES, CORED, SEEDED, AND CHOPPED

2 GARLIC CLOVES, FINELY CHOPPED

1 TSP GROUND CINNAMON

1 TSP GROUND GINGER

½ TSP GROUND CUMIN

½ TSP GROUND CORIANDER

1 TSP GROUND SWEET PAPRIKA

½ TSP RED PEPPER FLAKES

ONE 15-OZ/430-G CAN CHICKPEAS, RINSED AND DRAINED

3 CUPS/385 G CUBED PEELED BUTTERNUT SQUASH

2 CARROTS, PEELED, HALVED LENGTH-WISE, AND CUT INTO ½-IN/12-MM CHUNKS

¼ CUP/45 G GOLDEN RAISINS

2½ CUPS/600 ML VEGETABLE BROTH

KOSHER SALT AND FRESHLY GROUND BLACK PEPPER

2½ CUPS/600 ML WATER

2 CUPS/330 G COUSCOUS

ROUGHLY CHOPPED FRESH CILANTRO OR FLAT-LEAF PARSLEY, FOR SERVING

1. Heat the olive oil in a medium saucepan set over medium-high heat. Add the onions and cook, stirring occasionally, until softened and lightly browned, 7 to 10 minutes. Add the tomatoes and cook, stirring occasionally, until softened, about 5 minutes. Add the garlic, cinnamon, ginger, cumin, coriander, paprika, and red pepper flakes and cook, stirring often, until fragrant, 1 to 2 minutes.

2. Add the chickpeas, squash, carrots, raisins, broth, and 1 tsp salt. Season with pepper and bring the mixture to a simmer. Turn the heat to low, cover, and simmer until the squash and carrots are tender, about 15 minutes. Uncover and continue simmering, stirring occasionally, until very slightly thickened, about 5 minutes. Taste and season with more salt, if desired.

CONTINUED

3. Meanwhile, bring the water to a boil in a separate medium saucepan set over high heat. Once boiling, turn off the heat and immediately stir in the couscous. Cover the pan and let stand until the liquid is absorbed, 5 to 10 minutes.

4. Uncover the couscous and fluff with a fork. Mound the couscous onto a large serving platter. Make a wide well in the center and use a slotted spoon to fill it with the vegetables and chickpeas. Spoon a generous amount of the liquid over the couscous and sprinkle with cilantro. Serve immediately.

TOASTED ALMOND ISRAELI COUSCOUS

Unlike regular couscous, which is made up of tiny pasta granules formed from semolina flour and water, Israeli couscous (called *ptitim*, or "crumbles" in Hebrew) comes in larger, toasted pearls that make a satisfyingly chewy base for any number of side dishes. I almost exclusively cook Israeli couscous (like many grains) in broth instead of water, which gives it an added boost of flavor. Here, the cooked grain gets tossed with silky shallots, a bit of lemon juice, and a showering of crunchy sliced almonds.

SERVES 6 TO 8

¾ CUP/75 G SLICED ALMONDS

3½ CUPS/840 ML CHICKEN OR VEGETABLE BROTH

4 SPRIGS FRESH THYME

3 CUPS/445 G ISRAELI COUSCOUS

3 TBSP EXTRA-VIRGIN OLIVE OIL, PLUS MORE FOR DRIZZLING

6 MEDIUM SHALLOTS, HALVED LENGTH-WISE AND THINLY SLICED

KOSHER SALT AND FRESHLY GROUND BLACK PEPPER

1 TBSP FRESH LEMON JUICE

ROUGHLY CHOPPED FRESH FLAT-LEAF PARSLEY FOR SERVING

1. Place the almonds in a small pan set over medium heat. Cook, stirring occasionally, until fragrant and golden brown, 5 to 7 minutes. Remove from the heat and let cool completely.

2. Combine the broth and thyme in a medium pot set over high heat and bring to a boil. Stir in the couscous, turn the heat to low, cover, and cook until the liquid is absorbed, 8 to 12 minutes. Remove from the heat and let stand, covered, for 5 minutes. Uncover and fluff the couscous with a fork. Transfer the couscous to a large bowl and discard the thyme sprigs.

3. Meanwhile, heat the olive oil in a medium skillet set over medium heat. Add the shallots, season with salt and pepper, and cook, stirring frequently, until softened and browned, about 8 minutes. Add the cooked shallots, toasted almonds, and lemon juice to the couscous, drizzle with a little more oil, and toss to combine. Season again with salt and pepper, and top with parsley. Serve warm.

BULGUR WITH WALNUTS AND POMEGRANATE

When people see a bulgur-based salad, they tend to assume it's tabbouleh. But the nutty little grain is capable of so much more. This Middle Eastern–inspired mixture of tender bulgur, juicy pomegranate seeds, dried apricots, meaty walnuts, celery, and fresh herbs makes a perfect early fall side dish. A hint of cinnamon and allspice adds an unexpected dimension of sweetness that I love.

SERVES 6

NOTE

Seed a pomegranate quickly by filling a bowl about halfway with water and cutting the fruit into quarters. Working with one quarter at a time, use your fingers to remove the seeds, letting them drop into the water. Skim off any pith floating at the top of the water, then drain the seeds through a fine-mesh sieve.

¾ CUP/125 G FINE- OR MEDIUM-GRADE BULGUR (SEE NOTE, PAGE 71), RINSED AND DRAINED

1 TSP KOSHER SALT

1¼ CUPS/300 ML BOILING WATER

3 MEDIUM STALKS CELERY, VERY THINLY SLICED ON THE DIAGONAL

½ CUP/20 G ROUGHLY CHOPPED FRESH MINT

½ CUP/20 G ROUGHLY CHOPPED FRESH CILANTRO OR FLAT-LEAF PARSLEY

1 CUP/160 G POMEGRANATE SEEDS

1 CUP/115 G WALNUTS, ROUGHLY CHOPPED

½ CUP/100 G FINELY CHOPPED DRIED APRICOTS

¼ CUP/60 ML FRESH LEMON JUICE

¼ CUP/60 ML EXTRA-VIRGIN OLIVE OIL

1 TSP GROUND CINNAMON

½ TSP GROUND ALLSPICE

¼ TSP FRESHLY GROUND BLACK PEPPER

1. Combine the bulgur, salt, and boiling water in a medium bowl. Cover and let stand until the bulgur is tender but still chewy, 15 to 20 minutes. Drain well and transfer to a large bowl.

2. Add the celery, mint, cilantro, pomegranate seeds, walnuts, and apricots to the bulgur. In a separate medium bowl, whisk together the lemon juice, olive oil, cinnamon, allspice, and pepper. Drizzle over the salad and toss well to combine. Let stand for 10 to 15 minutes to allow the flavors to meld. Serve warm or at room temperature.

FARRO SALAD WITH CORN AND JALAPEÑO

This summery side dish follows the time-tested Jewish technique of "brown a pile of onions then . . ." Here, the quick-caramelized onions (helped along by a sprinkle of sugar) are tossed with farro—a deliciously nutty ancient grain grown as far back as biblical times—softened sweet corn (learn how to remove fresh corn kernels from the cob on page 18), and spicy minced jalapeño. If you like, swap barley or another grain for the farro, or add 1 cup/160 g quartered cherry tomatoes to the pan along with the corn and jalapeño.

SERVES 4

- 1 CUP/170 G SEMI-PEARLED FARRO, RINSED AND DRAINED
- ¼ CUP/60 ML EXTRA-VIRGIN OLIVE OIL, PLUS MORE FOR DRIZZLING
- 2 YELLOW ONIONS, FINELY CHOPPED
- 1 TSP SUGAR
- KERNELS FROM 2 EARS SWEET CORN, OR 1¼ CUPS/205 G THAWED FROZEN CORN KERNELS
- 1 JALAPEÑO, SEEDED AND FINELY CHOPPED (SEE NOTE, PAGE 149)
- KOSHER SALT AND FRESHLY GROUND BLACK PEPPER

1. Place the farro in a medium saucepan and cover with water by 3 in/7.5 cm. Bring to a boil, partially cover, and cook, adding more water as necessary, until the farro is tender but still chewy, 15 to 25 minutes. Drain well and transfer to a serving bowl.

2. Meanwhile, heat the olive oil in a medium pan set over medium heat. Add the onions and sugar and cook, stirring occasionally, until softened and browned, 10 to 15 minutes. Add the corn and jalapeño and cook, stirring occasionally, until softened, 3 to 5 minutes. Remove from the heat and season generously with salt and pepper.

3. Stir the corn mixture into the cooked farro. Taste and add a drizzle of oil or more salt and pepper, if desired. Serve warm.

FUL MEDAMES WITH POACHED EGGS

Ful medames, a dish of fava beans simmered with lemon juice and spices, is hugely popular all across Egypt. Egyptian Jews traditionally serve it for breakfast along with chopped salads, or at Shabbat lunch with sliced hard-boiled eggs. My version skews toward dinner, adding a glug of red wine to the mix and topping the beans with soupy poached eggs. The dish comes together in about half an hour and is a great way to use up the ends of that bottle of vino on your countertop. Serve it with plenty of warmed or grilled pita to scoop up all the delicious sauce.

SERVES 2 TO 4

NOTE

Canned fava beans, sometimes labeled as ful medames, *can be found at Middle Eastern and specialty food shops. See page 342 for an online source. Do not substitute frozen green fava beans.*

6 CUPS/1.4 L WATER

½ CUP/120 ML WHITE VINEGAR

2 TBSP EXTRA-VIRGIN OLIVE OIL, PLUS MORE FOR DRIZZLING

1 LARGE YELLOW ONION, FINELY CHOPPED

4 LARGE GARLIC CLOVES, FINELY CHOPPED

1½ TSP GROUND CUMIN

1 TSP SMOKED PAPRIKA

¼ TSP RED PEPPER FLAKES, OR MORE TO TASTE

2 RIPE PLUM TOMATOES, CORED, SEEDED, AND FINELY CHOPPED

¼ CUP/60 ML DRY RED WINE

TWO 15-OZ/430-G CANS FAVA BEANS, UNDRAINED

1 TBSP FRESH LEMON JUICE

KOSHER SALT

½ TSP FRESHLY GROUND BLACK PEPPER

4 EGGS

ROUGHLY CHOPPED FRESH FLAT-LEAF PARSLEY FOR SERVING

1. Combine the water and vinegar in a medium saucepan set over medium heat. Bring to a boil, then turn the heat to medium-low, and keep it at a gentle simmer.

2. Meanwhile, heat the olive oil in a medium pan set over medium heat. Add the onion and cook, stirring occasionally, until softened, 5 to 7 minutes. Add the garlic, cumin, paprika, red pepper flakes, and tomatoes and cook, stirring often, until fragrant, 1 to 2 minutes.

CONTINUED

3. Stir in the red wine and cook, stirring occasionally, until the tomatoes soften and most of the liquid has evaporated, 3 to 5 minutes. Add the fava beans with their liquid and bring to a simmer. Turn the heat to medium-low, cover, and simmer until the fava beans are tender, about 10 minutes. Uncover and continue simmering until the liquid thickens and reduces by about three-fourths, 8 to 12 minutes. Stir in the lemon juice, ½ tsp salt, and the pepper, then remove from the heat. Taste and season with more salt and pepper flakes, if desired. Keep warm.

4. Using a wooden spoon, stir the simmering water to create a whirlpool. Crack all 4 eggs directly into the whirlpool and cook (do not stir) until the whites are firm and the yolks are still soft, 3 to 5 minutes.

5. Divide the beans and sauce among bowls or plates. Gently remove the eggs with a slotted spoon and top each bowl or plate with 1 or 2 eggs, a drizzle of olive oil, and parsley. Serve hot.

VEGETARIAN PORCINI AND FARRO CHOLENT

Cholent, a traditional Ashkenazi Shabbat stew made with meat, barley, and beans, is traditionally cooked overnight at a very low temperature. The thing is, cholent is typically made with tough cuts of beef that require long cooking times to tenderize. Vegetarian cholent, on the other hand, is made with just beans, grains, and veggies, and really does not need such an extended simmering time. That is why I prefer to make meat-free cholent on the stovetop, instead of in the more conventional slow cooker.

This version gets its depth of flavor from dried porcini mushrooms and vegetarian baked beans, and its hearty texture from farro. Serve it directly from the pot. Or if you are making it on Friday afternoon for Shabbat lunch the next day, transfer the cooked cholent to a slow cooker (turned to the lowest "keep warm" setting) and let it hang out until lunchtime. Just make sure you schedule in time for a nap directly afterward.

SERVES 6 TO 8

- 1 OZ/30 G DRIED PORCINI MUSHROOMS
- 2 CUPS/480 ML BOILING WATER
- ¼ CUP/60 ML EXTRA-VIRGIN OLIVE OIL
- 2 LARGE YELLOW ONIONS, CHOPPED
- 3 MEDIUM CARROTS, PEELED AND CUT INTO ½-IN/12-MM ROUNDS
- 4 MEDIUM YUKON GOLD POTATOES, PEELED AND CUT INTO 1-IN/ 2.5-CM CHUNKS
- 1 MEDIUM SWEET POTATO, PEELED AND CUT INTO 1-IN/2.5-CM PIECES
- 5 LARGE GARLIC CLOVES, FINELY CHOPPED

- 2 TSP DRIED THYME
- ONE 15-OZ/430-G CAN VEGETARIAN BAKED BEANS, UNDRAINED
- ONE 15-OZ/430-G CAN PINTO BEANS, DRAINED AND RINSED
- 3 TBSP SOY SAUCE OR TAMARI
- ½ CUP/85 G SEMI-PEARLED FARRO, RINSED AND DRAINED
- 4 CUPS/960 ML VEGETABLE BROTH
- 1 TSP FRESHLY GROUND BLACK PEPPER
- HOT SAUCE, PREFERABLY SRIRACHA, FOR SERVING

1. Place the porcini in a small bowl and cover with the boiling water. Let stand for 20 minutes. Remove the mushrooms with tongs, rinse well to remove any lingering sediment, and coarsely chop. Strain the soaking liquid through a fine-mesh sieve into a small bowl, reserving the liquid and discarding any sediment.

2. Heat the olive oil in a large pot set over medium heat. Add the onions, carrots, potatoes, sweet potato, and garlic and cook, stirring occasionally, until slightly softened, 10 to 15 minutes. Add the thyme and cook, stirring often, until fragrant, 1 to 2 minutes.

3. Add the baked beans with their liquid, the pinto beans, soy sauce, farro, broth, chopped porcini mushrooms, and pepper. Carefully pour in the soaking liquid, making sure to leave behind any grit at the bottom of the bowl. Bring the mixture to a boil, turn the heat to medium-low, partially cover, and cook until the vegetables are very soft, the farro plumps, and the liquid thickens, 35 to 45 minutes. Serve warm, drizzled with hot sauce.

SLOW-COOKER SPICED BEEF AND CHICKPEA STEW

Nearly every Jewish community has its own version of cholent, a long-simmered stew that is traditionally served for Shabbat lunch. Typically, these one-pot meals are made with stew meat, barley (or another grain), potatoes, and beans, and are cooked overnight at very low heat without breaking the prohibition of kindling a new fire on Shabbat. Back in Eastern Europe, Jewish cooks would bring their cholent pots to the local baker, where they would sit in the hearth (still hot from Friday morning's challah baking) until lunchtime the following day. Today, people tend to use a slow cooker.

As much as I love the concept, Ashkenazi-style cholent has never been my thing. Too often, its flavor is muted and its heavy texture lands like concrete in my stomach. Instead, I prefer hamin, the Sephardi take on cholent, which tends to be made with wheat berries or rice instead of barley (resulting in a less dense, more saucy texture) and is flavored with an intoxicating array of spices. Hamin also typically includes whole eggs, which are cooked in their shell along with the stew. Peeling one at the table to reveal the beautiful, sepia-toned egg inside is a real treat.

SERVES 6

NOTE

If you are planning on cooking the stew overnight and serving it for Shabbat lunch, I highly recommend switching the slow cooker to "keep warm" after the 10-hour cooking time. If you observe the Shabbat laws, you can purchase a slow cooker with an automatic timer that will switch from "low" to "keep warm" for you at the right time.

2 TBSP EXTRA-VIRGIN OLIVE OIL

2 YELLOW ONIONS, HALVED THROUGH THE ROOT AND SLICED

8 GARLIC CLOVES, THINLY SLICED

1½ TSP GROUND CUMIN

1 TBSP SMOKED PAPRIKA

1½ TSP SWEET PAPRIKA

2 MEDIUM YUKON GOLD POTATOES, PEELED AND CUT INTO 2-IN/5-CM CHUNKS

1 LARGE SWEET POTATO, PEELED AND CUT INTO 2-IN/5-CM CHUNKS

½ CUP/100 G WHEAT BERRIES, RINSED AND DRAINED

TWO 15½-OZ/445-G CANS CHICKPEAS, RINSED AND DRAINED

2½ LB/1.2 KG FLANKEN (WITH BONES) OR CHUCK ROAST, TRIMMED OF EXCESS FAT AND CUT INTO 2-IN/ 5-CM CHUNKS

2½ TSP KOSHER SALT

½ TSP FRESHLY GROUND BLACK PEPPER

½ TSP RED PEPPER FLAKES

1 CINNAMON STICK

2 TBSP HONEY

6 CUPS/1.4 L WATER

6 EGGS IN THE SHELL (OPTIONAL)

1. Heat the olive oil in a large pot set over medium-high heat. Add the onions and cook, stirring occasionally, until softened and lightly browned, 8 to 10 minutes. Add the garlic, cumin, smoked paprika, and sweet paprika, and cook, stirring often, until fragrant, about 1 minute.

2. Transfer the onion mixture to a slow cooker set to low, and top with the potatoes, sweet potato, wheat berries, chickpeas, and flanken. Sprinkle the salt, pepper, and red pepper flakes over the top and nestle the cinnamon stick in the mixture. Drizzle the honey over the top and add the water, or enough to just cover the mixture. (Do not stir.) Place the eggs (if using) on top and gently submerge into the liquid. Cover the slow cooker and cook until the vegetables and wheat berries are very tender, about 10 hours. Spoon the stew into bowls, along with an egg. Serve hot, peeling the eggs at the table.

CHAPTER SIX

FISH, CHICKEN, AND MEAT

TILAPIA IN SPICY TOMATO SAUCE

The practice of serving fish cooked in tart sauces made with lemon, pomegranate, or tomato, among other things, is popular throughout Sephardi and Mizrahi cuisine. The slow simmer keeps the fish moist, while imparting a bright color and tangy flavor to the finished dish. This version pairs tilapia with a tangy tomato sauce that has a spicy kick, thanks to the addition of red pepper flakes. I love how the sauce transforms the rather inexpensive fillets into something special. If you are not a tilapia fan, however, you can substitute your favorite firm-fleshed white fish.

SERVES 4

¼ CUP/60 ML VEGETABLE OIL

1 LARGE YELLOW ONION, FINELY CHOPPED

6 GARLIC CLOVES, CHOPPED

½ TSP RED PEPPER FLAKES

ONE 14½-OZ/415-G CAN DICED TOMATOES

½ CUP/120 ML WATER

3 TBSP TOMATO PASTE

1 TSP SUGAR

1 BAY LEAF

1½ TSP KOSHER SALT

½ TSP FRESHLY GROUND BLACK PEPPER

4 TILAPIA FILLETS (ABOUT 6 OZ/170 G EACH), RINSED AND PATTED DRY

ROUGHLY CHOPPED FRESH FLAT-LEAF PARSLEY FOR SPRINKLING

LEMON WEDGES FOR SERVING

1. Heat the vegetable oil in a wide, deep saucepan set over medium heat. Add the onion and cook, stirring occasionally, until softened, 5 to 6 minutes. Add the garlic and red pepper flakes and cook, stirring often, until fragrant, 1 to 2 minutes. Stir in the diced tomatoes with their juice, water, tomato paste, sugar, bay leaf, salt, and pepper. Raise the heat to medium-high and bring the mixture to a boil.

2. Turn the heat to medium-low and nestle the fish fillets in the sauce, spooning the sauce over the top of the fillets to cover, if necessary. Cover the pan and simmer until the fish is cooked through, about 20 minutes. Using a flat spatula, carefully remove the fillets from the pan and transfer to a serving platter.

3. Continue to cook the remaining sauce in the pan, stirring often, until it thickens slightly, 3 to 5 minutes. Remove the pan from the heat, discard the bay leaf, and spoon the sauce over the fish. Sprinkle with parsley. Serve hot with lemon wedges on the side.

BAKED SOLE WITH BITTER GREENS

In *Cucina Ebraica: Flavors of the Italian Jewish Kitchen*, cookbook author Joyce Goldstein calls fish served with bitter greens (typically curly endive) a "classic dish" of the Italian Jewish repertoire. My take on this iconic pairing, which is inspired by Goldstein's, pairs buttery sole with escarole, chopped green olives, and lemon zest.

SERVES 6

- 2 TBSP EXTRA-VIRGIN OLIVE OIL, PLUS ¼ CUP/60 ML
- 1 LARGE YELLOW ONION, HALVED THROUGH THE ROOT AND THINLY SLICED
- KOSHER SALT
- 1 LARGE HEAD ESCAROLE, TRIMMED AND TORN INTO 3-IN/7.5-CM PIECES

- ZEST OF 2 LEMONS, PLUS LEMON WEDGES FOR SERVING
- ⅔ CUP/110 G PITTED GREEN OLIVES, ROUGHLY CHOPPED
- 6 GARLIC CLOVES, FINELY CHOPPED
- FRESHLY GROUND PEPPER
- 6 SOLE FILLETS (ABOUT 4 OZ/115 G EACH), RINSED AND PATTED DRY
- ¼ CUP/60 ML VEGETABLE BROTH

1. Preheat the oven to 375°F/190°C.

2. Heat the 2 Tbsp olive oil in a large saucepan set over medium heat. Add the onion and a generous pinch of salt and cook, stirring occasionally, until softened and lightly browned, 6 to 8 minutes. Add the escarole and cook, tossing occasionally with tongs, until wilted and tender, 3 to 5 minutes. If the escarole does not fit in your pan all at once, add it in batches and let it wilt a bit before adding more. Stir in the lemon zest, olives, and garlic. Season with salt and pepper, then remove the pan from the heat.

3. Layer about two-thirds of the escarole mixture in the bottom of a 9-by-13-in/ 23-by-33-cm baking dish. Top with the sole fillets (it's okay if they overlap a little), season with salt and pepper, and cover with the remaining escarole mixture. Drizzle the broth and remaining ¼ cup/60 ml olive oil over the top. Cover the baking dish with aluminum foil and bake until the fish is flaky and cooked through, 20 to 25 minutes.

4. Remove the baking dish from the oven and, with a flat spatula, transfer the fish and greens to a platter. Drizzle with 2 to 3 Tbsp of the cooking liquid. Serve hot with lemon wedges on the side.

GRILLED SALMON WITH ORANGE AND HERBS

This salmon dish was inspired by a bowl of oranges I had lying around. I usually eat the fruit out of hand, or make something sweet, but I got to thinking about the orange's savory potential. That initial brainstorm eventually morphed into this dish: smoky grilled salmon fillets topped with a Mediterranean-inspired mixture of orange and fresh herbs. Partnered with a salad, Pine Nut and Scallion Couscous (see page 157), and a glass of white wine, it makes a simple and flavor-packed weeknight meal. It is delicious warm, but is also great at room temperature for Shabbat lunch: grill the salmon ahead of time and make the orange sauce shortly before serving.

SERVES 4 TO 6

3 MEDIUM NAVEL ORANGES

ZEST AND JUICE OF 1 LIME

¼ CUP/40 G FINELY CHOPPED RED ONION

1 TSP DRIED OREGANO

2 TBSP FINELY CHOPPED FRESH MINT

2 TBSP FINELY CHOPPED FRESH FLAT-LEAF PARSLEY

½ TSP RED PEPPER FLAKES

2 TBSP EXTRA-VIRGIN OLIVE OIL

KOSHER SALT AND FRESHLY GROUND BLACK PEPPER

6 SKIN-ON SALMON FILLETS (ABOUT 6 OZ/170 G EACH), RINSED AND PATTED DRY

1. Zest 2 of the oranges over a medium bowl. Using a very sharp or serrated knife, cut off the top and bottom of each orange, so the fruit is exposed. Cut off the peel and pith with your knife, following the curve of the fruit. Cut the orange segments out of their membranes, letting them fall into the bowl, then use your fingers to break each segment in half (or thirds, if the segments are large). Add the lime zest and juice to the bowl, along with the onion, oregano, mint, parsley, red pepper flakes, and olive oil. Season with salt and pepper, and let stand to let the flavors meld.

2. Meanwhile, preheat a gas or charcoal grill, or set a grill pan over medium-high heat. Brush the grill rack or pan generously with vegetable oil, which will keep the fish from sticking. Season the salmon generously with salt and pepper. Grill the salmon, skin-side down, uncovered, until marks form, about 3 minutes. Carefully flip the fish with a flat spatula, cover the grill, and continue cooking until cooked through, 3 to 4 minutes more. Transfer the fish to a platter and top with the orange-herb mixture (or pass it in a bowl alongside). Serve immediately.

GREEK GODDESS SALMON

Before ranch dressing, there was green goddess, an indulgent mix of sour cream and mayonnaise tarted up with finely chopped olives, capers, and lots of herbs. The emerald-colored salad dressing was wildly popular in mid-twentieth-century America, but has since faded. Interestingly, it was a piece of roasted salmon, not a green salad, that got me thinking about possible ways to revitalize the dressing (which I happen to love). Salmon, which is a favorite fish within Ashkenazi Jewish cuisine, is often served with a creamy dill sauce. Green goddess seemed like the next logical progression. Since thick Greek yogurt is so prevalent, why not use it in place of the sour cream?

SERVES 4 TO 6

FOR THE DRESSING

1 CUP/240 ML FULL-FAT OR 2 PERCENT GREEK YOGURT (DO NOT USE 0 PERCENT)

¼ CUP/60 G MAYONNAISE

1 TSP DRIED TARRAGON

1 TBSP FRESH LEMON JUICE

½ CUP/20 G ROUGHLY CHOPPED FRESH MINT OR FLAT-LEAF PARSLEY

3 TBSP FINELY CHOPPED SWEET ONION, SUCH AS VIDALIA

1 TBSP BRINE-PACKED CAPERS, DRAINED AND PATTED DRY

2 TBSP FINELY CHOPPED PIMIENTO-STUFFED GREEN OLIVES

1 SMALL GARLIC CLOVE, ROUGHLY CHOPPED

⅛ TSP KOSHER SALT

⅛ TSP FRESHLY GROUND BLACK PEPPER

FOR THE SALMON

3 TBSP EXTRA-VIRGIN OLIVE OIL

3 GARLIC CLOVES, MINCED OR PUSHED THROUGH A PRESS

1 TSP LEMON ZEST

1 TSP FRESH LEMON JUICE

KOSHER SALT AND FRESHLY GROUND BLACK PEPPER

6 SKIN-ON SALMON FILLETS (ABOUT 6 OZ/170 G EACH), RINSED AND PATTED DRY

CHOPPED FRESH FLAT-LEAF PARSLEY FOR SERVING

1. Make the dressing: Combine all the ingredients in a blender or food processor and purée until smooth, scraping down the sides as necessary, 30 to 45 seconds. Transfer to a small bowl, cover, and refrigerate for at least 20 minutes. (Dressing can also be covered and refrigerated overnight.)

2. Meanwhile, make the salmon: Preheat the oven to 400°F/200°C and grease two ovenproof baking dishes. In a small bowl, stir together the olive oil, garlic, lemon zest, and lemon juice and season with salt and pepper. Rub or brush the salmon fillets on all sides with the oil mixture, then place them, skin-side down, in the prepared baking dishes. Roast until the fish is pale pink and cooked through, 10 to 15 minutes (longer for thicker pieces). Remove from the oven and divide among plates. Drizzle each fillet with dressing and sprinkle with parsley. Pass the remaining dressing at the table.

BROWN SUGAR– CITRUS GRAVLAX

Bagels and lox is undoubtedly the most recognizable Jewish food combination in America. And yet, when it comes to the fish we put on top of our bagels, the terms *lox* and *smoked salmon* tend to be used interchangeably. Don't be fooled, there is a difference. Lox, which comes from the Yiddish and German words for salmon (*laks/ lachs*), is cured in brine and has a vigorously salty flavor. Smoked salmon, which is confusingly sometimes referred to as *Nova lox*, is both lightly brined and also cold-smoked, giving it that woodsy taste many people mistakenly associate with regular lox.

And then there is gravlax, the Swedish take on cured fish that has made its way onto the Jewish fish platter. Like lox, gravlax is brined but not smoked. But instead of brining with salt alone, gravlax's cure tends to include sugar, herbs, and spices, which gives it a more nuanced, complex flavor. My version of gravlax adds citrus zest to the traditional cracked peppercorns, caraway, and dill. I have a feeling your bagel, or rye bread, or crackers will be quite pleased. When making gravlax, always use the freshest, best-quality salmon you can find.

SERVES 8

2 TBSP PEPPERCORNS

1 TBSP CARAWAY SEEDS

⅔ CUP/100 G KOSHER SALT

½ CUP/100 G PACKED LIGHT BROWN SUGAR

ZEST OF 2 LEMONS

ZEST OF 1 ORANGE

ONE 2-LB/910-G SKIN-ON SALMON FILLET, RINSED AND PATTED DRY

1½ CUPS/60 G ROUGHLY CHOPPED FRESH DILL

1. Use a mortar and pestle or a spice grinder to coarsely crack the peppercorns and caraway seeds. In a medium bowl, mix together the salt, brown sugar, peppercorns, caraway, lemon zest, and orange zest.

2. Stretch a layer of plastic wrap into a shallow baking dish large enough to hold the salmon, letting the plastic wrap hang over the edges. Sprinkle with half of the salt mixture. Using a sharp knife, make a few shallow cuts on the skin side of the salmon and place the fish, flesh-side up, on top of the salt mixture. Cover with the remaining salt mixture and about 1 cup/40 g of the dill.

CONTINUED

3. Fold the ends of the plastic wrap around the salmon and cover tightly with additional plastic wrap. Refrigerate the salmon for 48 to 72 hours, turning the package once a day and using your fingers to redistribute the herb-and-citrus brine. Drain off any liquid that accumulates in the dish by tipping it carefully into the sink. When cured, the salmon should feel firm to the touch at the thickest part.

4. Unwrap the salmon, rinse well under water, and pat dry. Discard the spices and brine in the baking dish. Spread the remaining ½ cup/20 g dill on a plate. Firmly press the flesh side of the salmon into the dill to coat it, brushing off any excess with your fingers. Use a sharp knife to thinly slice the gravlax against the grain and serve cold. Once cured, wrap the gravlax in plastic and store up to 2 weeks in the refrigerator.

APPETIZING: THE DELICATESSEN'S COUSIN

"Appetizing," the curiously named category of cured and smoked fish, cream cheese, and other foods served alongside bagels, is a culinary institution with a New York accent. In the early twentieth century, the appetizing shop reigned as the cousin of the meat-heavy Jewish delicatessen. Since meat and milk are not permitted to be served together in kosher establishments, there was an incentive to sell pastrami and farmer cheese out of separate shops.

All week long, and on Sunday mornings especially, hungry New Yorkers jostled at the counter while hardworking countermen filleted paper-thin slices of smoked salmon and tender-fleshed sable, fished herring fillets from a barrel, and doled out cream cheese as thick as a down comforter. These foods thrived in Jewish communities elsewhere, but the term *appetizing* (which was used as a noun, as in, "let's go buy some appetizing") never gained traction outside of New York City.

Appetizing shops have largely fallen by the wayside. They once numbered in the dozens in Manhattan, but as the Jewish population moved and assimilated, and supermarkets expanded to carry a wider array of goods, the need for a specific dairy foods shop disappeared along with the shops themselves. A few of the old-timers—century-old establishments like Russ & Daughters on the Lower East Side, and Zabar's, Barney Greengrass, and Murray's Sturgeon Shop on the Upper West Side—continue to thrive.

A few years ago in Brooklyn, a new appetizing shop, Shelsky's Smoked Fish, joined the pack, offering old-school charm and updated takes on nostalgic classics. Shops like Shelsky's give me hope that as long as people hanker for smoke and brine, and the chewy bite of pickled fish and cream cheese slathered onto seeded bagels, the appetizing store will be there to sate them.

GEFILTE FISH IN WHITE WINE– HERB BROTH

My take on gefilte fish strays from tradition, but with delicious results. I like to use mild-flavored whitefish fillets and lighten things up by swapping the typical fish broth used as a poaching liquid for a white wine- and herb-infused French broth called a court bouillon. I also infuse my gefilte fish with lemon zest, thyme, and oregano, giving it a lovely herbal flavor. Topped with grated horseradish or Creamy Horseradish Herb Sauce, it tastes just like tradition, but better.

MAKES ABOUT 20 GEFILTE FISH BALLS

FOR THE POACHING BROTH

9 CUPS/2.1 L WATER

1 TBSP KOSHER SALT

⅔ CUP/165 ML DRY WHITE WINE

1 LARGE YELLOW ONION, ROUGHLY CHOPPED

½ SMALL LEEK. WHITE AND LIGHT GREEN PARTS, ROUGHLY CHOPPED

1 STALK CELERY, ROUGHLY CHOPPED

1 MEDIUM CARROT, PEELED AND ROUGHLY CHOPPED

2 BAY LEAVES

2 SPRIGS FRESH THYME

2 LARGE GARLIC CLOVES, GENTLY SMASHED

½ CUP/20 G PACKED FRESH FLAT-LEAF PARSLEY, WITH STEMS AND LEAVES

1 TSP BLACK PEPPERCORNS, COARSELY CRACKED

1 LEMON, THINLY SLICED

FOR THE GEFILTE FISH

1½ TSP DRIED THYME

1 TSP DRIED OREGANO

1 SMALL YELLOW ONION, ROUGHLY CHOPPED

1 MEDIUM CARROT, PEELED AND CUT INTO CHUNKS

2½ LB/1.2 KG SKINNED WHITEFISH FILLETS, SUCH AS A MIX OF HALIBUT AND COD, RINSED, PATTED DRY, AND CUT INTO 1-IN/2.5-CM CHUNKS

¼ CUP/25 G MATZO MEAL (SEE PAGE 18)

3 EGGS, LIGHTLY BEATEN

1 TSP LEMON ZEST

1 TBSP KOSHER SALT

½ TSP FRESHLY GROUND BLACK PEPPER

CREAMY HORSERADISH HERB SAUCE (PAGE 319) OR PREPARED HORSE-RADISH FOR SERVING

CONTINUED

1. Make the poaching broth: Combine all the ingredients in a wide, deep pot set over high heat. Bring to a boil, then turn the heat to medium-low and simmer, partially covered, for 30 minutes. Strain the mixture through a fine-mesh sieve into a large bowl, then return the broth to the pot. Cover and set aside, off the heat. Discard the solids.

2. Make the gefilte fish: Use a mortar and pestle to crush the thyme and oregano.

3. Combine the onion and carrot in a food processor and process until the vegetables are finely chopped, scraping down the sides of the bowl as necessary. Transfer the vegetables to a large bowl. Working in two batches, add the fish to the food processor and process until it is finely chopped and begins to form a ball. Add the fish to the vegetables along with the matzo meal, eggs, lemon zest, thyme, oregano, salt, and pepper, and mix well to combine.

4. Return the poaching broth to a simmer over medium-low heat. Meanwhile, moisten your hands with water. Scoop out a scant ¼ cup/70 g of the mixture and form into an oval 3 in/7.5 cm long. Set aside on a plate and repeat with the remaining fish mixture.

5. Use a slotted spoon to place the fish balls in the gently simmering broth. Cover and simmer until firm and cooked through, 18 to 20 minutes. (If you cut one in half, it should be opaque at the center.) Remove the gefilte fish from the pot with a slotted spoon and transfer to a serving plate. Serve warm or at room temperature, topped with the horseradish herb sauce. (To make ahead, let cool and transfer to a large container. Pour over enough cooled poaching broth to submerge the gefilte fish. Cover the container and refrigerate for at least 2 hours, or up to overnight. Serve cold or at room temperature topped with the horseradish herb sauce.)

GEFILTE FISH: OLD SCHOOL AND NEW

Ask Jews of a certain age about their gefilte fish memories and they will likely start talking about fish and bathtubs. Most people today know gefilte fish as the fish quenelles floating in murky liquid inside glass jars at the supermarket. But according to anecdotal legend, and also Barbara Cohen's wonderful children's book *The Carp in the Bathtub*, Ashkenazi Jews in the not-so-distant past used to purchase whole live carps from their fishmongers and keep them swimming until Friday morning, when a gutsy cook would kill, clean, chop, shape, and poach them into the fish balls served with grated horseradish during the first course of Shabbat and holiday dinners. That, my friends, is hard-core.

Gefilte fish emerged from the fourteenth-century German practice of chopping up fish—typically freshwater varieties like carp, pike, or whitefish—seasoning it, and stuffing it back into the skin to roast. (*Gefilte* is Yiddish for "stuffed"). Within a few centuries, people had mostly abandoned the stuffing step and took to forming the fish into balls and poaching them in a pungent broth made from fish bones and heads.

Personally, I have always found traditional gefilte fish off-putting. It's just too old-world, too gray, and too, well, fishy. But in the last few years, gefilte fish has undergone something of a makeover. Take Gefilteria, a food company co-founded by my friends Jeff Yoskowitz and Liz Alpern. Gefilteria crafts artisanal versions of traditional Jewish foods, including a fantastic baked gefilte fish made with both whitefish and salmon. I usually keep a couple of their gefilte loaves in the freezer at all times.

MOROCCAN CHICKEN WITH PRESERVED LEMONS

This chicken dish, which Moroccan Jews serve on Shabbat and for the Yom Kippur break fast (see page 336), is packed with layers of flavor thanks to the host of spices, sliced green olives, and preserved lemon rind swimming in the sauce. It is traditionally cooked in an earthenware pot called a tagine, but if you do not have one, a Dutch oven also works beautifully.

SERVES 4 TO 6

- 3 TBSP EXTRA-VIRGIN OLIVE OIL
- 2 YELLOW ONIONS, HALVED THROUGH THE ROOT AND THINLY SLICED
- KOSHER SALT AND FRESHLY GROUND BLACK PEPPER
- 4 GARLIC CLOVES, THINLY SLICED
- 1 TBSP SWEET PAPRIKA
- 1 TSP GROUND CINNAMON
- ½ TSP GROUND GINGER
- ½ TSP TURMERIC
- ¼ TSP CAYENNE PEPPER

- 2 CUPS/480 ML CHICKEN OR VEGETABLE BROTH
- 4 LB/1.8 KG SKIN-ON CHICKEN LEGS AND THIGHS, TRIMMED OF EXCESS FAT
- 1 PRESERVED LEMON (PAGE 320), RINSED, PITH REMOVED, AND PEEL THINLY SLICED
- ½ CUP/80 G GREEN OLIVES, PITTED AND THINLY SLICED
- 2 TBSP FRESH LEMON JUICE
- ROUGHLY CHOPPED FRESH FLAT-LEAF PARSLEY OR CILANTRO FOR SPRINKLING

1. Heat the olive oil in a Dutch oven set over medium heat. Add the onions, season with salt and pepper, and cook, stirring occasionally, until softened and browned, 6 to 8 minutes. Add the garlic, paprika, cinnamon, ginger, turmeric, and cayenne and cook, stirring, until fragrant, about 1 minute.

2. Add the broth and bring the mixture to a boil. Meanwhile, sprinkle the chicken pieces with pepper, then add to the pot along with the preserved lemon. (It's okay if not all the chicken pieces are fully submerged in the broth.) Cover, turn the heat to medium-low, and simmer, stirring occasionally, until the chicken is tender and almost falling off the bone, 50 to 60 minutes. Use a pair of tongs to transfer the chicken to a platter.

3. Add the olives and lemon juice to the pot. Raise the heat to high, bring to a boil, and cook, uncovered, stirring occasionally, until slightly thickened, 5 to 10 minutes. Season with salt and pepper, and spoon the sauce over the chicken. Sprinkle with parsley. Serve hot.

APPLE CIDER–BRAISED CHICKEN

Autumn should be renamed braising season—there is simply no cozier or more warming way to cook during the year's chilly months. Fall is also peak season for apples and apple cider. This chicken dish combines the best of both, browning the chicken and then simmering it with sliced apples in a mixture of cider and savory broth. The resulting dish is saucy, lightly sweet, and deeply flavored. It also reheats well, making it a great make-ahead dish for Shabbat or the holidays.

SERVES 4 TO 6

4 LB/1.8 KG SKIN-ON CHICKEN LEGS AND THIGHS, TRIMMED OF EXCESS FAT

KOSHER SALT AND FRESHLY GROUND BLACK PEPPER

2 TO 4 TBSP EXTRA-VIRGIN OLIVE OIL

3 FIRM, SWEET APPLES, SUCH AS GALA, PEELED, QUARTERED, CORED, AND CUT INTO ½-IN/12-MM WEDGES

6 SPRIGS FRESH THYME, PLUS 1 TBSP FINELY CHOPPED FRESH THYME

6 MEDIUM SHALLOTS, THINLY SLICED

1 CUP/240 ML APPLE CIDER

½ CUP/120 ML APPLE CIDER VINEGAR

2 CUPS/480 ML CHICKEN OR VEGETABLE BROTH

1. Sprinkle the chicken pieces with salt and pepper. Heat 2 Tbsp of the olive oil in a large pan set over medium-high heat until shimmering. Working in batches, brown the chicken pieces, starting skin-side down and flipping once, until browned on both sides, about 10 minutes per batch. Add up to 2 Tbsp more oil, if needed. Transfer the chicken to a large ovenproof baking dish and top with the apples and thyme sprigs. Preheat the oven to 375°F/190°C.

2. Meanwhile, set the pan you cooked the chicken in over medium heat. Add the shallots, season with salt and pepper, and cook, stirring occasionally, until browned, about 5 minutes. Add the chopped thyme and cook, stirring often, for 1 minute. Stir in the apple cider and cider vinegar, scraping up any browned bits at the bottom of the pan. Raise the heat to high and cook until the liquid has reduced by half, 4 to 5 minutes. Stir in the broth and bring to a boil, then carefully pour the braising liquid over the chicken and apples. Cover the baking dish with aluminum foil. Braise in the oven until the chicken is fork-tender, 45 to 55 minutes. Use tongs or a slotted spoon to transfer the chicken and apples to a serving platter, and let rest.

3. Meanwhile, if desired, make a sauce by transferring 1½ cups/360 ml of the braising liquid to a saucepan set over high heat. Bring to a boil and cook, stirring often, until the liquid reduces by two-thirds, 10 to 15 minutes. Spoon the sauce over the chicken and serve warm.

ROAST CHICKEN WITH FENNEL AND ORANGE

With just a few simple additions, regular roast chicken becomes extraordinary. This version slips sweet fennel and slices of bright orange—both popular ingredients among Mediterranean Jewish communities—under chicken thighs and legs to soften and soak up the juices while the bird roasts. The result is a super-flavorful meal in a pan: tender vegetables, caramelized citrus fruit, and a gorgeously browned bird scented with thyme.

SERVES 4 TO 6

- 2 TBSP EXTRA-VIRGIN OLIVE OIL, PLUS ¼ CUP/60 ML
- 2 NAVEL ORANGES; 1 ZESTED AND JUICED, 1 CUT INTO ¼-IN/6-MM SLICES
- 1 TBSP DRIED THYME
- 3 MEDIUM FENNEL BULBS, HALVED, CORED, AND CUT INTO 8 WEDGES EACH

- 2 SMALL YELLOW ONIONS, QUARTERED THROUGH THE ROOT
- KOSHER SALT AND FRESHLY GROUND BLACK PEPPER
- 4 LB/1.8 KG SKIN-ON CHICKEN LEGS AND THIGHS, TRIMMED OF EXCESS FAT

1. Preheat the oven to 425°F/220°C. In a medium bowl, whisk together the 2 Tbsp of the olive oil, orange zest and juice, and thyme.

2. Arrange the fennel and onions evenly on the bottom of a roasting pan or on a large rimmed baking sheet, and top with a layer of orange slices. Drizzle with the remaining ¼ cup/60 ml oil and season with salt and pepper.

3. Sprinkle the chicken pieces with salt and pepper, then dip them into the oil–orange mixture, turning to coat. Arrange the chicken pieces, skin-side up, on top of the fennel and orange and roast for 30 minutes. Spoon the pan drippings over the chicken, then continue roasting until the skin is browned and an instant-read thermometer inserted into the thickest part of one of the thighs reaches 165°F/75°C, 25 to 30 minutes more. Transfer the chicken to a platter with the roasted fennel, onions, and orange, and drizzle with the pan juices. Serve hot.

ROSEMARY-MAPLE ROAST CHICKEN

Roast chicken is one of the most iconic dishes served for Shabbat dinner on Ashkenazi tables, and for good reason. Warm, golden, and perfumed with onions, it has all the comforting flavors of home. My version takes the classic dish and amplifies it with lots of rosemary and a glaze of maple syrup and balsamic vinegar. It has become a regular dinner fixture in my house, both for Shabbat and any weeknight when we are in the mood for something both familiar and extraordinary.

SERVES 4

4 GARLIC CLOVES, MINCED OR PUSHED THROUGH A PRESS

1 TBSP FINELY CHOPPED FRESH ROSEMARY, PLUS 3 SPRIGS

2 TBSP VEGETABLE OIL

1 WHOLE CHICKEN (ABOUT 3½ LB/ 1.6 KG)

KOSHER SALT AND FRESHLY GROUND BLACK PEPPER

3 SMALL YELLOW ONIONS, CUT INTO 8 WEDGES EACH

2 TBSP PURE MAPLE SYRUP

1 TBSP BALSAMIC VINEGAR

1. Preheat the oven to 450°F/230°C. In a small bowl, whisk together the garlic, chopped rosemary, and vegetable oil. Rub the mixture all over the entire chicken, including under the skin on each side of the breast and thigh. Sprinkle with salt and pepper.

2. Set a rack in a roasting pan. Fill the chicken cavity with as many onion wedges as comfortably fit (reserving the rest), plus the rosemary sprigs. Place the chicken, breast-side up, on the rack and tuck the wings under. Tie the legs together with kitchen twine. Roast the chicken for 40 minutes.

3. Meanwhile, whisk together the maple syrup and vinegar in a small bowl. After 40 minutes of roasting, add the remaining onion wedges to the roasting pan and brush the chicken all over with the maple syrup mixture.

4. Continue roasting, basting the chicken and onions once with the pan juices, until the juices run clear and an instant-read thermometer inserted into the thickest part of the thigh reaches 165°F/75°C, 20 to 25 minutes more. Let rest for 10 minutes before carving. Serve warm with the onions from the roasting pan.

CHICKEN SCHNITZEL WITH CAPER VINAIGRETTE

Schnitzel is straight-up Jewish comfort food. The practice of dredging meat (particularly veal) in flour and bread crumbs, then frying it in oil is popular throughout Europe, à la Austria's Wiener schnitzel and Italy's *cotoletta alla milanese*. Chicken schnitzel, which is the preferred variety among Jewish cooks, traveled with Central European Jews to Israel in the early twentieth century. There, schnitzel became a national obsession and a ubiquitous street snack on par with falafel. Schnitzel can be topped simply with a squeeze of lemon juice or more elaborately with a variety of sauces. Personally, I love this briny, herb-flecked caper vinaigrette, which brightens the cutlets without weighing them down. This dish is delicious paired with Toasted Almond Israeli Couscous (page 161).

SERVES 4 TO 6

NOTE

Serving fewer people? Cut this recipe in half: Make the same amount of vinaigrette and use the leftovers for a salad. For the schnitzel itself, use 2 eggs and halve everything else.

FOR THE VINAIGRETTE

1 TBSP RED WINE VINEGAR

1 TSP DIJON MUSTARD

1 GARLIC CLOVE, MINCED OR PUSHED THROUGH A PRESS

2 TBSP BRINE-PACKED CAPERS, DRAINED AND ROUGHLY CHOPPED

3 TBSP FINELY CHOPPED FRESH FLAT-LEAF PARSLEY

¼ CUP PLUS 2 TBSP/90 ML EXTRA-VIRGIN OLIVE OIL

½ TSP FRESHLY GROUND BLACK PEPPER

¼ TSP KOSHER SALT

FOR THE SCHNITZEL

1 CUP/125 G WHITE WHOLE-WHEAT FLOUR OR ALL-PURPOSE FLOUR

3 EGGS, LIGHTLY BEATEN

2 CUPS/160 G PANKO BREAD CRUMBS

4 BONELESS SKINLESS CHICKEN BREASTS (ABOUT 6 OZ/170 G EACH)

KOSHER SALT AND FRESHLY GROUND BLACK PEPPER

VEGETABLE OIL FOR FRYING

CONTINUED

1. Make the vinaigrette: Stir together the vinegar, mustard, garlic, capers, parsley, olive oil, pepper, and salt in a small bowl until well combined. (The mixture should look heavy on the herbs.) Set aside.

2. Make the schnitzel: Place the flour, eggs, and bread crumbs in three separate shallow bowls.

3. Use a sharp knife to carefully butterfly each chicken breast, then cut down the middle seam. Use a meat pounder to gently pound each half until it is ¼ in/6 mm thick. Sprinkle the chicken halves on both sides with salt and pepper. Working with one piece at a time, dredge the chicken in the flour and shake off the excess. Dip in the eggs, then coat well with bread crumbs, and set on a large plate.

4. Line a plate with paper towels. Heat ¼ in/6 mm of vegetable oil in a large skillet set over medium-high heat until shimmering. Working in batches, add the coated chicken pieces to the hot pan and cook, turning once, until crispy and cooked through, 5 to 6 minutes per batch. Transfer the chicken to the paper towel–lined plate to drain. Divide the chicken among plates and drizzle with the caper vinaigrette. Serve hot.

STEAK AND ZA'ATAR FAJITAS

I grew up eating my mom's take on fajitas—a savory mix of steak, peppers, and onion wrapped in warm flour tortillas that she likely learned to make while reading *Gourmet* or another one of the many food and women's magazines that populated our coffee table. My version marinates the smoky steak with lemony-scented za'atar in an unorthodox but delicious pairing. Think of it as a Middle Eastern spin on a Tex-Mex classic.

SERVES 4

FOR THE MARINADE

ZEST OF 1 LIME

3 TBSP EXTRA-VIRGIN OLIVE OIL

2 TSP HONEY

1 TBSP ZA'ATAR

¼ TSP GROUND CUMIN

¼ RED ONION, ROUGHLY CHOPPED

2 GARLIC CLOVES, ROUGHLY CHOPPED

½ TSP RED PEPPER FLAKES

½ TSP KOSHER SALT

½ TSP FRESHLY GROUND BLACK PEPPER

1 LB/455 G SKIRT STEAK

1 LARGE YELLOW ONION, HALVED THROUGH THE ROOT AND THINLY SLICED

3 BELL PEPPERS (ANY COLOR), SEEDED AND THINLY SLICED

1 TBSP EXTRA-VIRGIN OLIVE OIL

KOSHER SALT AND FRESHLY GROUND BLACK PEPPER

1 TBSP FRESH LIME JUICE

WARM FLOUR TORTILLAS, ROUGHLY CHOPPED FRESH CILANTRO, AND ZA'ATAR FOR SERVING

1. Make the marinade: Combine the lime zest, olive oil, honey, za'atar, cumin, onion, garlic, red pepper flakes, salt, and pepper in a blender and blend until smooth, scraping down the sides as necessary. If the mixture seems too thick to pour, add 1 to 3 tsp water and blend to combine.

2. Pour the marinade into a resealable plastic bag, add the steak, gently shake to coat, and refrigerate for at least 2 hours, or up to overnight. (You can do this step in the morning and keep it in the refrigerator all day until ready to grill.)

3. Preheat a gas or charcoal grill, or set a grill pan over medium-high heat. Brush the grill rack or pan generously with vegetable oil. Put the onion and bell peppers in a bowl, drizzle with the olive oil, and season with salt and pepper. Stir to coat.

4. Remove the steak from the marinade and wipe off excess marinade with a paper towel. Sprinkle the steak with the lime juice. Grill the steak until grill marks form, about 3 minutes. Turn and continue to cook 2 to 4 minutes more, depending on desired doneness. Transfer to a cutting board and let rest while you cook the vegetables.

5. Grill the onion and bell peppers, turning occasionally with tongs, until just tender, 6 to 7 minutes.

6. Slice the steak on the diagonal, against the grain, into thin strips. Serve hot in warm tortillas topped with the grilled vegetables, cilantro, and an additional sprinkle of za'atar.

RED WINE AND HONEY BRISKET

For many people, brisket is the Proustian madeleine of Jewish cooking. The rich, savory scent of caramelizing meat that perfumes the house as it cooks seems to stir people into a nostalgia-fueled fervor. There is no question that the brisket your bubbe made was the best ever, and you cannot compete with the layers of memories that flavor her version in your mind. That's okay, because you have a few tricks of your own up your sleeve. This version slow-cooks the meat in a sweet and tangy mixture of honey and red wine until it sighs and falls apart at the touch of a fork. I included the red wine as a nod to *stracotto*, the Roman Jewish take on brisket, which simmers beef in wine and spices. (Read more about stracotto and Rome's Jewish community on page 104.) Serve it for Rosh Hashanah dinner (see page 334), and start building the next generation of memories.

SERVES 8 TO 10

NOTE

This recipe calls for second-cut brisket, which is sometimes referred to as deckle. It can be difficult to find second-cut brisket packaged in the grocery store, so ask your butcher about it. While you're asking for things, see if the butcher will trim off any excess fat, too. Find more about deckle and an online source on page 343. If you have first-cut brisket on hand, go ahead and use it—the dish will still be delicious.

Brisket's flavor and texture improve with age, so while you can certainly serve it right away, it will taste best if you make it a day in advance. Once the brisket has chilled in the refrigerator overnight, spoon off and discard any excess fat congealed at the top and transfer the meat to a cutting board. Thinly slice the brisket against the grain (meat is easier to slice when it's cold), then place the slices back into the Dutch oven or roasting pan, spooning some of the saucy onion mixture over the top. Warm in a 300°F/150°C oven until hot and bubbling, 20 to 30 minutes.

4 TO 5 LB/1.8 TO 2.3 KG BRISKET, PREFERABLY SECOND CUT

KOSHER SALT AND FRESHLY GROUND BLACK PEPPER

1 TBSP VEGETABLE OIL

3 LARGE YELLOW ONIONS, HALVED THROUGH THE ROOT AND THINLY SLICED

8 SPRIGS FRESH THYME

8 GARLIC CLOVES, THINLY SLICED

2 BAY LEAVES

1½ CUPS/360 ML DRY RED WINE

3 TBSP BALSAMIC VINEGAR

¼ CUP/95 G HONEY

1 TSP ONION POWDER

1 TSP GARLIC POWDER

1 CUP/240 ML CHICKEN BROTH

CONTINUED

1. Preheat the oven to 325°F/165°C. Generously sprinkle both sides of the brisket with salt and pepper.

2. Heat the vegetable oil in a Dutch oven or large pot set over medium-high heat. Add the brisket and cook, turning once, until browned on both sides, 8 to 10 minutes total. (If the brisket does not fit all at once, cut it in half and sear it in batches.)

3. Remove the brisket from the pot and set aside on a cutting board. Add the onions, thyme, garlic, and bay leaves to the pot, followed by ½ cup/120 ml of the wine and the vinegar. Cook, stirring often, until the onions soften slightly and the mixture is fragrant, about 5 minutes.

4. Whisk together the remaining 1 cup/240 ml wine, honey, onion powder, garlic powder, broth, and 1 tsp salt in a medium bowl until fully combined. If you used a Dutch oven, lay the brisket on top of the onions and pour the wine mixture over the top. Cover and transfer to the oven. If you used a pot, transfer the onion mixture to a roasting pan and top with the brisket. Pour the wine mixture over the top. Cover tightly with aluminum foil and transfer to the oven.

5. Cook the brisket for 2 hours. Remove from the oven, uncover, and carefully turn the meat to the other side. Re-cover and continue cooking until the meat is fork-tender, 2 to 2½ hours more.

6. Remove from the oven and transfer the brisket to a cutting board. Cover loosely with foil and let rest for 10 to 15 minutes before slicing. Locate the thin lines running in one direction along the brisket and use a sharp knife to cut thin slices perpendicular to those lines. Remove and discard the thyme sprigs and bay leaves from the cooking liquid. Use a slotted spoon to remove the onions and arrange around the brisket. Spoon the desired amount of pan juices over the brisket. Serve hot.

SPICY CHORIZO AND RED PEPPER PENNE

Across the Middle East, including in Israel, cooks use a multilayered spice mixture called baharat to season grilled meats and dress up pilafs. Fittingly, *baharat* is the Arabic word for "spices." On a whim one evening, I sprinkled some into an Italian-inspired dish of penne pasta with sautéed onions, peppers, and chorizo, and was immediately glad I did. The complex mixture of sweet, savory, and smoky spices added a new dimension to a familiar dish, and turned a basic weeknight meal into something special. Find an online source for kosher chorizo on page 343. Vegetarians can substitute vegetarian chorizo, or another kind of firm, meat-free sausage.

SERVES 6

1 LB/455 G PENNE

EXTRA-VIRGIN OLIVE OIL FOR DRIZZLING, PLUS ¼ CUP/60 ML

2 YELLOW ONIONS, FINELY CHOPPED

KOSHER SALT

2 MEDIUM RED BELL PEPPERS, CUT INTO ½-IN/12-MM CHUNKS

8 OZ/225 G CHORIZO, CUT INTO ¼-IN/6-MM SLICES

4 GARLIC CLOVES, FINELY CHOPPED

2 TBSP BAHARAT (PAGE 323)

ROUGHLY CHOPPED FRESH FLAT-LEAF PARSLEY FOR SPRINKLING

1. Bring a pot of generously salted water to a boil. Add the penne and cook, stirring occasionally, until al dente, 10 to 12 minutes (or follow the timing instructions on the package). Drain well, transfer to a large bowl, drizzle with olive oil, toss to coat, and set aside.

2. Meanwhile, heat the remaining ¼ cup/60 ml olive oil in a large pan set over medium-low heat. Add the onions and a generous pinch of salt and cook, stirring occasionally, until softened and lightly browned, about 15 minutes. Raise the heat to medium and add the bell peppers and chorizo. Cook, stirring occasionally, until the peppers soften, 7 to 10 minutes. Add the garlic and baharat and cook, stirring often, until fragrant, 1 to 2 minutes. Taste and season with more salt, if desired.

3. Add the chorizo-pepper mixture to the pasta and drizzle with more oil, if needed; toss well to combine. Sprinkle with parsley. Serve hot.

POMEGRANATE MOLASSES MEATBALLS

Growing up, when my mom used to serve meatballs simmered in a sweet and tangy tomato sauce at holiday dinners, I always figured she was borrowing a recipe from the Italian playbook. I later learned that simmered meatballs are an important part of Eastern European Jewish cuisine as well. Old-world cooks would add mouth-puckering flavor to their sauce with sour salt (citric acid crystals), which was more readily available than fresh lemons. In America, Jewish home cooks started pouring canned cranberry sauce into the mix—a brilliantly simple way of incorporating tart and sweet flavor in one go. My recipe goes a slightly different route, incorporating a touch of Middle Eastern essence with the addition of tangy pomegranate molasses. It can be found in specialty food stores, or see page 342 for an online source.

SERVES 4 TO 6

NOTE

These meatballs have a wonderful lamby flavor. If that's not your thing, use all beef instead of half beef and half lamb.

If possible, make this dish a day before you need it, for richer flavor. Chill in the refrigerator and skim off the excess fat with a spoon. Warm in a 300°F/150°C oven until bubbling.

FOR THE SAUCE

2 TBSP VEGETABLE OIL

1 MEDIUM YELLOW ONION, FINELY CHOPPED

ONE 15-OZ/430-G CAN TOMATO SAUCE

½ CUP/120 ML WATER

1 TBSP POMEGRANATE MOLASSES

⅓ CUP/65 G PACKED LIGHT BROWN SUGAR

KOSHER SALT AND FRESHLY GROUND BLACK PEPPER

FOR THE MEATBALLS

1 LB/455 G GROUND BEEF

1 LB/455 G GROUND LAMB

1 MEDIUM YELLOW ONION, PEELED

1 EGG, LIGHTLY BEATEN

½ CUP/55 G PLAIN BREAD CRUMBS

1½ TSP KOSHER SALT

½ TSP FRESHLY GROUND BLACK PEPPER

1. Make the sauce: Heat the vegetable oil in a Dutch oven or large saucepan set over medium heat. Add the onion and cook, stirring occasionally, until softened and lightly browned, 6 to 8 minutes. Stir in the tomato sauce, water, pomegranate molasses, brown sugar, and a generous sprinkle of salt and pepper. Bring to a simmer, then remove from the heat.

2. Make the meatballs: Combine the beef and lamb in a large bowl and blend with your hands. Grate the onion on the large holes of a box grater and squeeze dry with your hands, discarding the liquid. Add the onion, egg, bread crumbs, salt, and pepper to the bowl and mix to combine.

3. Place the Dutch oven back over medium heat and let the sauce come to a gentle simmer. Meanwhile, form the meat mixture into golf ball–size balls (about 1½ in/4 cm) and gently nestle in the sauce. (It's okay if they do not all fit in one layer at first; they will shrink as they cook.) Turn the heat to medium-low, cover the pan, and simmer the meatballs, rotating halfway through to make sure both sides get fully covered in the sauce, until cooked through, 30 to 35 minutes. Serve the meatballs hot with the sauce spooned over the top.

MUSHROOM-AND-BEEF-STUFFED PEPPERS

Stuffed peppers are one of my favorite foods to make during the holiday of Sukkot (see page 338). Filled with herb-flecked rice, ground beef, and mushrooms, they epitomize the abundance celebrated during the harvest holiday. Simmered in an oregano- and thyme-spiced tomato sauce, they are simple and warm—a dish that comforts rather than challenges. And on a cool, early autumn night, particularly if you happen to be dining alfresco in a sukkah, that is just perfect. If you are serving a crowd, go ahead and double the recipe, letting the sauce simmer for 20 to 25 minutes.

SERVES 4

NOTE

The best peppers for this dish are squat and globe shaped, rather than thin and long ones.

FOR THE SAUCE

ONE 28-OZ/800-G CAN WHOLE TOMATOES

2 TBSP EXTRA-VIRGIN OLIVE OIL

1 YELLOW ONION, FINELY CHOPPED

4 GARLIC CLOVES, FINELY CHOPPED

1 TBSP FINELY CHOPPED FRESH THYME OR 1 TSP DRIED THYME

1½ TSP DRIED OREGANO

½ TSP RED PEPPER FLAKES

1 TSP SWEET PAPRIKA

1 TBSP APPLE CIDER VINEGAR

2 TSP KOSHER SALT

¼ CUP/50 G PACKED LIGHT BROWN SUGAR

¼ CUP/45 G LONG-GRAIN BROWN RICE

1½ TSP KOSHER SALT

2 TBSP EXTRA-VIRGIN OLIVE OIL

1 YELLOW ONION, FINELY CHOPPED

8 OZ/225 G WHITE MUSHROOMS, STEMMED AND FINELY CHOPPED

8 OZ/225 G GROUND BEEF

¼ CUP/10 G FINELY CHOPPED FRESH FLAT-LEAF PARSLEY

½ TSP FRESHLY GROUND BLACK PEPPER

4 MEDIUM BELL PEPPERS (ANY COLOR), HALVED LENGTHWISE, STEMMED, DERIBBED, AND SEEDED

1. Make the sauce: Pour the tomatoes with their juice into a large bowl and gently squeeze with your hands until they burst; set aside. Heat the olive oil in a medium saucepan set over medium heat. Add the onion and cook, stirring occasionally, until softened and lightly browned, 6 to 8 minutes. Add the garlic, thyme, oregano, red pepper flakes, and paprika and cook, stirring, until fragrant, 1 to 2 minutes. Stir in the tomatoes with their juice, vinegar, salt, and brown sugar. Bring to a boil and cook, stirring occasionally, until slightly thickened, 10 to 15 minutes. Remove from the heat and set aside.

2. Preheat the oven to 375°F/190°C. Combine the rice and ½ tsp of the salt in a small saucepan and cover with water by 1 in/2.5 cm. Bring to a boil over high heat, then turn the heat to medium and cook, uncovered, until the rice is partly cooked, about 10 minutes. Drain well and set aside.

3. Heat the olive oil in a medium pan set over medium heat. Add the onion and mushrooms and cook, stirring occasionally, until softened and the moisture is cooked out of the mushrooms, 8 to 10 minutes. Add the ground beef and cook, breaking up the meat into small pieces with a wooden spoon, until the beef is just browned, 3 to 4 minutes. Remove from the heat and stir in the partially cooked rice, parsley, remaining 1 tsp salt, and pepper. Let cool to the touch.

4. Pour most of the tomato sauce into the bottom of a 9-by-13-in/23-by-33-cm baking dish, reserving about ½ cup/120 ml. Spoon the filling into the pepper halves and arrange snugly in the baking dish. Spoon about 1 Tbsp of the remaining sauce on top of each pepper. Cover the dish with aluminum foil and bake until the peppers are tender, about 1 hour. Serve hot.

CHAPTER SEVEN

VEGETARIAN MAINS

BREADED EGGPLANT AND TOMATO STACKS

Coating eggplant in bread crumbs and baking it in the oven is a wonderful way to give the Mediterranean vegetable a meaty texture and transform it into main-course material. In this riff on eggplant parmigiana (a rustic Italian classic that has become popular among Jewish cooks), two bread crumb–and-Parmesan-coated eggplant rounds sandwich juicy roasted tomatoes and a slice of melted mozzarella. Instead of the traditional marinara, I top the stack with a light, lemony, herb-filled vinaigrette.

SERVES 4

1 TO 2 EGGPLANTS, CUT INTO SIXTEEN ¼-IN-/6-MM-THICK ROUNDS THAT ARE AT LEAST 3 IN/7.5 CM IN DIAMETER

KOSHER SALT

3 EGGS, LIGHTLY BEATEN

⅔ CUP/80 G ALL-PURPOSE FLOUR

1½ CUPS/120 G PANKO BREAD CRUMBS

½ CUP/40 G GRATED PARMESAN

5 MEDIUM TOMATOES, CORED AND SLICED HORIZONTALLY INTO ½-IN/12-MM ROUNDS

4 OZ/115 G FRESH MOZZARELLA, THINLY SLICED INTO 8 ROUNDS

FRESHLY GROUND BLACK PEPPER

1 DOUBLE RECIPE OF LEMON-MINT VINAIGRETTE (PAGE 44)

1. Place the eggplant rounds in a colander, sprinkle with 1 Tbsp salt, and mix with your hands to coat each round. Let stand for 30 minutes, then rinse well and thoroughly pat dry with paper towels. Fifteen minutes into the salting process, preheat the oven to 400°F/200°C and brush two large rimmed baking sheets with 1 Tbsp olive oil each.

2. Place the eggs in a shallow bowl. Place the flour on a plate, and mix the bread crumbs and Parmesan together on a separate plate. Working in batches, dip the eggplant rounds into the flour on both sides, followed by the eggs, shaking off any excess. Press the rounds into the bread crumb–Parmesan mixture, using your fingers to coat. Arrange the rounds in a single layer on one of the prepared baking sheets. Arrange the tomato slices in a single layer on the second baking sheet. Sprinkle the tomatoes with a little salt (the eggplants will already be salty) and sprinkle both generously with pepper.

3. Bake, flipping once with tongs, until the tomatoes are tender and the eggplant is golden on both sides, about 25 minutes. Layer half of the eggplant rounds with a slice of mozzarella and continue baking until the cheese melts, about 5 minutes. Remove the baking sheets from the oven.

4. Lay a cheese-covered eggplant round on a flat surface. Top with two or three tomato slices, followed by a cheeseless eggplant round. Repeat with the remaining eggplant and tomatoes. Arrange the stacks on a serving platter. Serve warm with the vinaigrette on the side.

SWEET POTATO– SCALLION FRITTATA

Frittatas are among my favorite vegetarian entrées. In addition to being hearty and simple to prepare, they make an elegant centerpiece to any dinner table or picnic spread. This version, which pairs spicy scallions, softened sweet potatoes, and woodsy rosemary, is perfect for early fall. For a rustic presentation, lay the frittata on a wooden cutting board and slice it at the table.

SERVES 6

2 TBSP EXTRA-VIRGIN OLIVE OIL

7 SCALLIONS, WHITE AND GREEN PARTS, SLICED DIAGONALLY INTO 1-IN/2.5-CM PIECES

1 MEDIUM SWEET POTATO, PEELED, HALVED LENGTHWISE, AND THINLY SLICED INTO HALF-MOONS

KOSHER SALT

12 EGGS

⅓ CUP/80 ML CRÈME FRAÎCHE

1 TBSP FINELY CHOPPED FRESH ROSEMARY

½ CUP/55 G GRATED SHARP CHEDDAR

½ TSP FRESHLY GROUND BLACK PEPPER

1. Preheat the oven to 400°F/200°C.

2. Heat the olive oil in a large nonstick ovenproof pan set over medium heat. Add the scallions, sweet potato, and a pinch of salt, cover, and cook, stirring occasionally, until the sweet potato softens, 10 to 12 minutes.

3. Meanwhile, in a medium bowl, whisk together the eggs, crème fraîche, rosemary, cheddar, pepper, and 1 tsp salt. Pour the egg mixture into the pan and stir gently to combine with the vegetables.

4. Transfer to the oven and bake until the frittata is cooked through and gently puffed, 10 to 15 minutes. Remove from the oven and let stand for a few minutes before slicing. Serve warm or at room temperature.

SPINACH SHAKSHUKA

Since I was little, I have thrilled at reading food-related passages in novels. But the food scenes in *Some Day* by Israeli novelist Shemi Zarhin are on another level. In one passage, Zarhin describes a dish so vividly, I felt compelled to re-create it in my own kitchen. He writes: "Ruchama . . . fried onions and sprinkled garlic cloves . . . seasoned it with spicy green pepper and coriander seeds and squeezed a lemon and placed a pile of beet leaves . . . in the middle, and within seconds the green pile sunk into the pot and became an aromatic green sauce, into which Ruchama chopped cubes of sheep's milk cheese and broke three eggs and dripped olive oil." As I read and my mouth watered, I realized that Ruchama is essentially making a tomato-free version of the North African poached egg dish, shakshuka. Riffing off the "recipe," I experimented with a spinach shakshuka and, like Ruchama, ended up mopping it up with pita "with great pleasure."

SERVES 2 OR 3

- 3 TBSP EXTRA-VIRGIN OLIVE OIL, PLUS MORE FOR DRIZZLING
- 1 LARGE YELLOW ONION, FINELY CHOPPED
- 1 SMALL JALAPEÑO, SEEDED AND FINELY CHOPPED
- 4 GARLIC CLOVES, FINELY CHOPPED
- ¼ TSP GROUND CORIANDER
- ¼ TSP GROUND CINNAMON
- 1 TSP KOSHER SALT
- 10 OZ/280 G BABY SPINACH
- 2 TSP FRESH LEMON JUICE
- 4 TO 6 EGGS
- FRESHLY GROUND BLACK PEPPER
- FETA CHEESE AND ROUGHLY CHOPPED FRESH CILANTRO, FOR SPRINKLING

1. Heat the olive oil in a large pan set over medium heat. Add the onion and jalapeño and cook, stirring occasionally, until softened, 6 to 8 minutes. Add the garlic, coriander, cinnamon, and salt and cook, stirring, until fragrant, 1 to 2 minutes.

2. Add the spinach and lemon juice to the pan, turn the heat to low, cover, and cook, tossing occasionally with tongs, until the spinach is very soft, 7 to 10 minutes. (If the spinach does not fit all at once in the pan, add a little at a time, adding more as the spinach in the pan wilts.) Uncover and evenly spread the mixture across the bottom of the pan. Use the back of the spoon to make four to six shallow indentations in the surface of the greens mixture to hold the eggs while they cook.

3. Break the eggs into small cups and gently slide them into the indentations. Raise the heat to medium, cover the pan, and cook until the whites are set but the yolks are still a bit runny, 4 to 5 minutes. Remove the pan from the heat. Drizzle a little more olive oil on top and sprinkle with pepper, feta, and cilantro. Serve hot, directly from the pan.

SPICED LENTIL PATTIES

Lentils go way back in Jewish history—all the way to the biblical story of Esau, who, in a moment of questionable judgment, agreed to sell his birthright to his brother, Jacob, in exchange for bread and a bowl of lentil stew. Not surprisingly, lentil dishes are scattered throughout Jewish cuisine, particularly on the Sephardi side. I happen to be only a moderate fan of lentils. I have encountered far more mediocre, and occasionally even dismal, lentil dishes than sublime ones. These spiced lentil patties help redeem the humble pulse. Threaded through with fresh mint, cinnamon, cumin, and a bit of red pepper flakes, then baked instead of fried, they are firm and flavorful, and far from dull. Pair them with Greek goddess dressing (see page 177), apple-date chutney (see page 119), or your favorite topping.

SERVES 4

- 1 CUP/190 G RED LENTILS, RINSED AND DRAINED
- 1 BAY LEAF
- 2 GARLIC CLOVES, MINCED OR PUSHED THROUGH A PRESS
- ½ MEDIUM RED ONION, FINELY CHOPPED
- ½ CUP/20 G FINELY CHOPPED FRESH MINT OR CILANTRO

- 2 EGGS, LIGHTLY BEATEN
- ½ CUP/55 G PLAIN BREAD CRUMBS
- ½ TSP GROUND CUMIN
- ½ TSP GROUND CINNAMON
- ¼ TSP TURMERIC
- ¼ TSP RED PEPPER FLAKES
- 1½ TSP KOSHER SALT
- FRESHLY GROUND BLACK PEPPER

1. Combine the lentils and bay leaf in a medium saucepan and cover with water by 2 in/5 cm. Bring to a simmer over medium-high heat, then turn the heat to low and gently simmer, partially covered and stirring occasionally, until the lentils grow soft and pulpy, 10 to 15 minutes. Drain well, discarding the bay leaf; let cool completely. (Store in an airtight container in the refrigerator for up to 2 days.)

2. Preheat the oven to 350°F/180°C and line a large rimmed baking sheet with parchment paper and brush with 1 Tbsp vegetable oil.

3. Transfer the cooled lentils to a large bowl and stir in the garlic, onion, mint, eggs, bread crumbs, cumin, cinnamon, turmeric, red pepper flakes, and salt. Season with pepper. Stir together until fully combined and set aside to let the ingredients meld, about 10 minutes.

4. Moisten your hands with water and shape the lentil mixture into 10 patties, each 2 to 3 in/5 to 7.5 cm wide and ½ in/12 mm thick. Place the patties on the prepared baking sheet.

5. Bake for 15 minutes. Gently flip the patties with a flat spatula and cook until firm and cooked through, about 10 minutes. Serve warm.

A VEGETARIAN MAIN-DISH MANIFESTO

During the nearly ten years I spent as a vegetarian, I ate very well. I got acquainted with the glories of cooking local produce from the farmers' market, and vigorously explored international cuisines that introduced a world of effortlessly meat-free dishes to my repertoire.

But I must admit, sometimes I really missed meat—not the taste or texture, per se, but the *decisiveness* of it. If you set a roast chicken or a platter of hamburgers on the table, you immediately know you are having a meal. But with vegetarian cooking, I often felt like I was cobbling together a bunch of side dishes. They were really delicious sides, but they lacked that sense of well-rounded completeness, that showy elegance of a main dish.

The problem was not the food itself, but poor meal planning skills on my part. As I developed as a home cook, I learned that vegetarian cooking works most successfully when it follows traditional meal planning logic: salad, main dish, starchy side, vegetable side. The main, of course, does not have to be a piece of steak. But it should command a certain amount of attention and respect at the table.

These days I do eat some meat, but my home kitchen is still vegetarian about 90 percent of the time. There are lots of meat-free dishes in other sections of this book that you could make the center of a meal. But for those of us who cook for vegetarian friends and family members (and ourselves!), I wanted to designate a group of recipes that stand out as entrées.

For simple, satisfying everyday dinners, I love making Spinach Shakshuka (page 208) or Spiced Lentil Patties (page 210). When feeding a crowd, I turn to a hearty casserole like Baked Ziti with Caramelized Cherry Tomatoes (page 218) or flavorful Porcini-, Tomato-, and Kale-Stuffed Peppers (page 213). And when I am entertaining for Shabbat or a dinner party, and need something particularly festive, I turn to Cinnamon-Roasted Seitan and Onions (page 223), Grilled Portobellos with Herbs and Mozzarella (page 215), or the beautiful Mushroom–Goat Cheese Tart (page 216) to deliver sophistication along with flavor.

PORCINI-, TOMATO-, AND KALE-STUFFED PEPPERS

This meat-free take on stuffed peppers is packed with overlapping layers of flavor, thanks to the dried porcini mushrooms, earthy kale, juicy tomatoes, fresh herbs, and salty Parmesan tucked inside. I like to serve them on Sukkot (see page 338) or Thanksgiving to celebrate the harvest, but just as often make them for a cozy weeknight dinner on a chilly fall or winter evening.

SERVES 4 TO 6

NOTE

The best peppers for this dish are squat and globe shaped, rather than thin and long ones.

1 OZ/30 G DRIED PORCINI MUSHROOMS

2 CUPS/480 ML BOILING WATER

½ CUP/90 G LONG-GRAIN WHITE OR BROWN RICE

KOSHER SALT

2 TBSP UNSALTED BUTTER OR EXTRA-VIRGIN OLIVE OIL

3 MEDIUM SHALLOTS, FINELY CHOPPED

3 GARLIC CLOVES, FINELY CHOPPED

2 RIPE PLUM TOMATOES, CORED, SEEDED, AND FINELY CHOPPED

2 CUPS/70 G LACINATO KALE, CUT INTO THIN RIBBONS

1 TBSP FINELY CHOPPED FRESH THYME

¼ CUP/10 G ROUGHLY CHOPPED FRESH BASIL

1 CUP/80 G GRATED PARMESAN

FRESHLY GROUND BLACK PEPPER

4 MEDIUM BELL PEPPERS (ANY COLOR), HALVED LENGTHWISE, STEMMED, DERIBBED, AND SEEDED

1. Place the porcini in a small bowl and cover with the boiling water. Let stand for 20 minutes. Remove the mushrooms with tongs, rinse well to remove any lingering sediment, and coarsely chop. Discard the soaking liquid.

2. Meanwhile, preheat the oven to 375°F/190°C. Combine the rice and ½ tsp salt in a small saucepan and cover with water by 1 in/2.5 cm. Bring to a boil over high heat, then turn the heat to medium and cook, uncovered, until the rice is partly cooked, about 10 minutes. Drain well and set aside.

CONTINUED

3. Melt the butter until foaming in a large pan set over medium heat. Add the shallots and cook until softened, 5 to 7 minutes. Add the garlic and cook, stirring often, until fragrant, 1 to 2 minutes Add the tomatoes, kale, and softened mushrooms, cover, and cook, stirring occasionally, until the kale wilts, 6 to 8 minutes. Remove the pan from the heat and stir in the thyme, basil, rice, and ½ cup/40 g of the Parmesan. Season generously with salt and pepper.

4. Spoon the filling into the bell pepper halves and arrange snugly in a 9-by-13-in/23-by-33-cm baking dish. Pour about ½ cup/120 ml water into the baking dish around the peppers. Cover the dish with aluminum foil and bake until the peppers are tender, about 50 minutes. Uncover and top each pepper with about 1 Tbsp Parmesan. Continue baking, uncovered, until the cheese melts, 5 to 10 minutes. Serve hot.

GRILLED PORTOBELLOS WITH HERBS AND MOZZARELLA

The grill is a portobello mushroom's best friend. Under the influence of heat and flame, they turn into smoky, meaty, lusciously tender dreams. Tucking some Parmesan and fresh herbs inside and melting mozzarella on top transforms them into a proper main course. Fire up a bunch of these stuffed mushrooms for an early summer barbecue, or swap out the bread crumbs for matzo meal and serve them as an unexpected dinner during Passover. Look for cup-shaped portobellos, which hold their shape better than the flatter ones while grilling.

SERVES 4 TO 6

½ CUP/40 G PANKO BREAD CRUMBS

½ CUP/120 ML EXTRA-VIRGIN OLIVE OIL

3 GARLIC CLOVES, FINELY CHOPPED

½ CUP/40 G GRATED PARMESAN

¼ CUP/10 G FINELY CHOPPED FRESH PARSLEY, PLUS MORE FOR SPRINKLING

3 TBSP ROUGHLY CHOPPED FRESH BASIL

1 TSP DRIED OREGANO

¼ TSP RED PEPPER FLAKES

½ TSP KOSHER SALT

⅛ TSP FRESHLY GROUND BLACK PEPPER

¼ CUP/60 ML BALSAMIC VINEGAR

6 PORTOBELLO MUSHROOMS, STEMMED AND GILLS SCOOPED OUT

SIX ¼-IN/6-MM SLICES FRESH MOZZARELLA

1. Preheat a gas or charcoal grill to medium heat, or set a grill pan over medium heat.

2. In a medium bowl, stir together the bread crumbs, ¼ cup/60 ml of the olive oil, the garlic, Parmesan, parsley, basil, oregano, red pepper flakes, salt, and pepper. In a small bowl, whisk together the vinegar and remaining ¼ cup/ 60 ml olive oil. Generously brush the mushroom caps on both sides with the oil-vinegar mixture.

3. Place the mushrooms, rounded-side up, on the grill. Close the grill and cook until grill marks form and the mushrooms soften slightly, about 3 minutes. Remove the mushrooms from the grill and gently fill with the bread crumb mixture, then top each with a slice of mozzarella. Place back on the grill (filling-side up, naturally!), close the grill, and cook until the mushrooms are tender and the cheese melts, about 5 minutes. Serve hot, topped with a sprinkling of parsley.

MUSHROOM–GOAT CHEESE TART

With its golden pastry encasing a layer of herb-flecked goat cheese, softened shallots, and earthy mushrooms, there is no mistaking this tart for a side dish. It is a vegetarian main dish that commands attention at the table, and delivers plenty of flavor. Switch up this tart by swapping the cremini mushrooms for shiitake, chanterelle, oyster, or your favorite mushrooms.

SERVES 4

4 TBSP/55 G UNSALTED BUTTER

6 SHALLOTS, HALVED LENGTHWISE AND THINLY SLICED

1 TSP SUGAR

KOSHER SALT AND FRESHLY GROUND BLACK PEPPER

1 LB/455 G CREMINI MUSHROOMS, STEMMED AND THINLY SLICED

4 GARLIC CLOVES, FINELY CHOPPED

6 OZ/170 G GOAT CHEESE, AT ROOM TEMPERATURE

1 EGG, LIGHTLY BEATEN

1 TBSP MILK

2 TSP FINELY CHOPPED FRESH THYME LEAVES

1 SHEET FROZEN PUFF PASTRY, THAWED

1. Preheat the oven to 375°F/190°C and lightly grease a large rimmed baking sheet. Melt 2 Tbsp of the butter until foaming in a medium pan set over medium heat. Add the shallots and sugar, and season with salt and pepper. Cook, stirring occasionally, until softened, 6 to 8 minutes. Transfer the shallots to a bowl and set aside.

2. Melt the remaining 2 Tbsp butter in the same pan. Add the mushrooms, season with salt and pepper, and cook, stirring occasionally, until softened and the moisture is cooked out of the mushrooms, 8 to 10 minutes. Add the garlic and cook, stirring often, until fragrant, about 1 minute. Remove from the heat and set aside.

3. In a stand mixer or using a handheld electric mixer and a medium bowl, beat together the goat cheese, egg, milk, and thyme on low speed until fully combined. Unroll the puff pastry on a lightly floured work surface and use a rolling pin to roll it into a 10-by-12-in/25-by-30.5-cm rectangle. Use a sturdy, flat spatula to carefully transfer it to the prepared baking sheet. Spread with an even layer of the goat cheese mixture, leaving a ¼-in/6-mm uncovered border. Top with the cooked shallots, followed by the cooked mushrooms. Bake until the pastry is puffed and brown, about 30 minutes. Serve hot.

BAKED ZITI WITH CARAMELIZED CHERRY TOMATOES

There is little more wonderful in this world than a bubbling dish of cheesy baked pasta, except perhaps a dish of baked pasta topped with a layer of sweet, lightly blistered cherry tomatoes. While not a traditionally Jewish dish, it is perfect for Shabbat dinner or anytime you are serving a crowd.

SERVES 8

NOTE

Here is my favorite trick for quickly slicing grape and cherry tomatoes, as well as other small, round fruits like grapes and blueberries: Lay a handful of the tomatoes in the well of a Tupperware lid. Cover with a second lid and gently press down to hold the tomatoes steady. Using a serrated knife, slice laterally between the lids, through the tomatoes. Lift the top lid and voilà: a bunch of perfectly halved tomatoes.

1 LB/455 G ZITI

EXTRA-VIRGIN OLIVE OIL FOR DRIZZLING, PLUS 2 TBSP

1 LARGE YELLOW ONION, FINELY CHOPPED

4 GARLIC CLOVES, FINELY CHOPPED

1 TSP DRIED OREGANO

1 TSP DRIED THYME

½ TSP RED PEPPER FLAKES

KOSHER SALT AND FRESHLY GROUND BLACK PEPPER

ONE 24-OZ/680-G JAR GOOD-QUALITY MARINARA

2 CUPS/455 G FULL-FAT OR LOW-FAT RICOTTA CHEESE

1 EGG, LIGHTLY BEATEN

10 FRESH BASIL LEAVES, CUT INTO THIN RIBBONS (SEE PAGE 18)

2 CUPS/210 G GRATED MOZZARELLA

¼ CUP/20 G GRATED PARMESAN

1½ CUPS/240 G HALVED CHERRY TOMATOES

1 TBSP SUGAR

1. Bring a large pot of generously salted water to a boil. Add the ziti and cook, stirring occasionally, until al dente, about 10 minutes (or follow the timing instructions on the package). Drain well, transfer to a large bowl, drizzle with olive oil, toss to coat, and set aside.

2. Meanwhile, preheat the oven to 375°F/190°C. Heat the 2 Tbsp olive oil in a medium pan set over medium heat. Add the onion and cook, stirring occasionally, until softened and lightly browned, 6 to 8 minutes. Add the garlic, oregano, thyme, and red pepper flakes and season with salt and pepper. Cook, stirring often, until fragrant, 1 to 2 minutes more. Stir in the marinara, turn the heat to low, and simmer until slightly thickened, about 5 minutes. Remove the pan from the heat.

3. In a medium bowl, stir together the ricotta, egg, basil, ½ tsp salt, ½ tsp pepper, and 1 cup/105 g of the mozzarella. Spoon about two-thirds of the sauce and all of the ricotta mixture into the drained pasta and stir to combine, making sure the pasta is evenly coated. Transfer the mixture to a 9-by-13-in/23-by-33-cm baking dish. Top evenly with the remaining sauce, and sprinkle with the remaining 1 cup/105 g mozzarella and the Parmesan.

4. In a small bowl, stir together the cherry tomatoes and sugar, and season with salt and pepper. Lay the tomatoes, cut-side up, all over the surface of the dish, pressing gently to nestle them into the cheese. Bake until bubbling, 30 to 35 minutes. If desired, turn on your broiler and broil until the cheese browns, 2 to 3 minutes. Serve hot.

SPINACH-MATZO LASAGNA

Over the last decade, matzo lasagna has quickly and emphatically entered the Passover mainstream. Its rise has partly to do with the need it fills for a substantive main dish to serve during the holiday's weeklong bread ban. The other reason for its popularity? It's delicious, and remarkably so. Softened matzo provides a convincingly noodle-like base for the rich ricotta and mozzarella, tangy marinara, and tender spinach threaded throughout the layers. I like to imagine that, fifty years from now, my future children and grandchildren will swear that Passover is not Passover without spinach-matzo lasagna.

SERVES 8 TO 10

3 TBSP EXTRA-VIRGIN OLIVE OIL

2 LARGE YELLOW ONIONS, FINELY CHOPPED

4 GARLIC CLOVES, FINELY CHOPPED

5 OZ/140 G BABY SPINACH

4 CUPS/910 G FULL-FAT OR LOW-FAT RICOTTA CHEESE

2 EGGS, LIGHTLY BEATEN

2 CUPS/200 G GRATED MOZZARELLA

¼ CUP/10 G ROUGHLY CHOPPED FRESH FLAT-LEAF PARSLEY

KOSHER SALT AND FRESHLY GROUND BLACK PEPPER

9 SHEETS MATZO

4 CUPS/960 ML GOOD-QUALITY MARINARA

¼ CUP/20 G GRATED PARMESAN

1. Preheat the oven to 350°F/180°C.

2. Heat the olive oil in a medium pan set over medium heat. Add the onions and cook, stirring occasionally, until softened and lightly browned, 5 to 7 minutes. Add the garlic and spinach and cook, tossing with tongs, until the garlic is fragrant and the spinach wilts, about 2 minutes. Remove from the heat and set aside.

3. In a medium bowl, stir together the ricotta, eggs, ½ cup/50 g of the mozzarella, and the parsley. Season generously with salt and pepper and set aside.

4. Fill a shallow baking dish with water. Dip 3 sheets of the matzo in the water and let soften for 1 to 2 minutes. (Not longer—you want the pieces to feel soft, but not mushy or soggy. They should still hold their shape.) Spoon half of the marinara into the bottom of a 9-by-13-in/23-by-33-cm baking dish. Shake the excess water off of the softened matzo pieces and arrange in the baking dish, breaking the sheets as necessary to fit. Top with about half of the ricotta mixture, followed by half of the spinach mixture. Repeat with half of the remaining marinara, another 3 softened sheets of matzo, and the remaining ricotta and spinach mixtures.

CONTINUED

5. Soften the remaining 3 sheets of matzo and arrange on top. Spoon the remaining marinara over the top, then sprinkle evenly with the remaining 1½ cups/150 g mozzarella and the Parmesan.

6. Cover with aluminum foil and bake until heated through, about 45 minutes. Uncover and continue baking until the cheese is lightly browned, 10 to 15 minutes more. Let stand for a few minutes. Serve hot.

CINNAMON-ROASTED SEITAN AND ONIONS

While there is nothing traditionally Jewish about this dish, whenever I make it, it starts to feel like Shabbat in our apartment. Maybe it is the perfume of cinnamon and onions wafting from the stovetop, or the notion that a warm, flavorful dish is about to emerge. Whatever it is, I am happy to enjoy that sense of nourishing comfort any night of the week. Serve the dish alongside Toasted Almond Israeli Couscous (page 161), mashed potatoes, or rice.

SERVES 4

¼ CUP/60 ML BALSAMIC VINEGAR

1 TBSP RED WINE VINEGAR

2 TBSP PURE MAPLE SYRUP

3 TBSP SOY SAUCE OR TAMARI

½ TSP FRESHLY GROUND BLACK PEPPER

2 TBSP EXTRA-VIRGIN OLIVE OIL

2 LARGE YELLOW ONIONS, HALVED THROUGH THE ROOT AND THINLY SLICED

TWO 8-OZ/225-G PACKAGES SEITAN, DRAINED AND CUT INTO 1-IN/ 2.5-CM CUBES

1 TSP GROUND CINNAMON

½ TSP CHILI POWDER

¼ TSP RED PEPPER FLAKES

1. In a medium bowl, whisk together the balsamic vinegar, red wine vinegar, maple syrup, soy sauce, and pepper until combined.

2. Heat the olive oil in a large pan set over medium-high heat. Add the onions and cook, stirring occasionally, until softened and lightly browned, 5 to 7 minutes. Add the seitan and cook, stirring occasionally, until lightly browned, 5 to 7 minutes. Add the cinnamon, chili powder, and red pepper flakes and cook, stirring often, until fragrant, about 1 minute.

3. Add the vinegar mixture, turn the heat to medium-low, and simmer, stirring occasionally, until the vinegar reduces and turns saucy, 3 to 5 minutes. Serve hot.

PANFRIED TOFU STEAKS WITH SHALLOT GRAVY

Many of my first cooking attempts in college were variations on basic tofu stir-fry—a mix of vegetables and cubed tofu doused in an improvised soy sauce and garlic concoction. Not surprisingly, very few of those early attempts ever tasted any good. Now I know that tofu can be wonderfully satisfying if it is treated well. This dish lightly coats and fries the tofu, which gives it a hearty texture, then tops it with rich gravy made with shallots, red wine, and thyme. It is a long way from those early stir-fries and good enough to write home about.

SERVES 4

FOR THE TOFU

ONE 14-OZ/400-G PACKAGE FIRM TOFU, DRAINED

½ CUP/55 G CORNSTARCH

1 TSP MUSTARD POWDER

½ TSP CAYENNE PEPPER

1 TSP FRESHLY GROUND BLACK PEPPER

VEGETABLE OIL FOR FRYING

FOR THE GRAVY

2 TBSP UNSALTED BUTTER OR VEGETABLE OIL

2 MEDIUM SHALLOTS, HALVED LENGTH-WISE AND THINLY SLICED

2 GARLIC CLOVES, FINELY CHOPPED

½ TSP DRIED THYME

¼ CUP/60 ML DRY RED WINE

2 TBSP SOY SAUCE OR TAMARI

1½ CUPS/360 ML VEGETABLE BROTH

FRESHLY GROUND BLACK PEPPER

2 TSP CORNSTARCH

ROUGHLY CHOPPED FRESH FLAT-LEAF PARSLEY FOR SERVING

1. Wrap the tofu in several layers of paper towels or a dish towel and set on a flat surface. Place a plate on top of the wrapped tofu and weigh it down with a couple of cans of beans. Let stand for 30 minutes, then unwrap and slice horizontally into ¼-in/6-mm steaks. In a shallow baking dish or bowl, stir together the cornstarch, mustard powder, cayenne, and pepper.

2. Line a large plate with two layers of paper towels. Heat ¼ in/6 mm of vegetable oil in a large skillet set over medium-high heat until shimmering. Working in batches, dip the tofu steaks into the cornstarch mixture, coating both sides and shaking off any excess. Add the coated tofu to the pan and cook, turning once, until both sides are crispy and lightly browned, 3 to 5 minutes per side. Transfer to the paper towel–lined plate to drain. Repeat with the remaining tofu steaks and cornstarch mixture.

3. Meanwhile, make the gravy: Melt the butter until foaming in a medium saucepan set over medium-high heat. Add the shallots and cook, stirring occasionally, until browned, 5 to 7 minutes. Add the garlic and thyme and cook, stirring often, until fragrant, about 1 minute. Add the wine and soy sauce and cook until the liquid is mostly evaporated, about 3 minutes. Add the broth, season with pepper, and bring to a boil. In a small bowl, stir together the cornstarch and about 2 Tbsp of the hot broth mixture until smooth. Add the cornstarch-broth mixture to the pan and cook, stirring frequently, until the gravy thickens slightly, 7 to 10 minutes.

4. Transfer the tofu to a serving platter and top with half of the gravy and the parsley. Serve hot with the remaining gravy on the side, to pass around the table.

CHAPTER EIGHT

BREADS AND PASTRIES

CHALLAH 101

I never met a homemade challah I did not like. Even the imperfect, dry, or lumpy loaves still manage to delight. And I should know; when I was first learning to make challah, I produced more than my fair share of imperfect, dry, and lumpy loaves. Even so, you could always taste the care that went into making them. (Plus, a slick of creamy hummus or a drizzle of honey makes pretty much anything taste good.) As I grew more confident in my challah baking, I learned that nothing beats the thrill of pulling two perfectly puffed braids from the oven or the satisfaction of slicing past a bronzed crust into a tender-centered loaf. I want to share that feeling with you.

Like everything, making good challah takes practice. Your first attempts might turn out great. But with many variables at play, including uncontrollable factors like the weather, chances are they will leave something to be desired, particularly if you are new to work-ing with yeast. Please promise me that you will not get disheartened and give up after your first attempt. If you keep baking, over time you begin to learn what dough should smell, look, and, most important, feel like at different stages along the process. Novice bakers and anyone looking for a refresher: Take a read through these tips, then get baking. Before long, you will have the power to make ambrosial challah at your fingertips.

HISTORY AND RITUAL SIGNIFICANCE

Challah sits at the center of every Shabbat and holiday table (except Passover, when you substitute unleavened matzo). In biblical times, *challah* referred to a loaf of bread given to the Kohanim (priests) as an offering. Observant Jews symbolically continue this practice today by pinching off and burning a small piece of dough before baking their challah. After the destruction of the Temple in Jerusalem, the home dining table came to symbolically represent the sacrificial altar. The bread blessed and eaten on Shabbat, then, represents the loaves of shewbread that were once left on view in the Temple.

For centuries, the bread consecrated on Shabbat did not have a specific form. But around the fifteenth century, Ashkenazi Jews in Germany and Austria began baking braided loaves modeled after a Teutonic ceremonial solstice bread. From those unex-pected beginnings, the braided loaves we bless and eat today emerged.

At the table, there are many customs for serving challah. It is typically covered with a cloth before being blessed as a sign of respect. Many communities sprinkle salt over the challah (or dip it directly into salt) after blessing it, a practice that connects back to the table as a representation of the Temple altar. On Rosh Hashanah, the salt is replaced with honey, which conveys hope for sweetness in the year ahead. Whether or not you personally connect to the ritual aspects of challah—whether you use it for Shabbat or Sunday morning French toast—every time you bite into an eggy loaf, you connect to a long and delicious tradition.

WORKING WITH YEAST

Want to feel like a sorcerer? Work with yeast. Unlike most ingredients, yeast is aggressively, excitingly alive. Bring active dry yeast into contact with warm water and within a few minutes it will be bubbling away, smelling like a loaf of bread in a bowl. When I first started baking bread, I was intimidated by yeast. After all, if I got that step wrong, the whole loaf was doomed. But once you know what to look for, there is nothing to fear. Here are a few tips to get you started:

Buying and storing. Active dry yeast is available at virtually every supermarket and is often sold in small jars or ¼-oz/7-g packets, which measure out to 2¼ tsp. Yeast grows less effective as it ages, so always start with fresh yeast. Store yeast in the freezer to extend its life, and check the expiration date before baking.

Water temperature matters. Use water that is too cold, and it won't activate the yeast; too hot and it kills it. The ideal temperature is 110°F/45°C. To get there, microwave tap water for 30 to 60 seconds or run the hot side of your faucet. Test the temperature with an instant-read thermometer or use the wrist trick: hold your wrist under the tap. If it feels noticeably hot but not burning hot, you are good to go. (Unless you have some otherworldly tolerance for heat. Then stick with the thermometer.)

Be patient. Your yeast won't activate immediately—it typically takes 5 to 10 minutes for yeast to fully proof once it comes into contact with warm water. Use this time to measure your flour and other ingredients, but keep an eye on the yeast because watching the thick, frothy bubbles bloom across the surface is one of baking's greatest pleasures. When ready, your yeast should look like the foamy head of a beer. If you're not sure whether your yeast is bubbling enough, it probably isn't. Give it another couple of minutes. Still nothing or just a few stray bubbles? Throw out the mixture and start again using fresh yeast and warm water.

MEASURING FLOUR

For the best, most consistent loaves of challah, I strongly suggest using the "spoon and sweep" method with measuring cups (find out how on page 18) or a scale for measuring out the flour and other dry ingredients.

KNEADING

Kneading is your chance to get to know your dough. Don't be shy and don't skimp—without proper kneading, your bread will turn out flat and dense. Remove any rings you are wearing. Sprinkle some flour over a dry, flat work surface and keep more flour nearby to add as needed. Turn the dough out onto the work surface. Sprinkle the dough with a little flour and use the heel of your hand to push it firmly forward and down. Fold the dough in half over itself, rotate it a quarter of a turn, and repeat.

Continue with this process, adding more flour as necessary. At first it will feel sticky and dense. But over time it should become buoyant, supple, and elastic. You will know it is ready when you shape the dough into a ball and it keeps its shape. If you poke the dough with your fingers, it should spring back at you.

It typically takes 8 to 12 minutes of kneading to get your dough to the right place. Put on some music to pass the time. If you have children, give them small pieces of the dough to knead along with you. Or use those minutes to daydream. There is no substitute for the wandering, contemplative thoughts that accompany 10 minutes of kneading.

RISING: STANDARD AND OVERNIGHT

Place your dough in a warm, draft-free spot to rise. It typically takes 60 to 90 minutes for your dough to approximately double in size. You will know it's ready when it appears swollen and puffy. It should release a small sigh of air when you (gently!) punch it down.

You can also let challah dough rise overnight in the refrigerator—a fantastic option for busy parents or anyone who is short on time. Follow the recipe through the kneading step, then place the dough in a lightly oiled bowl, cover, and place in the refrigerator. The dough slowly swells, while the gluten in the flour relaxes. The next day, when you are ready to bake, take out the dough and punch it down. Let it sit on the counter, covered, for 15 to 30 minutes to warm up enough to be shaped, then proceed with braiding and baking.

BRAIDING

There are many ways to form your challah dough into loaves. Here are a few of my favorites.

Three-String Braid: Divide the dough into three equal pieces and roll each piece into a long rope. Lay the ropes side by side and pinch at the top to connect them. Grab the rope on the right and cross it over the middle rope. (That now becomes the middle rope.) Take the rope on the left and cross it over the middle rope. (That now becomes the middle rope.) Continue braiding in this fashion until you reach the bottom of the ropes. Pinch the bottom to connect the ropes and gently transfer the braid to a baking sheet lined with parchment paper.

Four-String Braid: Divide the dough into four equal pieces and roll each piece into a long rope. Lay the ropes side by side and pinch at the top to connect them. Grab the rope farthest to the right and weave it toward the left, weaving over the rope closest to it, under the following rope, and over the final rope. Continue braiding in this fashion, always starting with the rope farthest to the right and weaving over, under, over, until you reach the bottom of the ropes. Pinch the bottom to connect the ropes and gently transfer the braid to a baking sheet lined with parchment paper.

Six-String Braid: Divide the dough into six equal pieces and roll each piece into a long rope. Lay the ropes side by side and pinch at the top to connect them. Grab the rope farthest to the right and weave it toward the left, passing over two ropes, under one rope, and over the final two ropes. Continue in this fashion, always starting with the rope farthest to the right, until you reach the bottom of the ropes. Pinch the bottom to connect the ropes and gently transfer the braid to a baking sheet lined with parchment paper.

Round/Spiral: Roll the dough into a long rope, about 24 in/61 cm long. Coil the rope in on itself and place in a lightly greased, 9-in/23-cm round baking pan, tucking the end underneath.

BAKING

A finished challah should have a deep golden sheen, be wonderfully fragrant, and sound hollow when tapped on the bottom with your finger. This sensory approach is decently reliable, but the best way to know that your challah is perfectly done is to check its internal temperature with an instant-read thermometer. Stick it into the center of the loaf: If it reads 195°F/90°C, remove it from the oven and let cool on a wire rack.

CLASSIC CHALLAH

Challah is one of the most recognizable Jewish foods. The braided loaves of bread are considered fundamental aspects of the Shabbat or holiday table, and their warm, yeasty scent has come to symbolize home. There are countless ways to make the ceremonial bread, but this is my go-to recipe for challah that is soft, tender, and subtly sweet. Find out more about challah's history and tips for making the perfect loaf on page 228.

MAKES 2 BRAIDED LOAVES

NOTE

A ¼-oz/7-g packet of yeast contains 2¼ tsp. So for 1 Tbsp, you will need all of one packet and a little bit of a second.

For this recipe, I strongly recommend using the "spoon and sweep" method for accurately measuring the flour with measuring cups. Find out how on page 18.

1 TBSP ACTIVE DRY YEAST

1 TSP SUGAR, PLUS ⅓ CUP/65 G

1 CUP/240 ML WARM WATER
    (110°F/45°C)

5½ CUPS/695 G ALL-PURPOSE FLOUR

2 TSP SALT

½ CUP/120 ML VEGETABLE OIL

4 EGGS

¼ CUP/95 G HONEY

SESAME SEEDS OR POPPY SEEDS FOR
    TOPPING (OPTIONAL)

1. Stir together the yeast, 1 tsp sugar, and warm water in a medium bowl. Let stand until foaming, 5 to 10 minutes.

2. Meanwhile, whisk together the remaining ⅓ cup/65 g sugar, flour, and salt in a large bowl.

3. Add the vegetable oil, 3 of the eggs, and the honey to the yeast mixture and whisk to combine. Make a well in the center of the flour mixture and pour in the yeast mixture. Gently stir until the dough begins to form, then turn out the dough onto a floured surface and knead well, adding more flour, a little at a time, as necessary, until a supple dough forms, 8 to 12 minutes. Rub about 1 tsp oil around the bottom of a large bowl, add the dough, and turn to coat. Cover with plastic wrap or a dish towel and let stand in a warm place until nearly doubled in size, 1 to 1½ hours.

CONTINUED

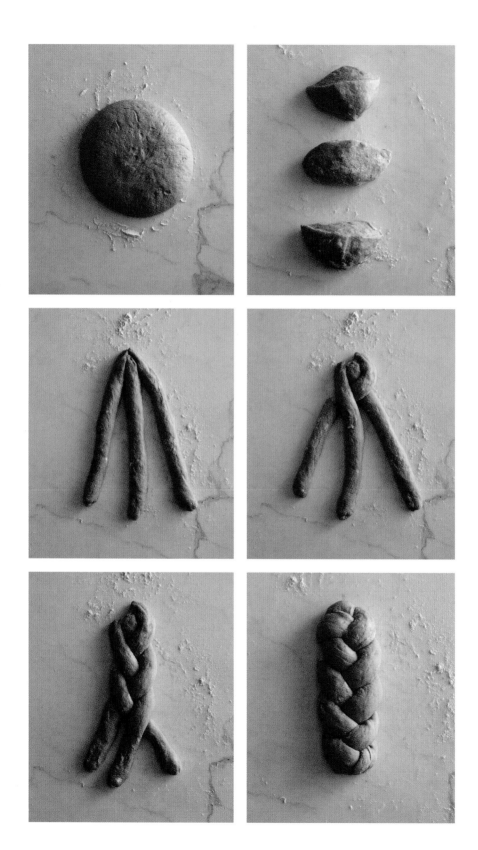

4. Gently deflate the dough with your hands by pressing it in the center and turning it out onto a lightly floured work surface. Divide the dough in half with a knife, then divide each half into thirds. Roll each third into a long rope. Pinch the top of three ropes together and braid, pinching at the bottom to seal. Repeat with the remaining three ropes.

5. Line a baking sheet with parchment paper. Place the braided challahs on the prepared baking sheet. Whisk the remaining egg in a small bowl and brush the loaves with one coat of egg wash. (Put the remaining egg wash in the refrigerator.) Cover the loaves loosely with lightly greased plastic wrap and let rise for 30 minutes more. Fifteen minutes before baking, preheat the oven to 375°F/190°C.

6. Uncover the loaves and brush with a second coat of egg wash. (Don't skip the second coat; it adds deep, beautiful color to the loaves.) Sprinkle with sesame seeds (if using). Bake the loaves until deep golden brown and cooked through, or an instant-read thermometer inserted into the center of the loaves registers 195°F/90°C, 30 to 40 minutes. Remove from the oven and let cool on a wire rack. Serve warm or at room temperature. Challah is best the day it is made, but will keep for up to 3 days and can be rewarmed in an oven or sliced and toasted.

CHALLAH WITH SAUTÉED LEEKS AND THYME

What could possibly be better than freshly made challah? How about freshly made challah hiding a fragrant mixture of sautéed leeks and thyme inside? These savory loaves are delicious all on their own, and also make a perfect base for a spread like Supremely Creamy Hummus (page 73), Matbucha (page 70), or Chopped Chicken Liver (page 76).

MAKES 2 BRAIDED LOAVES

NOTE

For this recipe, I strongly recommend using the "spoon and sweep" method for accurately measuring the flour with measuring cups. Find out how on page 18.

1 TBSP ACTIVE DRY YEAST

1 TSP SUGAR, PLUS ¼ CUP/50 G

1 CUP/240 ML WARM WATER
   (110°F/45°C)

5½ CUPS/695 G ALL-PURPOSE FLOUR

2 TSP KOSHER SALT

½ CUP/120 ML VEGETABLE OIL

4 EGGS

¼ CUP/95 G HONEY

FOR THE LEEK FILLING

2 TBSP EXTRA-VIRGIN OLIVE OIL

4 LARGE LEEKS, WHITE AND LIGHT
   GREEN PARTS, QUARTERED
   LENGTHWISE AND THINLY SLICED

KOSHER SALT

1 TBSP DRIED THYME, CRUSHED WITH A
   MORTAR AND PESTLE

SESAME SEEDS OR POPPY SEEDS, FOR
   TOPPING (OPTIONAL)

1. Stir together the yeast, 1 tsp sugar, and warm water in a medium bowl. Let stand until foaming, 5 to 10 minutes.

2. Meanwhile, whisk together the remaining ¼ cup/50 g sugar, flour, and salt in a large bowl.

3. Add the vegetable oil, 3 of the eggs, and the honey to the yeast mixture and whisk to combine. Make a well in the center of the flour mixture and pour in the yeast mixture. Gently stir until the dough begins to form, then turn out the dough onto a floured surface and knead well, adding more flour, a little at a time, as necessary, until a supple dough forms, 8 to 12 minutes. Rub 1 tsp oil around the bottom of a large bowl, add the dough, and turn to coat. Cover with plastic wrap or a dish towel and let stand in a warm place until nearly doubled in size, 1 to 1½ hours.

4. Meanwhile, make the leek filling: Heat the olive oil in a large pan set over medium heat. Add the leeks and a generous pinch of salt, cover, and cook until softened, about 10 minutes. Uncover and continue cooking, stirring often, until browned, about 5 minutes. Add the thyme and cook, stirring often, until fragrant, about 1 minute. Remove from the heat and divide the leek mixture into six equal piles in the pan. Let cool slightly.

5. Gently deflate the dough with your hands by pressing it in the center and turning it out onto a lightly floured work surface. Divide the dough in half with a knife, then divide each half into thirds. With a rolling pin, roll out one piece of dough into a long rectangle, about ⅛ in/4 mm thick (keeping the others covered with a dish towel). Spread one of the reserved leek piles in a straight line down one of the long edges, then tightly roll the dough like a jelly roll, tucking the filling inside. Gently stretch the filled rope into a long strand. Repeat the process with two more pieces of dough, then pinch the top of the three filled ropes together and braid, pinching at the bottom to seal. Repeat the rolling, filling, and braiding process with the remaining leek mixture and the remaining pieces of dough.

6. Place the braided challahs on the prepared baking sheet. Whisk the remaining egg in a small bowl and brush the loaves with one coat of egg wash. (Put the remaining egg wash in the refrigerator.) Cover the loaves loosely with lightly greased plastic wrap and let rise for 30 minutes more. Fifteen minutes before baking, preheat the oven to 375°F/190°C.

7. Uncover the loaves and brush with a second coat of egg wash. (Don't skip the second coat; it adds deep beautiful color to the loaves.) Sprinkle with sesame seeds (if using). Bake until deep golden brown and cooked through, or an instant-read thermometer inserted into the center of the loaves registers 195°F/90°C, 35 to 45 minutes. Remove from the oven and let cool on a wire rack. Serve warm or at room temperature. Challah is best the day it is made, but will keep for up to 3 days and can be rewarmed in an oven or sliced and toasted.

PUMPKIN-APPLE CHALLAH

This gorgeous, slightly sweet challah is inspired by the flavors of autumn. First, puréed pumpkin and spices get kneaded into the dough. The loaves are then filled with apple butter and finely chopped apple, and spiraled into a thick coil. People tend to be readily impressed by homemade challah, but my dinner guests audibly gasp every time I slice into the mahogany-colored loaves, threaded through with a ribbon of apple butter. Serve this challah on Sukkot (see page 338) or Thanksgiving, spread with Cinnamon-Honey Tahini Spread (page 313). And on the off chance that you have leftovers, it makes otherworldly French toast.

MAKES 2 SPIRAL-SHAPED LOAVES

NOTE

The apple butter and chopped apple add bulk and moisture to the dough, which tastes great but lengthens the baking time. If you prefer a quicker-baking pumpkin challah without all the extras, prepare the recipe through step 3, then follow the braiding and baking instructions from the Classic Challah recipe (page 233).

2¼ TSP ACTIVE DRY YEAST

1 TSP SUGAR, PLUS ⅓ CUP/65 G

1 CUP/240 ML WARM WATER
    (110°F/45°C)

4½ CUPS/570 G ALL-PURPOSE FLOUR

½ TSP GROUND CINNAMON

½ TSP GROUND CARDAMOM

1½ TSP KOSHER SALT

½ CUP/120 G FRESH OR CANNED
    PUMPKIN PURÉE

¼ CUP/60 ML VEGETABLE OIL

2 EGGS

⅔ CUP/160 G APPLE BUTTER

1 SMALL APPLE, PEELED, CORED, AND
    FINELY CHOPPED

1. Stir together the yeast, 1 tsp sugar, and warm water in a medium bowl. Let stand until foaming, 5 to 10 minutes.

2. Meanwhile, whisk together the remaining ⅓ cup/65 g sugar, flour, cinnamon, cardamom, and salt in a large bowl.

3. Add the pumpkin, vegetable oil, and 1 of the eggs to the yeast mixture and whisk to combine. Make a well in the center of the flour mixture and pour in the yeast mixture. Gently stir until the dough begins to form, then turn out the dough onto a floured surface and knead well, adding more flour, a little at a time, as necessary, until a supple dough forms, 8 to 12 minutes. Rub the 1 tsp oil around the bottom of a large bowl, add the dough, and turn to coat. Cover with plastic wrap or a dish towel and let stand in a warm place until nearly doubled in size, 1 to 1½ hours.

4. Line two 9-in/23-cm round cake pans with a circle of parchment paper and lightly grease the parchment. Gently deflate the dough with your hands by pressing it in the center and turning it out onto a lightly floured work surface. Divide the dough in half with a knife. Working with one piece of the dough (and keeping the other covered with a dish towel), use a rolling pin to roll it into a large rectangle, about ⅛ in/4 mm thick. Spread about half of the apple butter evenly over the top, and sprinkle with half of the chopped apple. Starting at one of the long ends, tightly roll the dough in on itself, like a jelly roll. Pinch the ends to seal and gently stretch into a rope 24 in/61 cm long. Coil the rope into a circle and place into one of the prepared pans, tucking the end underneath. Repeat with the second piece of dough and the remaining apple butter and chopped apple.

5. Whisk the remaining egg in a small bowl and brush the challahs with one coat of egg wash. (Put the remaining egg wash in the refrigerator.) Cover the loaves loosely with lightly greased plastic wrap and let rise for 30 minutes more. Fifteen minutes before baking, preheat the oven to 375°F/190°C.

6. Uncover the loaves and brush with a second coat of egg wash. (Don't skip the second coat; it adds deep beautiful color to the loaves.) Bake the loaves until deep golden brown and cooked through, or an instant-read thermometer inserted into the center of the loaves registers 195°F/90°C, 40 to 55 minutes. (The cooking time varies significantly depending on how thick the coil is. Start checking with your thermometer at 40 minutes, then every 5 minutes after that, as necessary.) Remove from the oven and let cool on a wire rack. Serve warm or at room temperature. Challah is best the day it is made, but will keep for up to 3 days and can be rewarmed in an oven or sliced and toasted.

HOMEMADE BAGELS

For years, I was scared to make bagels. I had successfully attempted pizza dough, chal-lah, and other yeast doughs, but when it came to bagels, one of the most widely recog-nized and revered foods in the Jewish canon, the stakes felt higher. When I finally went for it, my first batch was . . . okay. The flavor and texture were there, but they were as flat as pancakes. Turns out, I had let the dough rise too long, which caused the bagels to deflate when I dropped them into the hot water bath bagels traditionally take before getting baked.

Still, the experience buoyed my confidence enough to try again. I'm glad I did, because after a few more attempts, I opened the oven door to find a tray of beautiful, chubby bagels waiting for me. I felt triumphant. I may have danced a little in my kitchen before spreading them with a layer of homemade flavored cream cheese (see page 314). This recipe merges New York– and Montreal-style bagels. Some might call that sacrilege, but with the bagels' hint of sweet flavor and chewy crust, I call it delicious.

MAKES 12 BAGELS

NOTE

Barley malt syrup is a thick, molasses-colored sweetener made from sprouted barley. It can be found in health food stores, or see page 343 for an online source.

Vegans can keep these bagels that way by replacing the honey in the poaching liquid with more barley malt syrup, and omitting the egg wash. The sesame seeds will not stick quite as well, but the bagels will still taste great.

Bread flour has high levels of gluten, which helps to yield chewy, sturdy bagels. Do not substitute all-purpose or any other type of flour.

2¼ TSP ACTIVE DRY YEAST

2 TSP SUGAR

1½ CUPS/360 ML WARM WATER
    (110°F/45°C)

4 CUPS/500 G BREAD FLOUR

1 TBSP KOSHER SALT

1 TBSP BARLEY MALT SYRUP

1 TBSP BAKING SODA

2 TBSP HONEY

1 EGG, LIGHTLY BEATEN

SESAME SEEDS OR POPPY SEEDS FOR
    SPRINKLING

1. Stir together the yeast, sugar, and warm water in a small bowl. Let stand until foaming, 5 to 10 minutes.

2. Meanwhile, whisk together the flour and salt in a large bowl. Stir the malt syrup into the yeast mixture. Make a well in the center of the flour mixture and pour in the yeast mixture. Gently stir with a wooden spoon until the dough begins to form, then turn out the dough onto a flat, lightly floured surface and knead well, until a supple but not sticky dough forms, 8 to 10 minutes. Rub 1 tsp oil around the bottom of a large bowl, add the dough, and turn to coat. Cover with plastic wrap or a dish towel and let stand in a warm place until puffed, about 30 minutes.

3. Gently deflate the dough with the heel of your hand, turn it out onto a flat surface, and divide into twelve equal pieces with a knife. Working with one piece at a time (keeping the others covered with a dish towel), use your hands to roll a rope 8 in/20 cm long. Bring the ends together to form a circle, slightly overlapping one side, and pinch to seal. Repeat with the remaining pieces of dough. Place the bagels on a lightly floured flat surface, cover with a damp dish towel, and let stand for 15 minutes.

4. Meanwhile, preheat the oven to 425°F/220°C and line a large rimmed baking sheet with parchment paper. Fill a large saucepan with water, set it over high heat, and stir in the baking soda and honey. Bring to a boil, then turn the heat to medium-low and keep at a gentle simmer. Working in batches of three or four, gently drop the bagels into the simmering water. Cook for 30 seconds, flip with a slotted spoon, and cook for 30 seconds more. Transfer to the prepared baking sheet.

5. Lightly brush the tops of the boiled bagels with the beaten egg and generously sprinkle with sesame seeds. Bake, rotating the baking sheet halfway through, until the bagels are golden brown, 16 to 20 minutes. Remove from the oven and let cool on a wire rack. Serve warm or at room temperature. Store in an airtight container at room temperature for up to 5 days. Reheat leftovers in a toaster or toaster oven.

PLETZELS

You have undoubtedly eaten your fair share of pretzels, but what about pletzels? The flatbreads, which typically come topped with caramelized onions and poppy seeds, were a favorite among Eastern European Jews. Once they arrived in the States, pletzels continued to be sold in Jewish bakeries (where they were called onion boards, likely referring to their flat shape), but have since largely fallen out of fashion. Consider this recipe my contribution to help revive a worthy Jewish food. I like to serve the savory flatbreads spread with Salmon-Dill Cream Cheese (page 315), Chopped Chicken Liver (page 76), or Vegetarian Chopped "Liver" (page 77). They are also fantastic for mopping up soups like 20 Cloves of Garlic Borscht (page 80) and saucy dishes like Apple Cider–Braised Chicken (page 187). For a variation, sprinkle 1 Tbsp finely chopped fresh rosemary on the flatbread along with the poppy seeds.

SERVES 6

NOTE

I bake this flatbread in an 11-by-15-in/28-by-38-cm rimmed baking sheet, which yields a thin, crispy flatbread with a hint of fluffy chew at the center. If you want something closer to focaccia in texture and thickness, use a baking sheet with slightly smaller proportions (the bake time will be a bit longer). Do not use a larger baking sheet or the flatbread will be too thin.

2¼ TSP ACTIVE DRY YEAST

1 TSP SUGAR

1 CUP/240 ML WARM WATER
(110°F/45°C)

2½ CUPS/315 G ALL-PURPOSE FLOUR

1¾ TSP KOSHER SALT

¼ CUP/60 ML VEGETABLE OIL, PLUS
2 TBSP

2 YELLOW ONIONS, FINELY CHOPPED

1 TSP ONION POWDER

1 EGG, LIGHTLY BEATEN

1 TBSP POPPY SEEDS

1. Stir together the yeast, sugar, and warm water in a medium bowl. Let stand until foamy, 5 to 10 minutes.

2. Meanwhile, whisk together the flour and 1 tsp of the salt in a large bowl. Add the ¼ cup/60 ml vegetable oil to the yeast mixture and stir to combine. Make a well in the center of the flour mixture and pour in the yeast mixture. Gently stir with a wooden spoon until the dough begins to form, then turn out the dough onto a floured surface and knead well, adding more flour, a little at a time, as necessary, until a smooth, supple dough forms, about 10 minutes. Rub 1 tsp oil around the bottom of a large bowl, add the dough, and turn to coat. Cover with plastic wrap or a dish towel and let stand in a warm place until nearly doubled in size, about 1 hour.

CONTINUED

3. Meanwhile, heat the remaining 2 Tbsp vegetable oil in a large pan set over medium heat. Add the onions, cover, and cook, stirring occasionally, until softened, 10 to 12 minutes. Uncover and stir in the remaining ¾ tsp salt and the onion powder. Cook, stirring often, until browned, about 5 minutes. Remove from the heat and let cool slightly.

4. Brush an 11-by-15-in/28-by-38-cm rimmed baking sheet with 1 tsp oil. Gently deflate the dough with the heel of your hand. Remove the dough from the bowl and press it into the prepared baking sheet with your hands until it touches the edges on all sides. Using your fingertips, gently press indentations into the dough, all over the surface. Cover with lightly greased plastic wrap or a dish towel and let rest until slightly puffed, about 30 minutes. Fifteen minutes before baking, preheat the oven to 425°F/220°C.

5. Uncover the flatbread and use a fork to prick several small holes over the top (to prevent air bubbles from forming while it bakes). Brush one coat of the beaten egg all over the top of the dough (you will not use all of it). Top with an even layer of cooked onions and sprinkle with the poppy seeds. Bake the flatbread until golden and cooked through, 20 to 25 minutes. Transfer to a wire rack to cool slightly, then cut into squares or rectangles. Store in an airtight container at room temperature for up to 5 days. Reheat leftovers in the oven or a toaster oven.

SPINACH AND CHEESE BOUREKAS

Iraqi Jews traditionally serve bourekas—phyllo or puff pastry pockets stuffed with potato, cheese, spinach, or any number of other fillings—on Shabbat (Saturday) morning after synagogue. Today, these savory pastries are available in bakeries across Israel. The last time I visited the country, I bought a couple to nibble on while browsing in the shuk (Jerusalem's famous vegetable market) and felt powered for the whole morning. This version combines spinach and cheese inside a pocket of golden dough. Serve them for an on-the-go breakfast or as a dinner party appetizer, or pack them as a treat into your family's lunches.

MAKES 18 BOUREKAS

FOR THE FILLING

2 TBSP EXTRA-VIRGIN OLIVE OIL

1 SMALL YELLOW ONION, FINELY CHOPPED

KOSHER SALT

ONE 10-OZ/280-G PACKAGE FROZEN SPINACH, THAWED AND SQUEEZED OF EXCESS WATER

1 EGG, LIGHTLY BEATEN

1 GARLIC CLOVE, MINCED OR PUSHED THROUGH A PRESS

⅛ TSP GROUND NUTMEG

⅓ CUP/80 G RICOTTA CHEESE

⅓ CUP/40 G GRATED MOZZARELLA

¼ TSP FRESHLY GROUND BLACK PEPPER

2 SHEETS FROZEN PUFF PASTRY, THAWED

1 EGG, LIGHTLY BEATEN

SESAME SEEDS FOR SPRINKLING

1. Make the filling: Heat the olive oil in a small pan set over medium heat. Add the onion, season with salt, and cook, stirring occasionally, until softened and lightly browned, 5 to 7 minutes. Remove from the heat and let cool.

2. In a large bowl, combine the onion, spinach, egg, garlic, nutmeg, ricotta, mozzarella, pepper, and ½ tsp salt.

3. Preheat the oven to 350°F/180°C and grease two large rimmed baking sheets. Unroll the puff pastry on a lightly floured work surface. With a rolling pin, roll out one sheet of puff pastry into a 12-in/30.5-cm square, then cut into 4-in/10-cm squares. (There should be 9 squares total.) Spoon about 2 Tbsp of the filling near the corner of each square, and use your fingers or the back of a spoon to flatten the filling. Fold one corner over to meet its opposite corner, making a triangle and locking the filling inside. Press firmly all along the edges to seal. Repeat with the remaining sheet of puff pastry and filling.

4. Lay the filled bourekas on the prepared baking sheets. Brush the tops with the beaten egg and sprinkle with sesame seeds. Bake until puffed and golden brown, 30 to 35 minutes. Serve warm.

BUTTERNUT SQUASH AND SAGE BOUREKAS

I love this untraditional take on bourekas. The sweet squash mixed with crispy, browned onions and fragrant sage is the perfect embodiment of fall.

MAKES 18 BOUREKAS

FOR THE FILLING

1 MEDIUM BUTTERNUT SQUASH

2 TBSP UNSALTED BUTTER OR
    EXTRA-VIRGIN OLIVE OIL

1 LARGE RED ONION, HALVED AND
    THINLY SLICED

2 TBSP SUGAR

KOSHER SALT AND FRESHLY GROUND
    BLACK PEPPER

2 GARLIC CLOVES, MINCED

1 TBSP CHOPPED FRESH SAGE

⅓ CUP/55 G CRUMBLED FETA
    (OPTIONAL)

2 SHEETS FROZEN PUFF PASTRY,
    THAWED

1 EGG, LIGHTLY BEATEN

SESAME SEEDS FOR SPRINKLING

1. Preheat the oven to 400°F/200°C. Line a large rimmed baking sheet with aluminum foil. Cut the squash in half lengthwise and remove the seeds. Place the squash, cut-side down, on the prepared baking sheet and roast until tender and a knife can be easily inserted into the flesh, 40 to 50 minutes. Remove from the oven and use a pair of tongs to flip the squash. Let cool to the touch, then scoop the flesh into a medium bowl, discarding the skin. Let the squash cool completely. (Squash can be roasted up to 2 days in advance.)

2. Melt the butter until foaming in a pan set over medium heat. Add the onion and sugar and sprinkle generously with salt and pepper. Cook, stirring occasionally, until the onion softens, 6 to 8 minutes. Add the garlic and cook, stirring often, until fragrant, 1 to 2 minutes. Remove from the heat and let cool, then combine the squash, onion mixture, sage, and feta (if using).

3. Lower the oven temperature to 350°F/180°C and grease two large rimmed baking sheets. Unroll the puff pastry on a lightly floured work surface. With a rolling pin, roll out one sheet of puff pastry into a 12-in/30.5-cm square, then cut into 4-in/10-cm squares. (There should be 9 squares total.) Spoon about 2 Tbsp of the filling near the corner of each square, and use your fingers or the back of a spoon to flatten the filling. Fold one corner over to meet its opposite corner, making a triangle and locking the filling inside. Press firmly all along the edges to seal. Repeat with the remaining sheet of puff pastry and filling.

4. Lay the filled bourekas on the prepared baking sheets. Brush the tops with the beaten egg and sprinkle with sesame seeds. Bake until puffed and golden brown, 30 to 35 minutes. Serve warm.

PEACH AND RASPBERRY TART

Summertime cooking is all about ease and seasonality. The fresh fruits and vegetables available in abundance during the warmest months require few embellishments to taste great. Plus, it is simply too hot to hover near the oven. That's where this puff pastry tart comes in. Topped with juicy peaches and sweet raspberries, it captures the essence of summer with minimal kitchen time. It's a perfect recipe for beginning bakers or anyone who wants a low-fuss, high-impact dessert in their repertoire. For best results, use peaches that are ripe enough to taste sweet, but not so ripe that they verge on mushy and are hard to slice.

SERVES 4

1 SHEET FROZEN PUFF PASTRY, THAWED

2 TBSP APRICOT PRESERVES

3 MEDIUM PEACHES, HALVED, PITTED, AND THINLY SLICED INTO HALF-MOONS

⅓ CUP/50 G FRESH RASPBERRIES

2 TSP SUGAR

½ TSP GROUND CINNAMON

1. Preheat the oven to 400°F/200°C and line a large rimmed baking sheet with parchment paper.

2. Unroll the puff pastry onto the prepared baking sheet. Brush it evenly with the apricot preserves (it will be a very thin layer), leaving a ½-in/12-mm uncovered border. Fold the uncovered edges in on themselves on all sides. Arrange the peach slices in an overlapping pattern on top of the preserves, then dot the top with the raspberries.

3. Stir together the sugar and cinnamon in a small bowl and sprinkle it evenly over the fruit. Bake until the fruit is bubbling and the pastry is puffed and golden, 20 to 25 minutes. Serve warm or at room temperature.

CHOCOLATE-RASPBERRY BABKA

Named after the bubbes who made them (*babka* translates to "grandmother's loaf"), this twirled, butter-scented dessert is a beloved staple of the Eastern European Jewish pastry canon. My version looks a bit different from the chocolate and cinnamon babkas immortalized on "The Dinner Party" episode of *Seinfeld*. Instead of being bready and topped with streusel like many babkas, it is gooey and decadent, threaded through with a mix of cocoa powder and raspberry jam as well as chopped chocolate, and brushed with fresh raspberry syrup, giving it a rosy hue and gorgeous shine. Babka is not a quick pastry to whip up for dessert. It's a project. But if you have an afternoon free, I can think of no better way to satisfy a craving for butter and chocolate.

MAKES 2 LOAVES

FOR THE DOUGH

2¼ TSP ACTIVE DRY YEAST

1 TSP SUGAR, PLUS ½ CUP/100 G

1 CUP/240 ML WARM WATER
(110°F/45°C)

4 TO 5 CUPS/510 TO 635 G
ALL-PURPOSE FLOUR

1 TSP SALT

3 EGGS, LIGHTLY BEATEN

½ CUP/115 G UNSALTED BUTTER, CUT
INTO SMALL PIECES, AT ROOM
TEMPERATURE

FOR THE FILLING

¾ CUP/220 G RASPBERRY JAM

2 TBSP COCOA POWDER

8 OZ/225 G BITTERSWEET
BAKING CHOCOLATE, VERY
FINELY CHOPPED

¼ CUP/50 G SUGAR

2 TBSP UNSALTED BUTTER,
AT ROOM TEMPERATURE

FOR THE RASPBERRY SYRUP

1 CUP/150 G FRESH RASPBERRIES,
MASHED WITH A SPOON

2 TBSP WATER

¼ CUP/50 G SUGAR

1. Make the dough: Stir together the yeast, 1 tsp sugar, and warm water in a medium bowl. Let stand until foaming, 5 to 10 minutes.

2. Meanwhile, in a large bowl, whisk together 4 cups/510 g of the flour and the salt. Add the remaining ½ cup/100 g sugar and the eggs to the yeast mixture and whisk to combine. Make a well in the center of the flour mixture and pour in the yeast mixture. Gently stir until the dough begins to form, then turn out the dough onto a lightly floured work surface and knead well, adding the butter, a few pieces at a time, and up to 1 cup/125 g additional flour as needed, until a supple, slightly sticky dough forms, about 10 minutes. Rub 1 tsp oil around the bottom of a large bowl, add the dough, and turn to coat. Cover with plastic wrap or a dish towel and let stand in a warm place until nearly doubled in size, about 1 hour.

CONTINUED

3. Meanwhile, make the filling: In a medium bowl, stir together the jam and cocoa powder until combined. In a separate bowl, stir together the chocolate and sugar. Add the butter and use your fingers to combine until moist and crumbly.

4. Grease two 9-by-5-in/23-by-12-cm loaf pans. Gently deflate the dough by pressing on it in the center with the heel of your hand and turning it out onto a lightly floured work surface. Divide in half with a knife. Roll out one piece of dough into a large rectangle, about ⅛ in/4 mm thick (keeping the other piece covered with a dish towel). Use a knife to trim the dough into a 12-by-10-in/30.5-by-25-cm rectangle (I use a ruler as a guide).

5. Spread about half of the jam mixture onto the dough, leaving a ¼-in/6-mm uncovered border around the edges. Top with about half of the chocolate mixture and spread into an even layer. Starting at one of the short ends, roll the dough up tightly like a jelly roll, then trim about ½ in/12 mm off either end. Using a sharp knife, slice the roll in half down the center, leaving about ½ in/12 mm of dough uncut at the top end. You should now have two long strands of dough, connected at the top, with their layers of filling exposed. Twist the strands together and pinch at the bottom to seal; carefully place into the prepared baking pan. Repeat with the remaining piece of dough, the remaining jam mixture, and the remaining chocolate mixture. Loosely cover the loaf pans with plastic wrap or a dish towel and let rise for 45 minutes more until slightly puffed.

6. Fifteen minutes before baking, preheat the oven to 350°F/180°C. Bake the babkas, rotating the pans halfway through, until golden brown and cooked through, 45 to 60 minutes. (Start checking at 45 minutes, then every 5 minutes after that, as necessary. A tester inserted into the center of a babka should come out clean.)

7. Meanwhile, make the syrup: Combine the raspberries, water, and sugar in a small saucepan set over medium heat. Bring to a boil, then turn the heat to low and simmer, stirring and continuing to mash the raspberries, until the sugar dissolves, 1 to 2 minutes. Remove from the heat and let stand for 10 minutes, then strain through a fine-mesh sieve into a small bowl.

8. Remove the babkas from the oven and immediately brush the top of each generously with the raspberry syrup. (You might not use all of it.) Let the babkas cool in their pans for 20 minutes, then turn out onto a wire rack to cool completely. Serve at room temperature. (Store tightly in plastic wrap for up to 3 days at room temperature. Reheat leftovers in a toaster oven.)

BITTERSWEET GLAZED SUFGANIYOT WITH PEANUT BUTTER CREAM

Every winter when Hanukkah rolls around, the bakeries in Israel surrender to doughnut fever—particularly *sufganiyot*, the pillowy, filled doughnuts favored over potato latkes by Israelis during the eight-day Festival of Lights. Most sufganiyot come filled with fruit jams. Walking down the street in Tel Aviv or Jerusalem, you will see shop windows literally overflowing with deep-fried goodies, filled with everything from white chocolate to halvah to pistachio cream, and topped with a Technicolor array of glazes. This take on sufganiyot, which come filled with luscious peanut butter cream and dipped in a bittersweet chocolate glaze, are inspired by my favorite candy: chocolate peanut butter cups. When it comes to favorite Hanukkah foods, I am still a potato latke girl through and through. But there is always room for dessert.

MAKES ABOUT 15 DOUGHNUTS

NOTE

Commercial-brand peanut butters (Skippy, Jif, etc.) work better in this filling than natural peanut butters, which tend to separate. If you prefer more traditional sufganiyot, skip the peanut butter filling and pipe in apricot or raspberry jam instead. Give the jam a quick pulse in the food processor to make it easier to pipe.

FOR THE DOUGHNUTS

2½ CUPS/315 G ALL-PURPOSE FLOUR

½ TSP KOSHER SALT

2¼ TSP ACTIVE DRY YEAST

1 TSP GRANULATED SUGAR, PLUS ¼ CUP/50 G

½ CUP/120 ML WARM WATER (110°F/45°C)

2 EGG YOLKS

⅓ CUP/80 ML MILK

½ TSP VANILLA EXTRACT

2 TBSP UNSALTED BUTTER, CUT INTO SMALL PIECES, AT ROOM TEMPERATURE

8 CUPS/2 L VEGETABLE OIL

FOR THE PEANUT BUTTER CREAM

4 OZ/115 G CREAM CHEESE, AT ROOM TEMPERATURE

¼ CUP/70 G CREAMY PEANUT BUTTER

1 CUP/100 G CONFECTIONERS' SUGAR

1 TSP MILK

FOR THE CHOCOLATE GLAZE

½ CUP/50 G CONFECTIONERS' SUGAR

⅓ CUP/35 G COCOA POWDER, SIFTED

1 OZ/30 G BITTERSWEET BAKING CHOCOLATE, MELTED

½ TSP INSTANT COFFEE

3 TBSP MILK

1. Make the doughnuts: Whisk together the flour and salt in a large bowl.

2. Stir together the yeast, 1 tsp sugar, and warm water in a medium bowl. Let stand until foaming, 5 to 10 minutes. Add the remaining ¼ cup/50 g sugar, egg yolks, milk, and vanilla to the yeast mixture and whisk to combine. Make a well in the center of the flour mixture and pour in the yeast mixture. Gently stir until the dough begins to form a ball, then turn out the dough onto a lightly floured work surface. Scatter the butter pieces over the dough and knead, sprinkling additional flour as necessary, until the butter is fully incorporated and the dough is smooth, shiny, and elastic, about 8 minutes. Form the dough into a ball. Rub 1 tsp oil around the bottom of a large bowl, add the dough, and turn to coat. Cover with plastic wrap or a dish towel and let stand in a warm place until nearly doubled in size, 1½ to 2 hours.

3. Line one baking sheet with parchment paper, and fit a wire rack into a second baking sheet. Gently deflate the dough by pressing on it in the center with the heel of your hand. Transfer the dough to a lightly floured work surface and roll out to ¼-in/6-mm thickness. Use a 3-in/7.5-cm round biscuit cutter to cut out as many circles as possible and place them on the parchment-lined baking sheet. Gather the scraps and repeat the rolling and cutting process with the remaining dough. Cover the dough circles with a damp dish towel and let rise in a warm place until puffed, 30 to 45 minutes.

4. Heat the vegetable oil in a large heavy-bottomed pot set over medium heat until the temperature reaches 365°F/185°C on a deep-fry thermometer.

5. Meanwhile, make the peanut butter cream: In a stand mixer or using a hand-held electric mixer and a medium bowl, beat together the cream cheese and peanut butter on medium speed until smooth. Add the confectioners' sugar in three additions, beating after each addition until fully incorporated. Add the milk and beat until smooth and creamy. Spoon the filling into a pastry bag fit with a ¼-in/6-mm round tip.

6. Make the glaze: Whisk together the confectioners' sugar, cocoa powder, melted chocolate, instant coffee, and milk in a medium bowl until smooth.

7. When the oil reaches 365°F/185°C, gently add four of the dough rounds and fry, flipping once with a slotted spoon, until golden brown on both sides, about 2 minutes total. Transfer the doughnuts to the baking sheet fitted with the wire rack. Continue frying four more rounds. While the rounds from the second batch are frying, use tongs to pick up the doughnuts from the first batch and dip the bottom of each into the chocolate glaze. Return the doughnuts, glazed-side up, to the wire rack. Repeat the frying and glazing with the remaining dough rounds.

8. Use a small knife to cut a small hole into the side of each doughnut to form a pocket. Place the tip of the piping bag into each pocket and pipe about 1 tsp of filling inside. Serve warm or at room temperature. These are best eaten on the day they are made.

CHAPTER NINE

COOKIES, CAKES, AND OTHER SWEETS

SWEET HAMANTASCHEN

The first time I made hamantaschen—the traditional triangle-shaped Purim cookie—by myself, I was twenty-five and was working with a sketchy dough recipe I found on the Internet. The dough tasted fine but was super-delicate, and I ended up with a sorry-looking batch of cracked, leaky hamantaschen and two baking sheets caked with burnt jam. If only I had made this dough recipe instead. Bound with egg and oil and sweetened with orange juice, it rolls out and shapes with relative ease, making it ideal for beginners and skilled hamantaschen makers alike.

MAKES ABOUT 36 COOKIES

NOTE

For this recipe, I strongly recommend using the "spoon and sweep" method for accurately measuring the flour with measuring cups. Find out how on page 18.

2½ CUPS/315 G ALL-PURPOSE FLOUR

1 TSP BAKING POWDER

¼ TSP KOSHER SALT

1 TBSP FRESH ORANGE JUICE

¼ CUP/60 ML VEGETABLE OIL

⅔ CUP/130 G SUGAR

2 EGGS

1 TSP VANILLA EXTRACT

1 TSP LEMON ZEST

POSSIBLE FILLINGS: LEKVAR (PAGE 261), GOLDEN APRICOT FILLING (PAGE 262), CHOCOLATE-POPPY SEED FILLING (PAGE 263), RASPBERRY JAM, BLUEBERRY JAM, STRAWBERRY JAM, NUTELLA, PEANUT BUTTER, CHOCOLATE CHIPS

1. Whisk together the flour, baking powder, and salt in a medium bowl.

2. In a large bowl, whisk together the orange juice, vegetable oil, sugar, eggs, vanilla, and lemon zest until combined. Slowly stir in the flour mixture, mixing until the dough begins to come together. Turn the dough out onto a flat surface and knead a few times with your hands until it is smooth, but not sticky. (If the dough appears too dry, knead in more orange juice, 1 tsp—and no more!—at a time. If it looks too wet, knead in up to ¼ cup/30 g more flour, 1 Tbsp at a time, until you reach the right consistency.)

CONTINUED

3. Gather the dough, then divide it in half with a knife and form into two flat disks. Wrap each disk tightly in plastic wrap and refrigerate for at least 3 hours, or up to overnight.

4. Preheat the oven to 350°F/180°C and line a large rimmed baking sheet with parchment paper. Remove half of the dough from the refrigerator (keep the other half wrapped and chilled). On a lightly floured work surface, roll the dough to ⅛-in/4-mm thickness. Use a 3-in/7.5-cm round cookie cutter or glass to cut out as many circles as possible and carefully transfer them, about ½ in/12 mm apart, to the prepared baking sheet. Gather the dough scraps, reroll, cut out additional circles, and transfer them to the baking sheet.

5. Spoon 1 tsp of filling into the center of each dough circle. Fold the left side over on an angle, followed by the right side. Fold the bottom flap up, tucking one end under the side flap to make a triangle-shaped pocket (the filling should still be visible in the center); pinch the seams firmly to seal. Repeat the process with the remaining dough and filling.

6. Bake until lightly golden and browned at the corners, 15 to 20 minutes. Remove from the oven and let the cookies cool on the baking sheets for 5 minutes, then transfer to a wire rack to cool completely. Store in an airtight container at room temperature for up to 3 days.

LEKVAR

When I think about old-school Jewish food, prune lekvar is one of the first things that comes to mind. The thick Ashkenazi quick jam, which is made from fresh or dried plums, enhances all sorts of Jewish pastries, from strudel to cakes to Sweet Hamantaschen (page 259). This take on traditional prune lekvar livens up the filling with cinnamon, ginger, and orange zest. A night in the refrigerator allows the lekvar's flavors to mingle and deepen, so if possible prepare it the day before you plan to make hamantaschen.

MAKES ABOUT 1 CUP/300 G

1½ CUPS/225 G PITTED PRUNES

⅔ CUP/165 ML WATER

ZEST AND JUICE FROM 1 ORANGE

½ TSP GROUND CINNAMON

½ TSP GROUND GINGER

¼ CUP/50 G SUGAR

2 TBSP HONEY

1. Combine the prunes, water, orange zest and juice, cinnamon, and ginger in a small saucepan set over medium-high heat. Bring to a simmer, then turn the heat to low, cover, and cook, stirring occasionally, until the prunes are very soft and most of the liquid is absorbed, 15 to 20 minutes.

2. Remove from the heat and mash the prunes with a potato masher until a thick paste forms. While still hot, stir in the sugar and honey until dissolved. Let cool completely before filling hamantaschen. If desired, make up to 3 days ahead and store, covered, in the refrigerator.

GOLDEN APRICOT FILLING

Apricot jam is one of my favorite Sweet Hamantaschen (page 259) fillings. You can certainly use store-bought jam, but I prefer making this homemade version, which has an unexpected sweetness thanks to the addition of golden raisins.

MAKES ABOUT 1¼ CUPS/375 G

1 CUP/200 G DRIED APRICOTS, ROUGHLY CHOPPED

½ CUP/85 G GOLDEN RAISINS, ROUGHLY CHOPPED

¾ CUP/180 ML FRESH OR BOTTLED ORANGE JUICE (NOT FROM CONCENTRATE)

½ CUP/120 ML WATER

⅓ CUP/65 G SUGAR

1. Combine the apricots, raisins, orange juice, water, and sugar in a small saucepan set over medium-high heat. Bring to a simmer, then turn the heat to low, cover, and cook, stirring occasionally, until the fruit is very soft and most of the liquid is absorbed, 20 to 25 minutes.

2. Remove from the heat and use an immersion blender to blend the fruit into a chunky purée; or mash with a potato masher. Let cool completely before filling hamantaschen. If desired, make up to 3 days ahead and store, covered, in the refrigerator.

CHOCOLATE–POPPY SEED FILLING

There are two camps of hamantaschen eaters: those who love the poppy seed–filled version (called *mohn*), and those, like me, who do not. Never mind tradition—we no longer live in the shtetl. We have access to incredible jams, Nutella, and any number of other fillings that are superior to gritty ground poppy seeds. Or so I thought. Resigned to developing a recipe to include in this book, I did the only thing I could think of: I added chocolate. Fortunately I have learned to admit when I'm wrong, because this stuff was good. Like "sneak spoonfuls of the leftovers late at night" good. This recipe makes enough for two batches of Sweet Hamantaschen (page 259), or enough for one batch, plus copious snacking.

MAKES ABOUT 1¾ CUPS/455 G

NOTE

If you are a traditional poppy seed–filling fan, omit the chocolate in the recipe, and stir in ½ tsp lemon zest along with the juice.

1 CUP/130 G POPPY SEEDS

1 CUP/240 ML MILK

½ CUP/100 G SUGAR

⅓ CUP/60 G FINELY CHOPPED DRIED APRICOTS

1 TBSP FRESH ORANGE JUICE

1 TBSP FRESH LEMON JUICE

1 TBSP UNSALTED BUTTER

1 OZ/30 G BITTERSWEET BAKING CHOCOLATE OR SEMISWEET CHOCOLATE, ROUGHLY CHOPPED

2 TSP VANILLA EXTRACT

1. Use a spice or coffee grinder to grind the poppy seeds, working in batches if necessary, until powdery, 15 to 20 seconds.

2. In a small saucepan set over medium heat, combine the milk, sugar, ground poppy seeds, and apricots. Bring to a simmer, then turn the heat to low and cook, stirring frequently, until almost all the liquid is absorbed and the mixture thickens, 7 to 10 minutes.

3. Add the orange juice, lemon juice, and butter and cook until absorbed, 2 to 3 minutes. Stir in the chocolate and vanilla and cook, stirring continuously until the chocolate melts and the mixture is very thick, 2 to 3 minutes more. Remove from the heat and let cool slightly before filling hamantaschen. If desired, make up to 2 days ahead and store, covered, in the refrigerator.

SAVORY HAMANTASCHEN

Hamantaschen are cookies, and cookies are sweet. That's the conventional wisdom I followed for most of my life, until a few years ago when it occurred to me that, despite their distinct three-cornered shape, hamantaschen are not so different from empanadas, calzones, or any other stuffed pastry. Buoyed by this bit of insight, I tweaked my favorite recipe for sweet hamantaschen dough, dialing back the sugar and adding dried herbs to create a "cookie" worthy of a thick, sweet potato–Parmesan purée, a tangy tomato-beef mixture, or any other savory filling you dream up.

MAKES ABOUT 36 COOKIES

2½ CUPS/315 G ALL-PURPOSE FLOUR

1 TSP BAKING POWDER

1 TBSP DRIED HERBS, SUCH AS THYME, ROSEMARY, OR OREGANO, CRUSHED WITH A MORTAR AND PESTLE

½ TSP KOSHER SALT

1 TBSP WATER

¼ CUP/60 ML VEGETABLE OIL

½ CUP/100 G SUGAR

2 EGGS

POSSIBLE FILLINGS: SWEET POTATO– PARMESAN FILLING (PAGE 266), TOMATO-BEEF FILLING (PAGE 267)

1. Whisk together the flour, baking powder, dried herbs, and salt in a medium bowl.

2. In a large bowl, whisk together the water, vegetable oil, sugar, and eggs until combined. Slowly stir in the flour mixture, mixing until the dough begins to come together. Turn the dough out onto a flat surface and knead a few times with your hands until it is smooth, but not sticky. (If the dough appears too dry, knead in more water, 1 tsp—and no more!—at a time. If it looks too wet, knead in up to ¼ cup/30 g more flour, 1 Tbsp at a time, until you reach the right consistency.)

3. Gather the dough, then divide it in half with a knife and form into two flat disks. Wrap each disk tightly in plastic wrap and refrigerate for at least 3 hours, or up to overnight.

4. Preheat the oven to 350°F/180°C and line a large rimmed baking sheet with parchment paper. Remove half of the dough from the refrigerator (keep the other half wrapped and chilled). On a lightly floured work surface, roll the dough to ⅛-in/4-mm thickness. Use a 3-in/7.5-cm round cookie cutter or glass to cut out as many circles as possible and carefully transfer them, about ½ in/12 cm apart, to the prepared baking sheet. Gather the dough scraps, reroll, cut out additional circles, and transfer them to the baking sheet.

5. Spoon 1 tsp of filling into the center of each dough circle. Fold the left side over on an angle, followed by the right side. Fold the bottom flap up, tucking one end under the side flap to make a triangle-shaped pocket (the filling should still be visible in the center); pinch the seams firmly to seal. Repeat the process with the remaining dough and filling.

6. Bake until lightly golden and browned at the corners—15 to 18 minutes for the sweet potato–Parmesan and 18 to 20 minutes for the tomato-beef, until it is cooked through. Remove from the oven and let the cookies cool on the baking sheets for 5 minutes, then transfer to a wire rack to cool slightly. These are best served warm. Store in an airtight container in the refrigerator for up to 3 days. Reheat leftovers briefly in a toaster oven.

SWEET POTATO–PARMESAN FILLING

Mashed sweet potatoes make a delicious and unusual filling for either Sweet Hamantaschen (page 259) or Savory Hamantaschen (page 264). But the fresh thyme, garlic, and a hefty sprinkle of salty Parmesan in this filling place it squarely in the savory camp.

MAKES ABOUT 1⅓ CUPS/295 G

1 MEDIUM SWEET POTATO, PEELED AND
   CUT INTO 1-IN/2.5-CM PIECES

2 GARLIC CLOVES, PEELED

1 TBSP OLIVE OIL

1 SHALLOT, FINELY CHOPPED

KOSHER SALT AND FRESHLY GROUND
   BLACK PEPPER

1 TSP FINELY CHOPPED FRESH THYME

¼ CUP/20 G GRATED PARMESAN
   CHEESE

1. Place the sweet potato and garlic in a small saucepan and cover with cold water. Bring to a boil over high heat, then turn the heat to medium and simmer until the potato is very tender, 10 to 15 minutes. Drain well.

2. Meanwhile, heat the olive oil in a small pan set over medium heat. Add the shallot, season with salt and pepper, and cook, stirring occasionally, until browned, 3 to 5 minutes. Remove from the heat.

3. Using a potato masher or fork, mash the sweet potato and garlic into a thick purée. Stir in the thyme, shallot, and Parmesan. Season with more salt and pepper and let cool slightly before filling hamantaschen. If desired, make up to 2 days ahead and store, covered, in the refrigerator.

TOMATO-BEEF FILLING

I had savory Middle Eastern pastries like bourekas (see pages 245 and 246) on the brain when developing this "cookie" filling. The flavorful mixture of ground beef and tomato sauce spiked with chopped green olives and sweetened with just a touch of honey is the perfect filling for Savory Hamantaschen (page 264). These hamantaschen taste particularly good drizzled with a bright lemon-mint vinaigrette (see page 44).

MAKES ABOUT 1⅓ CUPS/260 G

NOTE

Bake until the filling is cooked through, 18 to 20 minutes.

8 OZ/225 G GROUND BEEF

½ SMALL YELLOW ONION, FINELY CHOPPED

1 GARLIC CLOVE, FINELY CHOPPED

¼ CUP/40 G FINELY CHOPPED PIMIENTO-STUFFED GREEN OLIVES

1 TSP DRIED OREGANO

1 TSP SWEET PAPRIKA

¼ CUP/60 ML TOMATO SAUCE

1 TBSP HONEY

KOSHER SALT AND FRESHLY GROUND BLACK PEPPER

Combine the ground beef, onion, garlic, olives, oregano, paprika, tomato sauce, and honey in a medium bowl. Sprinkle generously with salt and pepper, then mix the filling with your hands until well combined before filling hamantaschen.

VARIATION

Swap some of the sweet paprika for smoked paprika, or add cumin or a splash of hot sauce to the mixture.

HAMANTASCHEN: A PURIM PRIMER

Baking hamantaschen is one of my favorite parts of the Purim holiday (see page 329). The cookie's filling gets folded inside a triangle of dough, symbolizing the pocket of the Purim story's notorious villain, Haman. (The name translates from Yiddish as "Haman's pockets.") I love how the act of baking reminds me of the story, or at very least reminds me to Google "Purim" and refresh my memory. And to be honest, I am also just a sucker for jam-filled cookies.

Bakery-made hamantaschen tend to be disappointingly dry and crumbly, but good homemade hamantaschen are divine. They are also fun to bake with friends and kids. Make the dough ahead of time, then invite people over to help you roll, fill, bake, and eat. Here are some tips to get you rolling like a pro.

DOUGH

Like many doughs, hamantaschen dough can be fickle depending on the weather and humidity. You want a dough that is tender and pliable but not too wet or dry. If things seem a bit dry or crumbly after you have mixed all the ingredients together, stir in water, 1 tsp (and no more!) at a time, until you reach a smooth, supple consistency. Too wet? Add in flour, 1 tsp at a time, until the dough feels right. Also, letting your dough chill in the refrigerator makes it much easier to roll out later, so do not skip it.

ROLLING

When rolling out hamantaschen, you want to get the dough at least ⅛ in/4 mm thick, and a little bit thinner if possible. The reason? Thin dough equals a delicate, flaky cookie. Flour your work surface and rolling pin liberally, and work quickly so the dough does not have a chance to get too warm. If your dough does grow too soft to cut and form the hamantaschen, wrap it in plastic wrap and throw it in the refrigerator for 15 to 20 minutes to firm up.

FILLING

Back in Eastern Europe, hamantaschen were traditionally filled with either a sweet poppy seed mixture called *mohn*, or prune or apricot jam. In contemporary America, home bakers have expanded the options to include other jams like blueberry, strawberry, and raspberry; fruit butters; and less conventional fillings like Nutella, peanut butter, marzipan, and chocolate chips. I personally love mixing together raspberry jam with chocolate chips, or stirring apricot jam with finely chopped walnuts before spooning it onto the cookie.

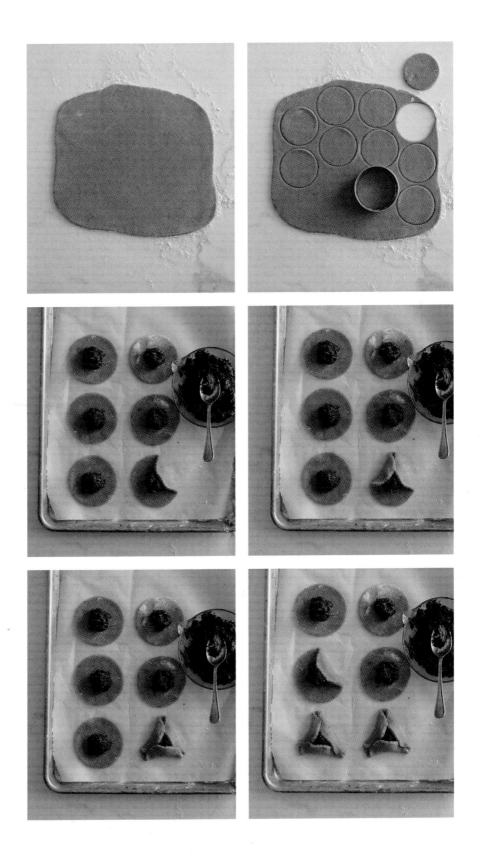

Some years, I am too busy to bother with homemade fillings. But whenever I have the time, I am so grateful I did. I am partial to my Chocolate–Poppy Seed Filling (page 263). I also love baking batches of truly unconventional Savory Hamantaschen (page 264) filled with either a Tomato-Beef Filling (page 267) or a Sweet Potato–Parmesan Filling (page 266). Whichever filling you use, make sure it errs on the thick side. Jammy fruit preserves, for example, work better than thin, watery jellies that tend to leak out during baking. And remember, less is always more. It can be tempting to heap a bunch of filling into the center, but it makes the cookies hard to form and encourages them to burst open in the oven; 1 tsp is typically the right amount for a 3-in/7.5-cm circle of dough.

FOLDING

For years I made hamantaschen the wrong way. I would fill the circle of dough, then awkwardly gather the corners together and pinch them closed. They looked nice enough on the baking tray, but tended to open up in the oven, leaving a sad round of dough and a baking tray covered in jam. Then a wise friend shared a secret that changed everything. Instead of just pinching, she told me, a successful hamantaschen starts with folding. Fill your circle, then fold one side over to the center at a slight angle. Fold the second side over to the center in the same way, slightly overlapping the dough over the first edge you created. Finally, fold the bottom of the circle up, tucking one side under the dough flap, and letting the other side hang over. (A small triangle of filling should still be visible in the center.) Wet your finger with a drop of water and *then* firmly pinch the folded corners.

CHOCOLATE-ALMOND-HAZELNUT HORNS

Old-school Jewish bakeries in New York make a wickedly good cookie called an almond horn. The crescent moon–shaped pastry is made with sweet almond paste and rolled in thinly sliced almonds (or chopped hazelnuts in this case), yielding a crunchy outside that gives way to a tender, chewy inside. Some bakeries up the ante by dipping them in melted chocolate at both ends (as pictured in the lower third of page 273). According to Stanley Ginsberg, co-author of the wonderful cookbook *Inside the Jewish Bakery,* "[almond horns] were expensive to make, high-priced, and absolutely worth it—one of the biggest sellers in the bakery." He's right, almond paste (see page 343) and almond flour can get a little pricey. But for almond lovers and gluten-free folks, they are more than worth the splurge.

MAKES 12 HORNS

6 OZ/170 G ALMOND PASTE, BROKEN INTO SMALL PIECES WITH YOUR FINGERS

⅓ CUP/30 G ALMOND FLOUR

¼ CUP/50 G SUGAR

2 EGG WHITES

1¼ CUPS/150 G HAZELNUTS, FINELY CHOPPED

3 OZ/85 G BITTERSWEET BAKING CHOCOLATE, ROUGHLY CHOPPED

1. Preheat the oven to 375°F/190°C and line a large baking sheet with parchment paper.

2. In a stand mixer or using a handheld electric mixer and a large bowl, mix the almond paste, almond flour, sugar, and 1 of the egg whites together on low speed until a moist dough forms.

3. Spread out the hazelnuts in a shallow dish. Moisten your hands lightly with water, then divide and roll the dough into twelve equal balls. Working one at a time, press each ball into the hazelnuts on all sides while shaping it into a 5-in/12-cm rope. Place the rope on the prepared baking sheet and gently form it into a "U" shape. The dough will feel fragile at this stage, but will firm up while baking. Repeat with the remaining dough balls, placing the cookies ½ in/12 mm apart.

CONTINUED

4. Whisk the remaining 1 egg white with about 1 tsp water. Gently brush the tops of the cookies with a little egg wash (you will not use all of it). Bake until lightly golden, 15 to 18 minutes. Let the cookies cool on the baking sheet for 10 minutes, then carefully transfer to a wire rack to cool completely.

5. Melt the chocolate in a double boiler set over simmering water. (Or melt in the microwave in a microwave-safe bowl at 30-second intervals, stirring between each interval until fully melted.) Dip the tips of the cookies into the chocolate and place back on the baking sheet. Chill in the refrigerator until the chocolate sets, about 15 minutes. Store in an airtight container at room temperature for up to 5 days.

CHOCOLATE-ALMOND MERINGUES

Every year when I was growing up, my mom would make meringues for Passover (see page 330). They were incredible—voluminous and airy with a crackly exterior and melt-in-your-mouth tenderness. And despite being a bona fide dessert, they were about 80 percent egg white, which meant I could eat lots and not feel stuffed or guilty for having too much dessert. And I did. Eat lots, I mean. My version (pictured in the upper left of page 273) takes her classic meringues and dips them in melted chocolate and finely chopped almonds for a treat that satisfies after the seder meal, or anytime.

MAKES ABOUT 30 COOKIES

NOTE

Make your own superfine sugar (also called castor sugar): Pulse granulated sugar in a food processor until finely ground but not powdery, about 30 seconds.

If you do not have a pastry bag, substitute a sturdy zip-top resealable bag. Spoon the meringue into the bag, then cut off about ¼ in/6 mm of one of the corners and pipe the meringue through it.

Avoid making these cookies in the middle of summer—the heat and humidity make the egg whites get weepy.

3 EGG WHITES, AT ROOM TEMPERATURE

⅛ TSP CREAM OF TARTAR

½ CUP/50 G CONFECTIONERS' SUGAR

¼ CUP/50 G SUPERFINE SUGAR

3 OZ/85 G BITTERSWEET BAKING CHOCOLATE, ROUGHLY CHOPPED

½ CUP/55 G ROASTED UNSALTED ALMONDS, FINELY CHOPPED

1. Preheat the oven to 250°F/120°C and line a baking sheet with parchment paper.

2. In a stand mixer or using a handheld electric mixer fitted with the whisk attachment and a large bowl, beat the egg whites on medium speed until foamy, 30 to 60 seconds. Beat in the cream of tartar until just combined. Beat in the confectioners' sugar in two additions, followed by the super-fine sugar, beating on medium-high speed for 1 minute after each addition. Continue beating until the mixture is stiff and shiny but not dry, about 1 minute more.

3. Spoon the meringue into a pastry bag fitted with a ½-in/12-mm plain or star tip. Pipe 1-in/2.5-cm rounds of meringue onto the prepared baking sheet, leaving ½ in/12 mm of space in between them. Bake until dry, about 1½ hours. (Meringues are done when they release easily from the parchment paper.) Turn off the heat, but allow the meringues to remain inside the oven to crisp up, about 1 hour. Remove from the oven and let cool completely.

4. Melt the chocolate in a double boiler set over simmering water. (Or melt in the microwave in a microwave-safe bowl at 30-second intervals, stirring between each interval until fully melted.) Spread the chopped almonds in a shallow dish. Once cool, dip the bottom of each meringue in the chocolate, then dip in the almonds. Place back onto the parchment-lined baking sheet and let stand until the chocolate sets. Store in the refrigerator between layers of parchment paper in an airtight container for up to 5 days, or freeze for up to 1 month. Let come to room temperature before serving.

RUGELACH TWO WAYS

Rugelach (pictured in the upper right of page 273) are a Jewish pastry so delicious, they have crossed over into the mainstream. The sweet, buttery Eastern European cookies (their name means "little twists" in Yiddish) come spiraled with a variety of delicious fillings and can be found at grocery stores and coffee shops across the country. When I was growing up, all the rugelach I ate came from bakeries, but they are surprisingly simple to make at home. Plus, the cream cheese– and butter-enriched dough puffs up in the oven, growing golden and flaky like a croissant. So there's that.

Chocolate-walnut filling is a total rugelach classic. If you want to get more experimental, try the alternative fig-ginger filling inspired by the clementine-ginger rugelach I buy from Shelsky's Smoked Fish, a nouveau appetizing store (see page 181) in Brooklyn. My version features fig jam spiced with cardamom, cinnamon, and orange zest, as well as heaps of finely chopped walnuts and crystallized ginger. Serve either cookie alongside tea or coffee for a sublime dessert or afternoon snack.

MAKES 32 COOKIES

FOR THE DOUGH

1 CUP/225 G UNSALTED BUTTER, AT ROOM TEMPERATURE

8 OZ/225 G CREAM CHEESE, AT ROOM TEMPERATURE

½ CUP/50 G CONFECTIONERS' SUGAR

½ TSP SALT

2 CUPS/255 G ALL-PURPOSE FLOUR

FOR THE CHOCOLATE-WALNUT FILLING

4 OZ/115 G SEMISWEET BAKING CHOCOLATE, ROUGHLY CHOPPED

1 CUP/115 G WALNUTS, FINELY CHOPPED

⅓ CUP/65 G GRANULATED SUGAR

1 TSP GROUND CINNAMON

¾ CUP/220 G APRICOT JAM

FOR THE FIG-GINGER FILLING

¾ CUP/225 G FIG JAM

¼ TSP GROUND CARDAMOM

½ TSP GROUND CINNAMON

½ TSP ORANGE ZEST

1 CUP/115 G FINELY CHOPPED WALNUTS

½ CUP/100 G FINELY CHOPPED CRYSTALLIZED GINGER

1 EGG, LIGHTLY BEATEN

2 TBSP GRANULATED SUGAR

1 TSP GROUND CINNAMON

1. Make the dough: In a stand mixer or using a handheld electric mixer and a large bowl, beat the butter, cream cheese, confectioners' sugar, and salt together on medium speed, scraping down the sides of the bowl as necessary, until smooth and creamy, about 2 minutes. Slowly add the flour, beating on low speed until just incorporated. Turn the dough out onto a lightly floured work surface and knead it a few times to bring the dough together. If necessary, sprinkle a little more flour over the dough while kneading until it feels soft and supple, but not sticky. Form the dough into two round disks, wrap both in plastic wrap, and refrigerate for at least 2 hours, or up to 1 day.

2. Make the chocolate-walnut filling: Use a food processor to pulse the chocolate into small pebbles. Transfer the chocolate to a medium bowl and stir in the walnuts, granulated sugar, and cinnamon until combined. In a separate small bowl, microwave the apricot jam until it is easily spreadable, about 30 seconds.

    Make the fig-ginger filling: Stir together the fig jam, cardamom, cinnamon, and orange zest in a small bowl. In a separate small bowl, stir together the walnuts and crystallized ginger.

3. Preheat the oven to 350°F/180°C and line two large rimmed baking sheets with parchment paper. Remove one disk of dough from the refrigerator and, on a lightly floured work surface, roll into a large circle that is ⅛ in/ 4 mm thick. (If you let the dough rest in the refrigerator overnight, it may need to warm up for 5 to 10 minutes before you roll it out.) Trim off the ragged edges with a knife, discarding the scraps, leaving a circle that is about 12 in/30.5 cm in diameter. (I like to use a ruler as a guide.)

4. Spread about half of the fig jam mixture or apricot jam evenly over the top of the dough, leaving about a ¼-in/6-mm uncovered border around the edges of the circle. Sprinkle with half of the chocolate-walnut or walnut-ginger mixture, and gently press the filling into the dough with your fingers. Using a pizza cutter or sharp knife, cut the dough into four equal wedges, then cut each wedge into four wedges (ending up with sixteen thin wedges). Starting from the outer edge, roll each wedge in on itself until you reach the center. Place the cookies on one of the prepared baking sheets at least ½ in/12 mm apart. Repeat the process with the remaining dough and filling.

5. Brush the tops of the cookies with the beaten egg (you will not use all of it). Stir together the 2 Tbsp granulated sugar and 1 tsp cinnamon, and sprinkle over the top of the cookies. Bake, rotating the pans halfway through, until golden brown and the tops are crisp like a croissant, 25 to 35 minutes. Immediately transfer the cookies to wire racks to cool completely. Store in an airtight container in the refrigerator for up to 1 week. Let come to room temperature before serving.

WALNUT MANDELBROT

Mandelbrot, which is Yiddish for "almond bread," is biscotti's Jewish cousin. Like biscotti they get baked twice. This particular recipe is the one my mom always makes, which she got from her late friend, Dr. Minnie Frank. And let me tell you, they are wonderful—crisp, nutty, and coated with a sweet dusting of cinnamon and sugar. Aside from swapping chopped walnuts for the more traditional almonds, I changed absolutely nothing about the recipe. No need—these cookies are already perfect.

MAKES 20 TO 22 COOKIES

1½ CUPS/185 G ALL-PURPOSE FLOUR

½ TSP BAKING POWDER

½ TSP BAKING SODA

¼ TSP KOSHER SALT

½ CUP/115 G UNSALTED BUTTER OR
NONHYDROGENATED MARGARINE,
AT ROOM TEMPERATURE

½ CUP/100 G SUGAR, PLUS ⅓ CUP/65 G

2 EGGS

½ TSP VANILLA EXTRACT

½ TSP FRESH LEMON JUICE

½ CUP/55 G FINELY CHOPPED WALNUTS

1 TBSP GROUND CINNAMON

1. Preheat the oven to 350°F/180°C and line a large rimmed baking sheet with parchment paper. Sift together the flour, baking powder, baking soda, and salt in a medium bowl.

2. In a stand mixer or using a handheld electric mixer and a large bowl, cream the butter and ½ cup/100 g sugar on medium speed until pale and fluffy, about 2 minutes. Add the eggs and beat to combine, followed by the vanilla and lemon juice. Add the flour mixture in two stages and beat on low speed until a moist, spreadable batter forms; stir in the walnuts.

3. Divide the dough in half and use a butter knife or offset spatula to spread each half into a long, flat log on the prepared baking sheet, leaving 2 in/ 5 cm in between. (Each log should be about 9 by 4 in/23 by 10 cm, and about ½ in/12 mm thick.) Bake until lightly browned, about 20 minutes, then remove from the oven and let cool slightly.

4. Meanwhile, stir together the remaining ⅓ cup/65 g sugar and the cinnamon in a small bowl. Slice the logs into ½-in-/12-mm-wide pieces, turn the pieces on their side, and sprinkle generously with half of the cinnamon-sugar. Bake for 10 minutes, then remove the pan from the oven, rotate the mandelbrot to the other side with tongs, sprinkle with the remaining cinnamon-sugar, and bake until firm, 10 to 15 minutes more. Remove from the oven and let cool completely on wire racks. The cookies will turn crunchy as they cool. Store in an airtight container in the refrigerator for up to 1 week. Let come to room temperature before serving.

COCONUT MACAROONS

Passover's best-known confection tends to get a bad rap for being cloying. But most people have only ever tried the mass-produced variety, which comes packed in a stuffy tin and is loaded with excess sugar. This homemade version, with its crunchy, caramelized outside and chewy, coconut-flavored center, tastes like an entirely different cookie. And that's a very welcome thing. Try them plain, enriched with cocoa powder and chocolate chips, or flavored with cinnamon, sweet almond extract, and crunchy sliced almonds.

MAKES ABOUT 2 DOZEN COOKIES

3 EGG WHITES

¼ TSP SALT

⅔ CUP/130 G SUGAR

1 TSP VANILLA EXTRACT

½ TSP ORANGE ZEST

2¼ CUPS/200 G COARSELY SHREDDED UNSWEETENED COCONUT

1. In a medium saucepan, stir together the egg whites, salt, sugar, vanilla, and orange zest until combined. Set the pan over low heat, stir in the coconut, and cook, stirring frequently, until the mixture thickens slightly and turns sticky, 5 to 6 minutes. Transfer the mixture to a large bowl and let stand, uncovered, for 20 minutes. Meanwhile, preheat the oven to 325°F/165°C and line two large rimmed baking sheets with parchment paper.

2. Mound slightly rounded tablespoons of batter onto the prepared baking sheets, moistening your fingers with water if the mixture is sticking. Bake, rotating the baking sheets halfway through, until the macaroons are golden around the edges, 20 to 25 minutes total. (Be careful not to overbake as the cookies will continue to firm up while they cool.) Carefully transfer to wire racks to cool completely. Store in an airtight container at room temperature for up to 4 days.

VARIATION

For Chocolate Macaroons: Stir ¼ cup/25 g sifted cocoa powder into the egg white mixture before placing the saucepan over the heat; increase the vanilla extract to 2 tsp and omit the orange zest. Just before forming the macaroons, stir ½ cup/90 g semisweet chocolate chips into the cooled batter.

For Cinnamon-Almond Macaroons: Replace the orange zest with ½ tsp almond extract; add ½ cup/50 g sliced almonds along with the coconut. Dust the tops of the cooled macaroons with a little ground cinnamon.

RHUBARB-OATMEAL CRUMBLE BARS

Every winter, I wait for rhubarb. Like a puppy staring out the window, longing for its owner to arrive home, I wait for those ruby-colored stalks to arrive at the farmers' market, ushering in the unbridled joy of spring. Then every year, I do the same old thing with rhubarb—stew it with sugar into a compote, or bake it with strawberries into a pie. The results are not necessarily disappointing (are you kidding? they are delicious), but I feel a twinge of guilt for not trying something new. This dessert is my antidote, a buttery cake base topped with pieces of soft, tart rhubarb and a just-sweet-enough oatmeal crumble. They are simple to make, but decadent enough to feel as if I have properly honored rhubarb's fleeting season. Serve them with vanilla ice cream or freshly whipped cream.

MAKES 16 BARS

NOTE

This recipe calls for white whole-wheat flour, which can be a confusing term because we tend to think of "white flour" as less wholesome and nutritious than whole wheat. White whole-wheat flour, however, is simply whole wheat (meaning it includes all the healthful stuff—bran, endosperm, and germ) made from softer, milder white wheat instead of the traditional harder red wheat. It is the best of all worlds. See page 343 for an online source.

FOR THE TOPPING

- ¼ CUP/30 G WHITE WHOLE-WHEAT FLOUR
- ¼ CUP/30 G OLD-FASHIONED ROLLED OATS
- ⅓ CUP/65 G PACKED LIGHT BROWN SUGAR
- ½ TSP KOSHER SALT
- 2 TBSP UNSALTED BUTTER, AT ROOM TEMPERATURE

FOR THE BARS

- 12 OZ/340 G RHUBARB, CUT INTO ½-IN/12-MM CHUNKS (ABOUT 3 CUPS)
- 3 TBSP GRANULATED SUGAR, PLUS ¾ CUP/150 G
- 2 TBSP WHITE WHOLE-WHEAT FLOUR, PLUS ¾ CUP/90 G
- ½ TSP BAKING POWDER
- ¼ TSP KOSHER SALT
- ½ CUP/115 G UNSALTED BUTTER, AT ROOM TEMPERATURE
- 2 EGGS
- 1 TSP VANILLA EXTRACT

1. Make the topping: Stir together the flour, oats, brown sugar, and salt in a large bowl. Add the butter and use your fingers to combine until crumbly. Set aside.

2. Make the bars: Preheat the oven to 375°F/190°C and grease an 8-in/20-cm square baking pan.

3. In a small bowl, stir together the rhubarb, 3 Tbsp granulated sugar, and 2 Tbsp flour. In a separate small bowl, whisk together the remaining ¾ cup/90 g flour, baking powder, and salt.

4. In a stand mixer or using a handheld electric mixer and a large bowl, cream the butter and remaining ¾ cup/150 g granulated sugar on medium speed until pale and fluffy, about 2 minutes. Beat in the eggs, one at a time, followed by the vanilla, scraping down the sides of the bowl as necessary. Beat in the flour mixture on low speed until just combined.

5. Pour the batter into the prepared pan and smooth with a rubber spatula. Top with the rhubarb mixture and sprinkle with the crumble topping. Bake until golden and a tester inserted into the center comes out mostly clean with a few moist crumbs, 40 to 50 minutes. Remove from the oven, set the pan on a wire rack, and let cool completely before slicing into squares. Store tightly wrapped in the refrigerator for up to 5 days. Let come to room temperature before serving.

CHOCOLATE CUPCAKES WITH APRICOT JAM FROSTING

These cupcakes are inspired by the chocolate-dipped apricots my mom would make each year for Passover. The moist, chocolaty cake gets topped with a sweet-tart frosting amped up with apricot jam. A sprinkle of chopped dried apricots seals the deal. They are not kosher for Passover (see page 330), so stick with the chocolate-dipped fruit during the holiday, and enjoy these cupcakes the other 51 weeks of the year.

MAKES 12 CUPCAKES

NOTE

You can substitute ½ cup/120 ml of hot brewed coffee for the instant if you prefer. I like using instant because it saves me from brewing a whole pot of coffee and I honestly don't taste a difference.

FOR THE CUPCAKES

1 CUP/125 G ALL-PURPOSE FLOUR

½ TSP BAKING POWDER

½ TSP BAKING SODA

½ TSP KOSHER SALT

⅓ CUP/35 G COCOA POWDER

1 CUP/200 G GRANULATED SUGAR

1 TBSP INSTANT COFFEE

½ CUP/120 ML BOILING WATER

½ CUP/120 ML VEGETABLE OIL

½ CUP/120 ML MILK

½ TSP VANILLA EXTRACT

1 EGG, LIGHTLY BEATEN

FOR THE FROSTING

3 TBSP UNSALTED BUTTER, AT ROOM TEMPERATURE

3 TBSP APRICOT JAM

2 TBSP MILK, PLUS MORE AS NEEDED

1½ CUPS/150 G CONFECTIONERS' SUGAR

FINELY CHOPPED DRIED APRICOTS FOR TOPPING

1. Make the cupcakes: Preheat the oven to 350°F/180°C and line a 12-cup muffin tin with paper liners.

2. In a large bowl, whisk together the flour, baking powder, baking soda, salt, cocoa powder, and granulated sugar. In a small bowl, stir together the instant coffee and boiling water, then add it to the flour mixture along with the vegetable oil, milk, vanilla, and egg and stir well to combine.

3. Divide the batter evenly among the muffin cups. Bake until the tops are firm to the touch and a tester inserted into the center of a cupcake comes out clean, 20 to 22 minutes. Remove from the oven and let cool completely on a wire rack.

4. Meanwhile, make the frosting: In a stand mixer or using a handheld electric mixer and a medium bowl, beat the butter, apricot jam, milk, and ½ cup/50 g of the confectioners' sugar together on medium speed until smooth. Slowly add the remaining 1 cup/100 g confectioners' sugar, beating until creamy.

5. Spread a generous amount of frosting on top of the cooled cupcakes and sprinkle with chopped dried apricot. Serve at room temperature.

ORANGE-GLAZED CORNMEAL CAKE

I would never claim to be an expert on gluten-free baking, but sometimes you just get a lucky baking break. Take this cake. It is naturally gluten-free (and dairy-free to boot), but lacking in absolutely nothing. The cornmeal gives it a rich, nubby texture, while the almond flour adds heft and flavor. Finished with a sweet and citrusy glaze that gets painted right on top of the still-warm cake and with a sprinkle of toasted pistachios for crunch, all of the parts come together in one gorgeous dessert.

SERVES 8 TO 10

⅓ CUP/40 G SHELLED UNSALTED PISTACHIOS, ROUGHLY CHOPPED

1 CUP/150 G FINELY GROUND YELLOW CORNMEAL

1 CUP/95 G ALMOND FLOUR

2½ TSP BAKING POWDER

¼ TSP KOSHER SALT

3 EGGS

⅔ CUP/130 G SUGAR

½ CUP/120 ML VEGETABLE OIL

ZEST AND JUICE OF 1 ORANGE

1 TSP VANILLA EXTRACT

FOR THE GLAZE

½ CUP/120 ML FRESH ORANGE JUICE

3 TBSP SUGAR

1. Preheat the oven to 350°F/180°C and grease a 9-in/23-cm round cake pan.

2. Place the pistachios in a small pan set over medium heat. Cook, stirring occasionally, until fragrant and lightly browned, about 5 minutes. Transfer to a small bowl to cool completely.

3. Whisk together the cornmeal, almond flour, baking powder, and salt in a medium bowl.

4. Whisk together the eggs, sugar, vegetable oil, orange zest and juice, and vanilla in a separate bowl until fully combined. Slowly add the cornmeal mixture, whisking until just combined. Let stand for 20 minutes. Pour the batter into the prepared pan. Bake until a tester inserted into the center comes out clean, 35 to 40 minutes. Remove from the oven and let cool slightly on a wire rack.

5. Meanwhile, make the glaze: Combine the orange juice and sugar in a small saucepan set over medium heat. Bring to a simmer and cook, stirring occasionally, until the sugar completely dissolves and the mixture thickens slightly, 3 to 4 minutes. Remove from the heat.

6. Using a toothpick, poke holes all over the surface of the cake. Use a pastry brush to slowly brush the entire top of the cake with the glaze until all the glaze is used. (Don't rush, or your cake will turn out soggy!) Let cool completely, then sprinkle with toasted pistachios before slicing and serving.

HONEY-CINNAMON POUND CAKE

Honey cake is to Rosh Hashanah (see page 334) what fruitcake is to Christmas. It is an icon that everyone agrees is integral to the holiday, but usually comes out so dense and dry that nobody really enjoys it much. But since honey is one of the Jewish New Year's most important foods (the sweetness symbolizes our hopes for a sweet year ahead), it is worth getting right. That is where this pound cake comes in. It is made with ultrasoft cake flour (find an online source on page 343), which produces a cake that is deliciously moist with a tender crumb and beautiful golden coloring. This is not the most traditional honey cake, but sometimes that's a good thing. Serve it with Maple-Cardamom Roasted Pears (page 307) and expect to have your friends invite themselves over for next year's Rosh Hashanah dinner.

SERVES 8

1½ CUPS/185 G CAKE FLOUR

½ TSP BAKING POWDER

½ TSP KOSHER SALT

1 TSP GROUND CINNAMON

1 CUP/225 G UNSALTED BUTTER, AT
    ROOM TEMPERATURE, OR
    ½ CUP/120 ML VEGETABLE OIL

1 CUP/200 G SUGAR

¼ CUP/95 G HONEY

4 EGGS

1 TSP VANILLA EXTRACT

¼ CUP FRESH ORANGE JUICE

1. Preheat the oven to 325°F/165°C and grease and flour a 9-by-5-in/23-by-12-cm loaf pan, tapping out any excess flour.

2. Sift together the flour, baking powder, salt, and cinnamon in a small bowl.

3. In a stand mixer or using a handheld electric mixer and a large bowl, cream the butter, sugar, and honey on high speed until pale and fluffy, about 3 minutes. (If using the oil, beat until combined, about 1 minute. The mixture may look grainy until you add the eggs—that's fine.) Add the eggs, one at a time, followed by the vanilla and orange juice, beating to combine after each addition and scraping down the sides as necessary. Add the flour mixture in two stages, beating on low speed until just combined.

4. Pour the batter into the prepared pan. Bake until a tester inserted into the center comes out clean, 60 to 70 minutes. Let cool in the pan for 15 minutes, then run a butter knife around the edges, turn out the cake onto a wire rack, and let cool completely. Serve at room temperature.

VARIATION

Add ½ tsp orange zest to the batter, along with the vanilla and orange juice.

PASSOVER PEAR CAKE

Time was, when dessert rolled around after the Passover seder (see page 330), people would dutifully choke down flavorless sponge cakes, tinned macaroons, and alarmingly neon jellied fruit rings as if it were part of their holiday obligation. My mom's family used to call these sweet atrocities "Pesadrek," a combination of the Hebrew name for Passover, Pesach, and the Yiddish word *drek*. (Look it up.) But dreadful Passover desserts are increasingly becoming a thing of the past. Take this moist, full-bodied cake. Layered with juicy pears and perfumed with cinnamon, it makes a great Passover dessert, yes, but would be equally welcome any day of the year.

SERVES 8

½ CUP/55 G PECANS, ROUGHLY CHOPPED

½ CUP/100 G PACKED LIGHT BROWN SUGAR

2 TSP GROUND CINNAMON

½ TSP GROUND NUTMEG

4 EGGS

1 CUP/200 G GRANULATED SUGAR

½ CUP/120 ML VEGETABLE OIL

1 TSP VANILLA EXTRACT

1 CUP/125 G MATZO CAKE MEAL

4 MEDIUM RIPE, FIRM-FLESHED PEARS, SUCH AS BARTLETT, PEELED, QUARTERED, CORED, AND CUT INTO ¼-IN/6-MM SLICES

1. Preheat the oven to 350°F/180°C and lightly grease an 8-in/20-cm square baking pan.

2. Mix together the pecans, brown sugar, cinnamon, and nutmeg in a small bowl.

3. In a stand mixer or using a handheld electric mixer fitted with a whisk attachment and a large bowl, beat the eggs on medium speed until well combined and bubbly, 1 full minute. Add the granulated sugar, 2 Tbsp at a time, beating until the mixture is thick and billowy. (The gradual additions impact the cake's final texture.) Add the vegetable oil in a steady stream, followed by the vanilla, and beat until combined. Add the matzo cake meal and beat on low speed until just combined.

4. Pour about half of the batter into the prepared pan. Sprinkle with half of the pecan mixture and arrange about half of the pears on top. Add the remaining batter, smoothing the top with a rubber spatula. Top with the remaining pears, followed by the remaining pecan mixture.

5. Bake until a tester inserted into the center comes out clean, 60 to 75 minutes. (Start checking with the cake tester at 60 minutes, then every 5 minutes after that, as necessary). Transfer to a wire rack and let cool completely before slicing and serving.

PLUM-ALMOND CAKE

Plum cake, or *pflaumenkuchen,* is a lesser-known gem of Ashkenazi Jewish cuisine. This naturally dairy-free version is topped with softened plums, sliced almonds, and a snow-fall sprinkling of sugar, making it as gorgeous to look at as it is delicious to eat. My friend Avigail, who makes a mean plum cake of her own, taught me the trick of sprinkling a layer of bread crumbs over the batter before arranging the plums on top. The crumbs disappear while the cake bakes, but help keep the plums from sinking into the batter. Pure genius! If you don't need this cake to be dairy-free, serve with freshly whipped cream or ice cream, or eat it for breakfast with yogurt and a drizzle of maple syrup.

SERVES 8

NOTE

Use plums that are just ripe and still a little firm, and stick with sweeter varieties.

1¼ CUPS/155 G ALL-PURPOSE FLOUR

1 TSP BAKING POWDER

½ TSP BAKING SODA

½ TSP KOSHER SALT

1 CUP/200 G SUGAR, PLUS MORE FOR SPRINKLING

¾ CUP/180 ML VEGETABLE OIL

¼ CUP/60 ML FRESH ORANGE JUICE

3 EGGS

1 TSP VANILLA EXTRACT

1 TSP ALMOND EXTRACT

¼ CUP/25 G PLAIN BREAD CRUMBS

1¼ LB/570 G PLUMS, HALVED, PITTED, AND CUT INTO EIGHTHS

⅓ CUP/30 G SLICED ALMONDS

1. Preheat the oven to 350°F/180°C and grease a 9-in/23-cm round cake pan or springform pan.

2. Stir together the flour, baking powder, baking soda, and salt into a medium bowl.

3. In a stand mixer or using a handheld electric mixer and a large bowl, beat together the sugar, vegetable oil, and orange juice on medium speed until fully combined and thick, 1 to 2 minutes. Add the eggs, one at a time, followed by the vanilla and almond extract, beating to incorporate. Add the flour mixture in two stages, beating on low speed until just incorporated and scraping down the sides of the bowl as necessary.

4. Pour the batter into the prepared pan and smooth with a rubber spatula. Scatter the top evenly with the bread crumbs. Arrange the plum pieces on top of the cake in a circular pattern, and sprinkle with the almonds and 2 to 3 Tbsp sugar (depending on how sweet or sour your plums are). Bake until the cake begins to pull away from the sides of the pan, and a tester inserted into the center comes out clean, 45 to 55 minutes. Let cool completely on a wire rack, then remove from the pan, slice, and serve.

UPSIDE-DOWN APPLE CAKE

Along with honey cake, apple cake is one of the most popular desserts for Rosh Hashanah (see page 334). My mom makes the best version I have ever tasted. No, really! It's more of a quick bread than a true cake, but it is super-moist and filled with an almost obscene amount of juicy apple pieces. Since that recipe made it into my first cookbook, *The Hadassah Everyday Cookbook: Daily Meals for the Contemporary Jewish Kitchen*, I thought I would try something a little different. Riffing off of the retro-classic pineapple upside-down cake, I swapped out the canned pineapple rings for sweet apple slices nestled in a pool of caramel atop a layer of tender cake. The result is gorgeous to look at and so good, it might (almost) rival my mom's!

SERVES 8

NOTE

Use firm, sweet apples like Galas or Empires that will hold their shape during baking. Depending on the size of your apples, you may not end up using all the slices.

This cake really tastes best when made with butter. You can substitute non-hydrogenated margarine, but I don't recommend it. If you are looking for a delicious dairy-free cake for Rosh Hashanah, try the Honey-Cinnamon Pound Cake (page 286).

FOR THE APPLES

3 TBSP UNSALTED BUTTER, MELTED

⅓ CUP/65 G SUGAR

1 TSP GROUND CINNAMON

3 MEDIUM APPLES, PEELED, CORED, AND CUT INTO 12 WEDGES EACH

1¼ CUPS/155 G ALL-PURPOSE FLOUR

1 TSP BAKING POWDER

1 TSP GROUND CINNAMON

½ TSP KOSHER SALT

½ CUP/115 G UNSALTED BUTTER, AT ROOM TEMPERATURE

½ CUP/100 G SUGAR

2 EGGS

1 TSP VANILLA EXTRACT

½ CUP/120 ML APPLE CIDER OR APPLE JUICE

1. Preheat the oven to 350°F/180°C and grease a 9-in/23-cm round cake pan.

2. Make the apples: Combine the melted butter, sugar, and cinnamon in the prepared pan, mix well to combine, and use a rubber spatula to spread it in the bottom of the pan. Arrange the apple wedges in an overlapping circle all over the bottom of the pan, on top of the butter-sugar mixture.

3. Whisk together the flour, baking powder, cinnamon, and salt in a small bowl. In a stand mixer or using a handheld electric mixer and a large bowl, cream the butter and sugar on medium speed until pale and creamy, 2 to 3 minutes. Add the eggs, one at a time, followed by the vanilla, beating until incorporated. Add one-third of the flour mixture, followed by half of the cider, beating on low speed until just combined. (Don't beat too long at this stage or your cake might turn out tough). Repeat the process, adding another one-third of the flour, the remaining cider, and the final one-third of flour.

4. Spoon the batter over the apples and smooth the top with the spatula. Bake until a tester inserted into the center comes out clean, 35 to 45 minutes. Remove from the oven and set the cake on a wire rack. Let cool for at least 30 minutes, then run a knife along the sides of the pan and invert the cake onto a plate. Serve warm or at room temperature.

KABOCHA SQUASH–CHOCOLATE CHIP CAKE

Kabocha, an Asian variety of winter squash that is becoming increasingly popular at farmers' markets, looks like a small, slightly flattened, dark green pumpkin. The matte orange flesh inside is supremely creamy and dense. Like pumpkin and butternut squash, it makes a wonderful addition to baked goods—particularly this moist, naturally dairy-free cake. Sweetened with maple syrup and flavored with a delicate, floral hint of coconut from the unrefined coconut oil in the batter, it is unlike any other cake I have ever made. I bake it on Sukkot (see page 338), for Shabbat during the winter, or whenever I notice the squash piled high at the market.

SERVES 8

NOTE

Unrefined coconut oil (also referred to as "virgin" or "pure") is trans fat–free and full of nutrients. It is increasingly available at grocery stores, and should be stored in the cupboard or pantry. Coconut oil has a melting point of 76°F/24°C, so depending on the temperature in your home, you may open your pantry to find it in liquid or solid form. For this cake, it is best to measure in its liquid state. If necessary, place the jar in the microwave (make sure there is no foil on the package!) or stick it in a pot of warm water until it melts.

1 MEDIUM KABOCHA SQUASH

2 CUPS/255 G ALL-PURPOSE FLOUR

2 TSP BAKING POWDER

½ TSP KOSHER SALT

½ TSP GROUND CINNAMON

⅛ TSP GROUND NUTMEG

½ CUP/55 G PECANS, ROUGHLY CHOPPED

½ CUP/90 G SEMISWEET CHOCOLATE CHIPS

⅓ CUP/80 ML MELTED UNREFINED COCONUT OIL (SEE NOTE)

½ CUP/100 G PACKED LIGHT BROWN SUGAR

½ CUP/120 ML PURE MAPLE SYRUP

3 EGGS

1 TSP VANILLA EXTRACT

1. Preheat the oven to 400°F/200°C and line a rimmed baking sheet with aluminum foil. Use a sharp knife to poke several deep slits into the squash and place on the prepared baking sheet. Bake until the flesh pierces easily with a fork, 45 to 60 minutes. Remove from the oven and gently cut the squash in half, then allow to cool to the touch. Scoop out and discard the seeds, then scoop out packed 1¼ cups/250 g of flesh and mash with a potato masher until smooth. Set aside, reserving the remaining squash for another use. (Store, covered, in the refrigerator for up to 2 days.)

2. Lower the oven temperature to 350°F/180°C. Grease and lightly flour a 9-in/23-cm round springform pan. Whisk together the flour, baking powder, salt, cinnamon, and nutmeg in a medium bowl. Stir in the pecans and chocolate chips.

3. Whisk together the coconut oil, brown sugar, and maple syrup in a large bowl until smooth and combined, about 1 minute. Add the eggs, one at a time, followed by the squash and vanilla, whisking until incorporated. Add the flour mixture in three stages, stirring with a wooden spoon until just combined after each addition, and scraping down the sides of the bowl as necessary.

4. Pour the batter into the prepared pan and smooth with a spatula. Bake until a tester inserted into the center comes out clean, 50 to 60 minutes. Transfer the cake to a wire rack and let cool for at least 30 minutes before removing from the pan. Serve warm or at room temperature.

CHOCOLATE-BANANA BUNDT CAKE

Imagine chocolate chip–banana bread. Now imagine the dense chocolate Bundt cake your bubbe used to serve at bridge games (or was it mah-jongg?). Put them together, then stop imagining and start making this supremely moist, chocolaty cake with chocolate chips and luscious banana flavor infused throughout.

SERVES 10 TO 12

1¾ CUPS/215 G ALL-PURPOSE FLOUR

1 TSP BAKING POWDER

1 TSP BAKING SODA

½ CUP/50 G COCOA POWDER

½ TSP KOSHER SALT

1 CUP/180 G SEMISWEET
CHOCOLATE CHIPS

½ CUP/115 G UNSALTED BUTTER, AT
ROOM TEMPERATURE

1 CUP/200 G GRANULATED SUGAR

3 EGGS

2 TSP VANILLA EXTRACT

1½ CUPS/345 G MASHED RIPE BANANA
(FROM 3 OR 4 BANANAS)

¾ CUP/180 ML BUTTERMILK

CONFECTIONERS' SUGAR FOR DUSTING

1. Preheat the oven to 350°F/180°C and generously grease a Bundt pan.

2. Sift together the flour, baking powder, baking soda, cocoa powder, and salt in a medium bowl. Stir in the chocolate chips.

3. In a stand mixer or using a handheld electric mixture and a large bowl, cream the butter and granulated sugar on medium speed until pale and fluffy, 2 to 3 minutes. Add the eggs, one at a time, followed by the vanilla, beating on medium-low speed after each addition until combined.

4. Stir together the banana and buttermilk in a medium bowl until combined. Add half of the banana mixture to the butter mixture, followed by half of the flour mixture, beating on low speed after each addition until just combined. Repeat with the remaining banana mixture and flour mixture.

5. Pour the batter into the prepared pan and smooth with a rubber spatula. Bake until a tester inserted into the cake comes out mostly clean with a few moist crumbs, 45 to 50 minutes. Remove the cake from the oven and transfer to a wire rack. Let cool for 15 minutes, then run a knife around the edges of the pan and invert the cake onto the rack. Let cool completely. Just before serving, dust the top of the cake with confectioners' sugar.

RICOTTA–VANILLA BEAN CHEESECAKE WITH RASPBERRY SAUCE

When Yoshie and I visited Italy (see page 104), we made sure to stop at Pasticceria il Boccione, a 200-year-old kosher bakery located in Rome's historic Jewish ghetto neighborhood. Everything that comes out of the shop's ancient ovens is delicious, but I was particularly enamored with their crostata di ricotta, a rich ricotta tart filled with sour cherry preserves. This Shavuot-friendly (see page 333) cake is my riff on Boccione's classic. I call it the "cheesecake for people who don't like cheesecake," thanks to its delicate flavor, which is mild and fresh compared to traditional cheesecake's typical tartness. The eggs in the batter cause the cake to puff up handsomely in the oven, then settle back into place like a down comforter being fluffed and floated over a bed. The fresh raspberry sauce, which can either be poured directly over the top of the cake before serving or drizzled on individual slices, lends a tangy sweetness and Technicolor hue.

SERVES 8 TO 10

FOR THE CRUST

¾ CUP/75 G GRAHAM CRACKER CRUMBS

1 TBSP LIGHT BROWN SUGAR

3 TBSP UNSALTED BUTTER, MELTED

⅛ TSP KOSHER SALT

FOR THE CHEESECAKE

3½ CUPS/800 G FULL-FAT OR LOW-FAT RICOTTA CHEESE, AT ROOM TEMPERATURE

¾ CUP/150 G GRANULATED SUGAR

¼ CUP/30 G ALL-PURPOSE FLOUR

2 EGGS

1 VANILLA BEAN, SPLIT LENGTHWISE AND SEEDS SCRAPED OUT

2 TSP VANILLA EXTRACT

¼ TSP KOSHER SALT

FOR THE RASPBERRY SAUCE

2 CUPS/300 G FRESH RASPBERRIES, RINSED AND PATTED DRY

¼ CUP/60 ML FRESH ORANGE JUICE

¼ CUP/50 G GRANULATED SUGAR

½ TSP LEMON ZEST

CONTINUED

1. Preheat the oven to 350°F/180°C.

2. Make the crust: Whisk together the graham cracker crumbs, brown sugar, butter, and salt in a medium bowl until combined. Press the moistened crumb mixture into the bottom of a 9-in/23-cm round springform pan. Place in the freezer to set.

3. Make the cheesecake: Put the ricotta in a food processor and process until smooth and creamy. Add the granulated sugar and flour and pulse until incorporated, stopping to scrape down the sides of the bowl as necessary. With the motor running, add the eggs, one at a time, followed by the vanilla seeds, vanilla extract, and salt.

4. Pour the batter into the prepared crust and smooth the top with a rubber spatula. Bake until the cake is puffed, the center is set, and the edges are golden, 55 to 65 minutes. (The cake will still quiver slightly, but shouldn't feel runny at the center.) Remove from the oven and let cool completely on a wire rack.

5. While the cake bakes, make the raspberry sauce: Combine the raspberries, orange juice, granulated sugar, and lemon zest in a small saucepan set over medium heat. Bring to a simmer and cook, stirring occasionally, until it thickens and turns deep red, 10 to 12 minutes. Remove from the heat and let cool completely (the sauce will continue to thicken as it cools).

6. Shortly before serving, pour the sauce over the top of the cheesecake and smooth with a rubber spatula. Gently remove the cheesecake from the springform pan and transfer to a serving plate. Alternately, slice the cheesecake and serve with a drizzle of sauce.

A FEW THOUGHTS ABOUT MARGARINE

In the early twentieth century, food marketers introduced margarine and vegetable short-ening to the mainstream market. Jewish cooks were immediately smitten. Kosher-keeping Jews observe the prohibition against serving meat and dairy at the same meal, which limits them from using butter in baked goods when cooking chicken, beef, or another type of meat for dinner. (Fish, which is considered neither meat nor dairy according to Jewish law, is an exception.) For these cooks, dairy-free margarine opened up a world of buttery-tasting cookies, flaky piecrusts, and other exciting dessert possibilities.

When I was growing up in the 1980s and 1990s, margarine was widely touted as a healthier alternative to butter. But in recent years, research about the trans fats and hydrogenated oils found in most margarine brands has tarnished its reputation. The good news is, public favor has widely swung back toward butter, which deserves to be celebrated as the delicious, natural food that it is. But for kosher keepers, the conun-drum remains.

As the author of a Jewish cookbook, I feel the need to take a definitive stand on marga-rine. The problem is, like any good Jew, I have more than one opinion about it. On the one hand, I am a loyal member of the pro-butter camp. And when I do make dairy-free desserts, I try to focus on ones that just happen to be made with coconut oil, vegetable oil, fruit, or eggs instead of butter, milk, or cream. But in some cases, no other fat can do what butter can. And in those instances, I turn to margarine. When I do, I always use a brand that is nonhydrogenated and trans fat–free, like Earth Balance.

I draw a much firmer line for nondairy creamers—the corn syrup and artificial flavor cocktails that try to pass off as cream, and that have traditionally been staples of kosher-friendly cookbooks. I can't think of a single redeeming quality about them, taste or otherwise, and so avoid them completely. Instead, I save real whipped cream for desserts served after vegetarian meals, and use a natural alternative like almond or coconut milk when I need a nondairy milk for baking.

The bottom line is, whether you bake with butter or margarine, cow's milk or coconut, keep the old-school advice "everything in moderation" close to heart. For easy reference, here is a list of the desserts in *Modern Jewish Cooking* that are naturally dairy-free:

CHOCOLATE-ALMOND-HAZELNUT HORNS
(also gluten-free) (page 271)

CHOCOLATE-ALMOND MERINGUES
(also gluten-free) (page 274)

CHOCOLATE-DIPPED FIGS
(also gluten-free and vegan) (page 308)

HONEY-CINNAMON POUND CAKE
(page 286)

JEWELED RICE PUDDING
(also gluten-free and vegan) (page 303)

KABOCHA SQUASH–CHOCOLATE CHIP CAKE
(page 292)

MAPLE-CARDAMOM ROASTED PEARS
(also gluten-free and vegan) (page 307)

ORANGE-GLAZED CORNMEAL CAKE
(also gluten-free) (page 284)

PASSOVER PEAR CAKE
(page 287)

PLUM-ALMOND CAKE
(page 288)

SWEET HAMANTASCHEN
(page 259)

COCONUT MACAROONS
(also gluten-free) (page 279)

CHOCOLATE CHIP CHEESECAKE WITH CARAMEL WHIPPED CREAM

This recipe amps up a traditional graham-cracker-crust cheesecake by adding chocolate chips and dollops of rich, caramel-scented whipped cream. The whipped cream is technically optional, but shouldn't be. You may almost decide to ditch the cheesecake and spoon the whipped cream straight from the bowl. Almost.

SERVES 8 TO 10

FOR THE CRUST

1½ CUPS/150 G GRAHAM CRACKER CRUMBS

3 TBSP LIGHT BROWN SUGAR

6 TBSP/85 G UNSALTED BUTTER, MELTED

¼ TSP KOSHER SALT

FOR THE CHEESECAKE

1 LB/455 G CREAM CHEESE, AT ROOM TEMPERATURE

⅓ CUP/65 G GRANULATED SUGAR

¼ CUP/50 G PACKED LIGHT BROWN SUGAR

2 EGGS

1 TSP VANILLA EXTRACT

1 CUP/170 G MINI SEMISWEET CHOCOLATE CHIPS

FOR THE WHIPPED CREAM

¼ CUP/85 G JARRED DULCE DE LECHE (SEE PAGE 343 FOR AN ONLINE SOURCE)

1 CUP/240 ML HEAVY WHIPPING CREAM

1. Preheat the oven to 350°F/180°C.

2. Make the crust: Whisk together the graham cracker crumbs, brown sugar, butter, and salt in a large bowl until combined. Press the moistened crumb mixture onto the bottom and sides of a 9-in/23-cm pie plate. Place in the freezer to set.

3. Make the cheesecake: In a stand mixer or using a handheld electric mixer and a large bowl, beat the cream cheese, granulated sugar, and brown sugar together on medium speed until smooth, scraping down the sides as necessary. Add the eggs, one at a time, followed by the vanilla, beating until smooth. Fold in about half of the chocolate chips, then pour the batter into the crust. Sprinkle the top with the remaining chocolate chips.

4. Bake until mostly set with a slightly jiggly center, 35 to 40 minutes. Let cool on a wire rack, then cover and refrigerate at least 4 hours, or up to overnight. Place the bowl of a stand mixer or a large mixing bowl in the refrigerator to chill.

5. Shortly before serving, make the whipped cream: Combine the dulce de leche and ½ cup/120 ml of the whipping cream in the chilled bowl. Using a stand mixer or handheld electric mixer fitted with a whisk attachment, beat on medium speed until combined. Add the remaining ½ cup/120 ml whipping cream and continue beating at medium-high speed until soft peaks form.

6. Slice the cheesecake into wedges and divide onto plates. Serve chilled, topped with a dollop of whipped cream.

LEMON CHEESECAKE WITH ALMOND SHORTBREAD CRUST

One of my favorite things about cheesecake is how easily it goes from being simple to sublime. Just a few simple tweaks—a fluffy pile of lemon zest in the filling, say, a few drops of almond extract, or swapping in buttery shortbread crumbs for the more traditional graham crackers—and the familiar dessert becomes a thing of unexpected beauty.

SERVES 8 TO 10

NOTE

To make shortbread crumbs, pulse your favorite store-bought shortbread in a food processor until powdery crumbs form.

FOR THE CRUST

1¼ CUPS/140 G SHORTBREAD COOKIE CRUMBS

2 TBSP LIGHT BROWN SUGAR

3 TBSP UNSALTED BUTTER, MELTED

1 TSP ALMOND EXTRACT

¼ TSP KOSHER SALT

FOR THE CHEESECAKE

1 LB/455 G CREAM CHEESE, AT ROOM TEMPERATURE

¾ CUP/150 G GRANULATED SUGAR

2 EGGS

1 TSP VANILLA EXTRACT

2 TSP LEMON ZEST

2 TBSP FRESH LEMON JUICE

FRESH BERRIES FOR SERVING

1. Preheat the oven to 350°F/180°C.

2. Make the crust: Stir together the shortbread crumbs, brown sugar, butter, almond extract, and salt in a bowl until combined. Press the mixture into the bottom of a 9-in/23-cm pie plate. Bake until browned around the edges, 25 to 30 minutes. Remove from the oven and let cool slightly.

3. Make the cheesecake: In a stand mixer or using a handheld electric mixer and a large bowl, beat the cream cheese and granulated sugar together on medium speed until smooth, scraping down the sides as necessary. Add the eggs, one at a time, followed by the vanilla, lemon zest, and lemon juice, beating until smooth.

4. Pour the batter into the crust and smooth the top with a rubber spatula. Bake until mostly set with a slightly jiggly center, 35 to 40 minutes. Let cool on a wire rack, then cover and refrigerate at least 4 hours, or up to overnight.

5. Cut cheesecake into wedges and divide onto plates. Serve topped with berries.

JEWELED RICE PUDDING

Persian Jews serve jeweled rice, a sumptuous rice pilaf, at weddings and other festive occasions. The dish gets its name from the pistachios, barberries (a tart berry similar to a currant), and other jewel-like goodies nestled throughout the golden, saffron-flavored rice. As a serious rice pudding fiend, I knew I wanted to include a recipe for it in this cookbook, but I also wanted it to be special and unexpected. Then, in a stroke of late-night insight (isn't that when all good insight happens?) it came to me: Jeweled rice pudding! Flavored with rose water instead of saffron, this creamy, surprisingly light pudding comes crowned with an array of dazzling garnishes.

SERVES 6

¾ CUP/145 G BASMATI RICE

1½ CUPS/360 ML WATER

1 CINNAMON STICK

4 CUPS/960 ML MILK OR ALMOND MILK

1 TSP VANILLA EXTRACT

1 VANILLA BEAN, SPLIT LENGTHWISE
AND SEEDS SCRAPED

⅓ CUP/80 ML HEAVY CREAM OR
COCONUT MILK

½ CUP/100 G SUGAR

2 TSP ROSE WATER (SEE PAGE 343 FOR
AN ONLINE SOURCE)

OPTIONAL MIX-AND-MATCH GARNISHES:
TOASTED CHOPPED PISTACHIOS,
TOASTED SLIVERED ALMONDS,
GOLDEN RAISINS, DRIED CRAN-
BERRIES, FINELY CHOPPED DRIED
APRICOTS, POMEGRANATE SEEDS,
CANDIED ORANGE PEEL, GROUND
CINNAMON, GROUND CARDAMOM

1. Stir together the rice, water, and cinnamon stick in a large saucepan set over medium-high heat. Bring to a boil, then stir, turn the heat to low, cover, and cook until the rice is tender and the water is absorbed, 13 to 15 minutes. Stir in the milk, vanilla extract, and vanilla seeds. Raise the heat to medium and bring to a simmer, then turn the heat to low and cook, uncovered, stirring often, until it thickens into a soupy porridge, about 15 minutes. (The mixture should still be rather loose and liquidy. It will continue to thicken as it cools.)

2. Meanwhile, whisk together the heavy cream, sugar, and rose water in a medium bowl. Pour the mixture into the pudding and stir until the sugar dissolves, 1 to 2 minutes. Remove from the heat and let cool to room temperature, stirring occasionally. Cover and refrigerate until chilled, 3 to 4 hours. Discard the cinnamon stick. Serve chilled, topped with any desired garnishes.

CARAMEL-CHOCOLATE MATZO CLUSTERS WITH PISTACHIO

Marcy Goldman, author of the wonderful cookbook *A Treasury of Jewish Holiday Baking*, gave the world a huge gift when she created her matzo caramel butter crunch, a mix of rich caramel and melted chocolate layered on top of sheets of matzo. Over the last decade, her recipe has spread like crazy across the Internet. It's called different things—matzo brittle, matzo toffee, and (my favorite) matzo crack—because it's so addictive. Whatever the name, it's become a true Passover icon. Riffing on Goldman's classic, I combined it with matzo clusters, another beloved Passover sweet, to make an intensely chocolaty no-bake confection that will make the holiday taste much sweeter.

MAKES ABOUT 24 CLUSTERS

½ CUP/70 G SHELLED PISTACHIOS, RAW OR SALTED, ROUGHLY CHOPPED

3 SHEETS MATZO, CRUMBLED INTO ¼-IN/6-MM PIECES

¾ CUP/170 G UNSALTED BUTTER OR NONHYDROGENATED MARGARINE, CUT INTO CHUNKS

¾ CUP/150 G PACKED LIGHT BROWN SUGAR

¼ TSP KOSHER SALT

1 TSP VANILLA EXTRACT

¾ CUP/135 G SEMISWEET CHOCOLATE CHIPS

1. Line a large rimmed baking sheet with parchment paper. Place the pistachios in a small pan set over medium heat. Cook, stirring occasionally, until fragrant and golden brown, 5 to 7 minutes. Transfer to a small bowl to cool completely. Put the pistachios and matzo in a large bowl and stir to combine.

2. Combine the butter and brown sugar in a small saucepan set over medium heat. Bring the mixture to a boil, then cook, stirring constantly, until bubbling and thickened, 1 to 2 minutes. Remove from the heat, stir in the salt and vanilla, then immediately pour over the pistachios and matzo and stir to coat.

3. Melt the chocolate chips in a double boiler set over simmering water. (Or melt in the microwave in a microwave-safe bowl at 30-second intervals, stirring between each interval until fully melted.) Pour the chocolate over the matzo mixture and stir to evenly coat. Drop level tablespoons of the mixture onto the prepared baking sheet (no need to make them bigger—these suckers are rich!) and refrigerate until set, about 30 minutes. Store, between layers of waxed paper or aluminum foil, in an airtight container in the refrigerator. Serve chilled or at room temperature.

VARIATION

Substitute chopped hazelnuts, almonds, walnuts, or pecans for the pistachios. Sprinkle the clusters with finely chopped nuts, or dust them with flaky sea salt, cinnamon, or cayenne pepper before putting them in the refrigerator to firm up.

TAHINI, ROASTED FIG, AND PISTACHIO SUNDAES

Fresh figs roasted with cinnamon, honey, and orange zest make a sultry, late-summer topping for ice cream. I like to round out this Middle Eastern–inspired sundae by pairing scoops of vanilla ice cream with the warm figs, a spoonful of fragrant syrup from the roasting pan, a sprinkle of toasted pistachios, and a decadent drizzle of tahini.

SERVES 6

¼ CUP/95 G HONEY

½ TSP ORANGE ZEST

2 TBSP FRESH ORANGE JUICE

½ TSP GROUND CINNAMON

9 MEDIUM FRESH FIGS, STEMS TRIMMED AND HALVED LENGTHWISE

VANILLA ICE CREAM (DAIRY OR COCONUT MILK–BASED) FOR SERVING

⅓ CUP/40 G ROASTED SALTED PISTACHIOS, ROUGHLY CHOPPED

TAHINI FOR DRIZZLING

1. Preheat the oven to 375°F/190°C and line a 9-by-13-in/23-by-33-cm baking dish with aluminum foil.

2. Whisk together the honey, orange zest, orange juice, and cinnamon in a medium bowl. Arrange the figs, cut-side up, in the prepared baking dish and drizzle evenly with the honey mixture. Roast until the figs are tender and juicy, but not falling apart, 15 to 20 minutes. Remove from the oven and let cool slightly.

3. Scoop the desired amount of ice cream into six bowls. Divide the figs among the bowls, sprinkle with the pistachios, and drizzle with juices from the baking pan and the tahini. Serve immediately.

MAPLE-CARDAMOM ROASTED PEARS

For my bubbe's generation, nothing quite captured the flavors of fall like an apple filled with nuts and raisins and baked until wrinkled and spoon-soft. I adore baked apples, but on Sukkot (see page 338) a few years ago, my friends Anna and Naf upped the ante, serving a dish of roasted pears that completely blew my mind. What set the pears apart was the intoxicatingly fragrant mixture of maple syrup, honey, and cinnamon they were cooked in. Here is my ode to roasted pears, spiked with cardamom and lemon juice to offset the sweetness. Serve them alongside Honey-Cinnamon Pound Cake (page 286) and vanilla ice cream, then pair any leftovers with yogurt for breakfast. Any type of pear will work for this dessert. You can even use slightly unripe pears, but the cooking time might be a little longer. Leave the peels on for a gorgeous, rustic look.

SERVES 6

NOTE

I use a small sharp knife to remove the pears' stems and a melon baller or metal teaspoon to hollow out the cores.

6 MEDIUM PEARS, HALVED LENGTH-
WISE, STEMMED, AND CORED

⅓ CUP/115 G HONEY

⅓ CUP/80 ML PURE MAPLE SYRUP

1 TBSP FRESH LEMON JUICE

1 TBSP WATER

1 TSP GROUND CINNAMON

½ TSP GROUND CARDAMOM

¼ TSP KOSHER SALT

1. Preheat the oven to 375°F/190°C.

2. Arrange the pears, cut-side up, in a 9-by-13-in/23-by-33-cm baking dish. Whisk together the honey, maple syrup, lemon juice, water, cinnamon, cardamom, and salt in a small bowl and pour over the pears.

3. Roast, uncovered and occasionally basting the pears with the pan juices, until slightly softened, about 30 minutes. Flip the pears with tongs and continue roasting until completely tender when pierced with a knife, 25 to 35 minutes more. Serve the pears warm or at room temperature drizzled with the cooking syrup.

CHOCOLATE-DIPPED FIGS

Lots of fruits get dipped in chocolate—strawberries, cherries, apricots—but none of them competes with a chocolate-dipped fig. There is just something magical that happens when you combine the dried fruit's jammy sweetness and light crunch of seeds with a layer of bittersweet chocolate. It is also ridiculously simple to make, while making a big impact. As in, bring them to a party and you will immediately become the life of it. The sprinkle of sea salt brings everything together, so don't skip it! Dried Calimyrna figs are caramel colored and have a deep, sweet flavor. If you cannot find them, substitute smaller, darker dried Black Mission figs, or your favorite variety.

SERVES 4

2 OZ/55 G BITTERSWEET BAKING
CHOCOLATE, ROUGHLY CHOPPED

12 DRIED CALIMYRNA FIGS

FLAKY SEA SALT FOR DUSTING

1. Line a large rimmed baking sheet with parchment paper. Melt the chocolate in a double boiler set over simmering water. (Or melt in the microwave in a microwave-safe bowl at 30-second intervals, stirring between each interval until fully melted.)

2. Use your fingers to reshape any figs that got flattened in their package. Dip the rounded bottom half of each fig in the melted chocolate and lay them on their sides on the prepared baking sheet. Sprinkle each fig bottom with a little sea salt. Refrigerate the figs until the chocolate sets, about 15 minutes. Serve chilled or at room temperature.

CHOCOLATE- STRAWBERRY EGG CREAM

The egg cream is one of the most curious drinks in Jewish food history. For one, it contains neither eggs nor cream. And despite its humble ingredient list (milk, Fox's U-Bet chocolate syrup, and seltzer water), the soda fountain drink, likely invented in the 1890s in New York City by a Jewish candy store owner named Louis Auster, endures.

Over the years, egg creams have been swilled by countless stars of the Yiddish theater, including Jack Kerouac (he supposedly preferred the ones made at Gem Spa, a newspaper stand that still mixes up the drink in the East Village) and rocker Lou Reed, who wrote a song about them. "When I was a young man, no bigger than this / a chocolate egg cream was not to be missed. / Some U-Bet's chocolate syrup, seltzer water mixed with milk / you stir it up into a heady fro, tasted just like silk." My version of the egg cream stays true to the original recipe with one addition: fresh strawberries. The ruby fruit helps bring a drink beloved by many into sweet new territory.

MAKES 1 EGG CREAM

NOTE

If you don't have a cocktail muddler, mash the strawberries in a bowl with a potato masher, then add to the glass.

For the tastiest results, the seltzer and milk should both be straight-from-the-refrigerator cold.

3 RIPE STRAWBERRIES, STEMMED

2 TBSP CHOCOLATE SYRUP, PREFERABLY FOX'S U-BET

3 TBSP MILK, PREFERABLY WHOLE

½ CUP/120 ML SELTZER WATER

Put the strawberries in a pint glass and thoroughly muddle with a cocktail muddler. Add the chocolate syrup and milk and stir to combine. While continuing to stir, add the seltzer (use more if desired). Serve immediately.

VARIATION

Replace the strawberries with a handful of fresh raspberries.

CHAPTER TEN

FILLINGS AND EXTRAS

ROSEMARY– ROASTED GARLIC FOR CHALLAH

Great challah (see page 233) deserves a great topping, and rosemary-roasted garlic is one of my absolute favorites. The golden heads of garlic look beautifully rustic sitting next to the challah on my Shabbat table. And the herb-scented cloves melt into the bread as you spread it. This roasted garlic also makes a fantastic topping for pizza, a savory addition to vegetable soups, and a wonderful accompaniment to roasted meat or chicken.

MAKES ENOUGH FOR 2 LOAVES OF CHALLAH

4 HEADS GARLIC, UNPEELED, TOPS TRIMMED TO EXPOSE CLOVES

4 TSP EXTRA-VIRGIN OLIVE OIL

1 TBSP FRESH ROSEMARY LEAVES

1. Preheat the oven to 400°F/200°C.

2. Place each head of garlic on a square of aluminum foil. Drizzle each with 1 tsp olive oil and sprinkle the rosemary leaves evenly among the four heads. Wrap the garlic heads tightly in their foil and place in a small baking dish.

3. Roast until the cloves are very soft and lightly browned, 35 to 45 minutes. Remove from the oven and let cool to the touch. Serve whole heads of garlic alongside challah, and instruct your guests to squeeze out the soft cloves and spread them on their bread. Store, covered, in the refrigerator for up to 2 days. Let come to room temperature before using.

CINNAMON-HONEY TAHINI SPREAD

Several years ago, my friends Rachel and Dan introduced me to a little something they call crack butter. It's a mix of softened butter and honey that they spread on challah and, true to its name, it is seriously addictive. One Friday afternoon, I started to make it but realized I did not have any butter in the house. (Shocking, but somehow true.) Fortunately, I did have a jar of tahini and the substitution turned out to be equally crave-worthy. This rich, sweet, and spicy spread makes the perfect topping for Pumpkin-Apple Challah (page 238), and the leftovers are delightful slathered on your morning toast. There's no need for measuring; just mix, taste, and adjust until it tastes so good you want to eat the entire bowl in one sitting.

TAHINI

HONEY

GROUND CINNAMON

TOASTED SESAME SEEDS

CAYENNE PEPPER (OPTIONAL)

Stir together the desired amount of tahini with a generous squeeze of honey in a small bowl until well combined. Sprinkle with cinnamon, toasted sesame seeds, and a little cayenne, if desired, before using.

CREAM CHEESE MANY WAYS

Over the years, I have developed a few tricks for hosting a successful brunch or Yom Kippur break fast gathering: (1) Make one large main dish like a baked French toast, a killer noodle kugel (see page 139), or a couple of large frittatas (see page 41) that can serve a crowd. (2) Have plenty of bagels, coffee, and orange juice on hand (ask your friends to bring the bubbly to make mimosas). (3) Keep everything else simple. Breakfast, after all, is hardly a time for fussing. That's where these cream cheese riffs come in. They can be made ahead of time and deliver a lot of bagel-enhancing flavor with minimal work. Think of the following combinations as guidelines rather than hard-and-fast recipes. Be sure to start with room-temperature cream cheese so the mix-ins blend in easily, and tweak to your taste.

VEGGIE CREAM CHEESE

Mix together one room-temperature 8-oz/225-g package cream cheese with 2 Tbsp finely chopped carrots, 2 Tbsp finely chopped celery, 2 Tbsp finely chopped bell pepper (any color), and 2 thinly sliced scallions in a medium bowl. Season with salt and pepper and stir until combined. Cover and refrigerate until ready to use.

SHALLOT-CHIVE CREAM CHEESE

Finely chop 2 medium shallots. Heat 1 Tbsp extra-virgin olive oil in a pan set over medium heat. Add the shallots and 1 tsp sugar and cook, stirring occasionally, until softened and lightly browned. Remove from the heat and let cool, then mix together with one room-temperature 8-oz/225-g package cream cheese and 2 Tbsp finely chopped fresh chives in a medium bowl. Season with salt and pepper. Cover and refrigerate until ready to use.

ROASTED RED PEPPER CREAM CHEESE

Place 1 peeled and seeded roasted red bell pepper (thoroughly patted dry with paper towels) in a food processor along with one room-temperature 8-oz/225-g package cream cheese and 2 Tbsp grated Parmesan. Season with pepper and process until combined. Transfer to a medium bowl. Cover and refrigerate until ready to use. (Learn how to roast peppers on page 68.)

HERBED CREAM CHEESE

Mix together one room-temperature 8-oz/225-g package cream cheese with 1 Tbsp finely chopped fresh thyme, 1 Tbsp finely chopped fresh oregano, 2 Tbsp finely chopped fresh flat-leaf parsley, and 2 thinly sliced scallions in a medium bowl. Season with salt and pepper and stir until combined. Cover and refrigerate until ready to use.

SALMON-DILL CREAM CHEESE

Mix together one room-temperature 8-oz/225-g package cream cheese with 4 oz/115 g finely chopped smoked salmon and 3 Tbsp finely chopped fresh dill in a medium bowl. Season with salt and pepper and stir until combined. Cover and refrigerate until ready to use.

OLIVE-BASIL CREAM CHEESE

Place 6 roughly chopped fresh basil leaves in a food processor along with one room-temperature 8-oz/225-g package cream cheese and 1 small garlic clove. Season with pepper and process until combined. Transfer to a bowl and stir in the desired amount of thinly sliced pitted olives (any kind). Cover and refrigerate until ready to use.

HONEY-ORANGE CREAM CHEESE

Mix together one room-temperature 8-oz/225-g package cream cheese with 1 Tbsp honey (or more to taste) and ½ tsp orange zest in a medium bowl. Cover and refrigerate until ready to use.

MAPLE-CINNAMON CREAM CHEESE

Place one room-temperature 8-oz/225-g package cream cheese in a food processor along with 1 Tbsp pure maple syrup (or more to taste) and ½ tsp ground cinnamon, and process until combined. Transfer to a medium bowl. Cover and refrigerate until ready to use.

ASHKENAZI CHAROSET

Charoset—the fruit-and-nut mixture that symbolizes the brick mortar used by the Israelites enslaved in ancient Egypt—holds a dear place in my heart. As a kid, it was one of the few dishes I was tasked with as part of my family's Passover seder preparations, and I remember taking great care to chop the walnuts and apples just so. Decades later, when my husband, Yoshie, and I were first dating, he showed up unexpectedly at my apartment the night before the seder holding a bottle of sweet wine to use in my charoset. More than flowers or chocolates, I realized, this was the sign I needed in order to know he liked me. This charoset version is fairly traditional, using toasted nuts, crisp apples, and a little sweet wine to hold things together. If you're feeling more adventurous, add one or more of the following ingredients along with the cinnamon: ⅛ tsp ground nutmeg, ½ tsp ground ginger, or ½ tsp orange zest.

MAKES ABOUT 5 CUPS/900 G

1½ CUPS/170 G WALNUTS

3 MEDIUM CRISP, SWEET APPLES,
    SUCH AS GALA OR FUJI, PEELED,
    QUARTERED, CORED, AND FINELY
    CHOPPED

1½ TSP GROUND CINNAMON

1 TBSP FRESH LEMON JUICE

2 TBSP HONEY

¼ CUP/60 ML SWEET RED WINE
    OR GRAPE JUICE, OR MORE
    AS NEEDED

1. Place the walnuts in a small pan set over medium-low heat. Cook, stirring occasionally, until fragrant and lightly browned, 5 to 7 minutes. Transfer to a small bowl to cool completely, then finely chop.

2. Combine the apples, cinnamon, lemon juice, honey, and walnuts in a large bowl and stir to combine. Stir in the sweet wine. Taste and add a little more wine, about 1 tsp at a time, until the mixture glistens. Cover and refrigerate until ready to serve, or up to 1 day.

SEPHARDI CHAROSET

When it comes to charoset, the Sephardi world thrives on creativity. Ashkenazi charoset tends to be a fixed formula of apples, walnuts, and wine. But each Sephardi culture has its own take on the symbolic "mortar" eaten during Passover. Most use some array of dried fruits (like dates, figs, or raisins) and nuts, and many are perfumed with heady spices like cloves and cinnamon.

MAKES ABOUT 2½ CUPS/610G

1 CUP/240 ML DRY RED WINE

2 TBSP HONEY

1 CUP/160 G ROUGHLY CHOPPED DRIED PITTED DEGLET NOOR DATES

1 CUP/140 G ROUGHLY CHOPPED DRIED BLACK MISSION FIGS

½ CUP/85 G BLACK RAISINS

1½ TSP GROUND CINNAMON

½ TSP GROUND CLOVES

1 CUP/115 G ROASTED UNSALTED ALMONDS

2 TBSP FRESH OR BOTTLED ORANGE JUICE

1. Whisk together the wine and honey in a medium saucepan set over medium-high heat. Bring to a boil, then turn the heat to low and stir in the dates, figs, raisins, cinnamon, and cloves. Partially cover and cook, stirring occasionally, until the dried fruit softens and most of the liquid is absorbed, 6 to 7 minutes. Remove from the heat.

2. Place the almonds in the bowl of a food processor and pulse until crumbly with a few larger pieces. Transfer to a medium bowl.

3. Transfer the cooked fruit mixture and the orange juice to the food processor and pulse until the desired consistency is reached (less time will yield a chunkier charoset with visible fruit pieces; more time will turn the mixture into a thick paste). Add the puréed fruit to the nuts and stir until combined. Cover and refrigerate until ready to serve, or up to 2 days. Bring to room temperature before using.

VARIATION

Make Moroccan-style charoset balls by puréeing the fruit until thick and pasty. Stir in the nuts, let the mixture cool to the touch, then carefully roll heaping tablespoons of the mixture into 1-in/2.5-cm balls. If desired, roll the balls in finely shredded coconut or finely chopped almonds. Serve at room temperature.

SCHMALTZ AND GRIBENES

Schmaltz, the savory rendered chicken fat used as a cooking oil in countless Ashkenazi dishes, was born out of necessity. Mediterranean Jews had access to olive oil for cooking, but the Jews of Eastern and Central Europe had to be more creative. They took a cue from their non-Jewish neighbors, who fried foods in nonkosher lard (pig fat), and began rendering fat from kosher poultry, including geese and, later, chickens. It is a good thing they did because schmaltz adds incredible flavor to matzo balls (see pages 148 and 149), Savory Matzo Farfel (page 147), Chopped Chicken Liver (page 76), Potato-Leek Kugel (page 127), and Kasha Varnishkes (page 142). And gribenes, the little cracklings left behind in the pan, make an incomparable snack. Case in point: My mother, who is typically a major proponent of healthful eating, kept a jar of rendered schmaltz in the refrigerator every Passover. These days, I do, too.

MAKES ABOUT ½ CUP/110 G SCHMALTZ

1 LB/455 G CHICKEN FAT AND SKIN, RINSED, DRIED, AND CUT WITH KITCHEN SHEARS INTO ¼-IN/6-MM PIECES

KOSHER SALT

1 LARGE YELLOW ONION, HALVED AND VERY THINLY SLICED

1. Place the chicken fat and skin in a large nonstick pan set over medium-low heat and season with a little salt. Cook, uncovered and stirring often, until the fat melts and pools at the bottom of the pan and the skin darkens and begins to curl up at the edges, 20 to 30 minutes. Add the onion and cook for 5 minutes, just long enough for the flavor to release into the fat. Remove the pan from the heat and strain the fat through a fine-mesh sieve into a glass jar. Let cool completely, then cover and refrigerate or freeze for up to 6 months.

2. Line a plate with paper towels. Return the skin and onion to the pan, season with salt, and set over medium heat. Cook, stirring often, until the skin and onions are deeply browned and crispy, 15 to 25 minutes. (Watch carefully so they don't burn.) Transfer the gribenes to the paper towel–lined plate to drain. Serve warm.

CREAMY HORSERADISH HERB SAUCE

Serve this creamy, piquant sauce with Gefilte Fish in White Wine–Herb Broth (page 182), or dollop it over chicken schnitzel (see page 191) or grilled steak.

MAKES 1½ CUPS/280 G

- ¾ CUP/180 G MAYONNAISE
- ⅓ CUP/80 G PREPARED WHITE HORSERADISH
- ¼ CUP/10 G FINELY CHOPPED FRESH DILL
- ¼ CUP/10 G SNIPPED FRESH CHIVES
- 1 TSP FRESH LEMON JUICE
- ⅛ TSP FRESHLY GROUND BLACK PEPPER

Stir together the mayonnaise, horseradish, dill, chives, lemon juice, and pepper in a medium bowl. Cover and refrigerate until ready to serve, or up to 2 days.

PRESERVED LEMONS

I had the good fortune of traveling with Jewish cookbook maven Joan Nathan and a few other journalists on a culinary tour of Israel. I remember a lot of things about that trip, of course, but one of my most vibrant memories is hearing Joan gush about the tart, briny preserved lemon rind we kept encountering in dishes at restaurants. "I always keep a jar of preserved lemons at home," she said. "They go with everything." It's advice I have followed since. Preserved lemons (pictured on the left of the following page) take about a month to cure, but then last for up to a year in the refrigerator. And they do indeed add a special brightness to just about anything they touch. Try them on the Roasted Beet Salad with Preserved Lemon (page 67) or the Moroccan Chicken with Preserved Lemons (page 186).

MAKES ONE 1-QT/960-ML JAR

NOTE

To use the preserved lemon: Remove a lemon from the jar and rinse with water. Remove the pulp and seeds and discard, then slice the rind as needed. Make sure the lemons left in the jar stay submerged under the lemon juice.

KOSHER SALT

6 TO 8 LEMONS, SCRUBBED AND PATTED DRY, PLUS JUICE FROM 3 TO 5 ADDITIONAL LEMONS

OPTIONAL ADD-INS: CINNAMON STICK, BAY LEAF, RED PEPPER FLAKES, MUSTARD SEEDS, PEPPERCORNS

1. Sprinkle a thin layer of salt in the bottom of a clean, dry 1-qt/960-ml glass jar with a tight-fitting lid.

2. Prepare each lemon by slicing the tips off of each end and quartering lengthwise, but not cutting all the way through to the opposite side. Gently open the lemon and fill the crevices with salt, then place in the jar. Push the lemons down as you go, packing them in as tightly as possible, and adding a small amount of one or more of the add-ins (if using). Once all the lemons are in the jar, pour over the additional lemon juice. Press down until the lemons are completely submerged in juice. Cover and let stand at room temperature for 3 days, turning the jar upside down occasionally.

3. Transfer the jar to the refrigerator and let cure for 3 to 4 weeks before using. Store in the refrigerator for up to 1 year.

SPICY DILL PICKLES

There was a time in American Jewish history, roughly from the late 1800s through the mid-1900s, when pickles were the highlight of Jewish cuisine. Pushcart peddlers sold half and full sours by the barrel, and just about everything from beets to cabbage to apples got preserved in brine. These salt-and-vinegar-cured cucumber pickles (pictured on the right of page 321) have all the sour, crunchy, dill-flecked appeal of the ones you would find at a delicatessen, plus a complex hit of spice, thanks to the cinnamon sticks and hot red pepper flakes resting in the jar.

MAKES TWO 1-QT/960-ML JARS

NOTE

Make sure your cucumbers are all about the same size, so they cure at the same rate. I like cucumbers that err on the short, thin side.

If you are not a fan of heat, decrease the amount of red pepper flakes or omit them entirely.

4 CUPS/960 ML WATER

½ CUP/120 ML WHITE VINEGAR

¼ CUP/40 G KOSHER SALT

2 TSP RED PEPPER FLAKES

1 TSP CORIANDER SEEDS

1 TSP BLACK PEPPERCORNS

1 TSP MUSTARD SEEDS

8 TO 12 SMALL OR MEDIUM KIRBY CUCUMBERS, SCRUBBED

2 CINNAMON STICKS

6 GARLIC CLOVES, THINLY SLICED

2 BAY LEAVES

1 SMALL BUNCH FRESH DILL, WASHED, PATTED DRY, AND TOUGH STEMS TRIMMED OFF

1. Bring a medium pot of water to a boil. Dip in two 1-qt/960-ml jars and their lids so they are fully submerged, then remove with tongs. Let dry on the counter.

2. Combine the 4 cups/960 ml water, vinegar, and salt in a pot set over medium-high heat. Bring to a boil and stir until the salt dissolves, about 1 minute. Remove from the heat.

3. In a small bowl, stir together the red pepper flakes, coriander seeds, peppercorns, and mustard seeds. Pack the cucumbers vertically and snugly into the jars, dividing the spices, cinnamon sticks, garlic, bay leaves, and as much dill as you can comfortably cram in as you go.

4. Fill the prepared jars with the brine until the cucumbers are fully submerged. Let the brine cool completely, then cover the jars with their lids and refrigerate for at least 2 days before eating. Remove the cinnamon sticks after 1 week. Store in the refrigerator for up to 2 months. The spiciness and flavor will continue to develop over time.

BAHARAT

Baharat (pictured at the bottom of page 321) is a Middle Eastern spice mix that tastes complex, but is made from basic pantry spices and comes together surprisingly quickly. I like to make more of it than I need for one recipe, like Spicy Chorizo and Red Pepper Penne (page 199), then sprinkle the extra on grilled fish or vegetables, stir it into chili or lentil dishes, or mix it into hamburgers. For the most potent mixture, start with very fresh spices.

MAKES ABOUT ½ CUP/50 G

2 TBSP GROUND CUMIN

2 TBSP SWEET PAPRIKA

1 TBSP FRESHLY GROUND BLACK
PEPPER

1 TBSP GROUND CORIANDER

1 TBSP GROUND CINNAMON

1 TSP ALLSPICE

1 TSP GROUND CARDAMOM

1 TSP SMOKED PAPRIKA

½ TSP GROUND NUTMEG

¼ TSP CAYENNE PEPPER

Combine the cumin, sweet paprika, pepper, coriander, cinnamon, allspice, cardamom, smoked paprika, nutmeg, and cayenne in a container with a tight-fitting lid, and shake or stir to combine. Store in an airtight container in a cool, dark place for up to 3 months.

CHAPTER ELEVEN

THE HOLIDAYS

The holidays lie at the heart of all Jewish cuisine. All cultures share a desire to gather together with friends, family, and food, but the Jewish calendar is particularly filled with festive meals. For starters, there is Shabbat, the weekly day of rest that begins with what is essentially a Friday night dinner party. Then there is the annual cycle of festivals that dot the year, bringing with them a rich and beautiful variety of symbolic foods.

From Passover's matzo balls to the cheesecake traditionally eaten on Shavuot, these dishes add significance and sweetness to the holidays themselves. And since many of these foods are seasonal (fried potato latkes during Hanukkah in winter, apple cake in fall for Rosh Hashanah), they also help root the holidays in a specific time and place. But most important, the holidays have played an incomparable role in shaping, enriching, and diversifying Jewish cuisine.

Regardless of whether you observe these days traditionally, or simply love the foods associated with them, their contribution to Jewish eating is worth celebrating.

SHABBAT

EVERY WEEK: FRIDAY AT SUNSET THROUGH SATURDAY AT SUNDOWN

On most Friday evenings when I was growing up, my mom lit Shabbat candles in our kitchen. She would set out two candlesticks, fit them with taper candles, and drape a cloth over the top of her head. The cloth was white with smears of pastel paint running across it—a Hebrew school art project my brother or I made as toddlers. She uses the same one today.

Once ready, she would call out to us to join her. Sometimes we balked, reluctant to leave whatever TV program had us enthralled. But other times the stars lined up and we would head into the kitchen to watch her light the candles, cover her eyes, and recite the blessings traditionally said to usher in Shabbat. My dad, who is not Jewish but had picked up enough Hebrew to chant along, would occasionally join in, ending with a dramatic baritone "a-a-men." Since we were not traditionally observant, life more or less picked up as usual shortly after the candles were lit. But while I did not appreciate it at the time, those brief moments, when they happened, were so peaceful. A tiny bit of stillness amidst the din.

When I moved to New York City after college and started attending Shabbat dinners, and later when I met Yoshie, who grew up in an observant Jewish household, I learned more about the ancient day of rest that arrives every Friday at sunset and continues through the following day until nightfall. Shabbat commemorates the seventh day of biblical creation, when the Torah says God stopped to rest and appreciate the world. I learned that traditional Jews honor this rest by abstaining from driving, spending money, checking their email, and engaging in the thirty-nine types of broadly defined "creative work" identified in the Torah. So instead of plugging in, they slow down. They go to synagogue, take walks outside, sing together, reflect, learn, spend time with family, and eat meals filled with foods designed to nourish, comfort, and delight.

Historically, Jewish cooks around the world pulled out all the stops for Shabbat meals. The foods they ate throughout the week would typically be humble and simple, but even in times of poverty, people made a special effort to mark the occasion through food. Ashkenazi Jews baked savory kugels, simmered pots of chicken soup, slow-cooked brisket, and splurged on harder-to-find white flour to bake loaves of challah. Sephardi and Mizrahi cooks, who generally lived in warmer climates than their Eastern European cousins and had more access to fresh produce, would lay out sumptuous spreads of salads and dips, followed by fish, chicken, or meat cooked in tangy sauces, and spiced rice dishes.

Because actively cooking over a fire or with electricity is one of the types of creative work prohibited during Shabbat, most food prep is traditionally completed before sundown on Friday. Many of the foods eaten on Shabbat, like the Sephardi-filled pastries called bourekas, can be made in advance and served at room temperature. The no-cooking restriction also gave rise to creative solutions, like the long-simmered stew cholent and its Sephardi equivalent, hamin. Cooked in a prelit oven (in Eastern Europe, Jewish women used to bring their cholent pots to the local baker, where they sat in the hearth all night) or today in a slow cooker, these hearty meat, bean, and grain stews are traditionally served for Saturday lunch after synagogue.

To me, the pinnacle of Shabbat is Friday night dinner, which offers a weekly excuse to throw a dinner party. I love the flurry of cooking that typically begins Thursday night and continues amidst attempts to get other deadlines taken care of right up until Shabbat begins. I like to incorporate as many seasonal flavors and ingredients into the meal as possible, weaving them into traditional dishes and improvising around them to make each Shabbat dinner different and special.

As the sun dips, the frenetic rush suddenly gives way to a deep calm. I light candles, while Yoshie provides the harmony and the "a-a-men." Shortly after, friends arrive toting bottles of wine and stories from the week. By the time we make it to the table and say blessings over the wine and challah, I am exhausted, but in a wonderful way. Because at that point, there is nothing left to do but rest, eat, and enjoy. Washing the dishes can wait.

WINTER SHABBAT DINNER MENU

Pumpkin-Apple Challah (page 238) with Cinnamon-Honey Tahini Spread (page 313)

20 Cloves of Garlic Borscht (page 80; kosher keepers: skip the sour cream)

Carrot Salad with Mint and Dates (page 58)

Roast Chicken with Fennel and Orange (page 188)

Potato-Leek Kugel (page 127)

Kabocha Squash–Chocolate Chip Cake (page 292)

SPRING SHABBAT DINNER MENU

Classic Challah (page 233) with Supremely Creamy Hummus (page 73)

Creamy Sorrel Soup with Harissa (page 86)

Spring Pea Salad with Browned Butter Vinaigrette (page 54)

Baked Sole with Bitter Greens (page 175)

Pine Nut and Scallion Couscous (page 157)

Puréed Carrots with Orange and Ginger (page 105)

Rhubarb-Oatmeal Crumble Bars (page 280)

SUMMER SHABBAT DINNER MENU

Classic Challah (page 233) with Garlic-Marinated Zucchini (page 100)

Sourdough Gazpacho (page 81)

Fattoush (page 72)

Moroccan Chicken with Preserved Lemons (page 186)

Farro Salad with Corn and Jalapeño (page 164)

Peach and Raspberry Tart (page 248)

FALL SHABBAT DINNER MENU

Challah with Sautéed Leeks and Thyme (page 236)

Classic Chicken Soup (page 93)

Grilled Pear, Fennel, and Toasted Walnut Salad (page 62)

Rosemary-Maple Roast Chicken (page 190)

Butternut Squash Kugel with Crispy Shallots (page 128; kosher keepers: use coconut oil)

Roasted Cauliflower and Red Onion (page 115)

Plum-Almond Cake (page 288)

VEGETARIAN SHABBAT DINNER MENU

Classic Challah (page 233) with Vegetarian Chopped "Liver" (page 77)

Wild Mushroom and Barley Soup (page 90)

Roasted Beet Salad with Preserved Lemon (page 67)

Cinnamon-Roasted Seitan and Onions (page 223)

Toasted Almond Israeli Couscous (page 161)

Chocolate-Banana Bundt Cake (page 294)

PURIM

BEGINS THE 14TH OF ADAR/FEBRUARY OR MARCH

Purim, which arrives in the late winter, is a holiday of revelry. I like to think of it as the Jewish calendar's biggest annual party—a night where dressing up in costumes and drinking in excess are not only tolerated, but encouraged.

Purim celebrates the heroism of Queen Esther, a Jewish woman who rose to become the Queen of Persia and saved her people from destruction at the hands of her husband's ill-intentioned adviser, Haman. Each year, people gather in synagogues to read Esther's story aloud from a *megillah* (scroll), stamping their feet and shaking noisemakers called *graggers* every time Haman's name is mentioned. As far as religious services go, it's pretty raucous. Afterward, people head to parties to celebrate the ancient victory by wearing costumes and getting tipsy.

The most widely known food eaten on Purim are the three-cornered cookies called *hamantaschen* (the name translates to "Haman's pockets" in Yiddish). The golden pastries, which traditionally come stuffed with either ground poppy seeds or jam, are a sweet reminder of Esther's success. In recent years, I have taken to baking a batch of untraditional-but-tasty savory hamantaschen to go along with the sweet ones.

In one of my favorite Purim traditions, called *mishloach manot*, people prepare small gifts of food (usually some hamantaschen and another edible goodie or two) and deliver them to friends, family, and neighbors. The idea is that Purim is supposed to be joyous, and giving people these gift bags ensures everyone will have enough food to enjoy. Delivering mishloach manot (which literally means "sending of portions" in Hebrew) is also a great opportunity to drop by for an impromptu visit with friends.

On Purim day, once everyone has recovered from the previous night, people traditionally hold a festive Purim lunch. Pretty much anything goes for these meals, though it is traditional to serve the filled dough pockets called *kreplach*. Whatever you serve, make sure to have plenty of hamantaschen around. With a cookie in one hand and a cocktail in the other, the holiday is destined to be sweet.

SWEET HAMANTASCHEN

Sweet Hamantaschen (page 259) with Chocolate–Poppy Seed Filling (page 263)

Sweet Hamantaschen (page 259) with Golden Apricot Filling (page 262)

Sweet Hamantaschen (page 259) with Lekvar (page 261)

SAVORY HAMANTASCHEN

Savory Hamantaschen (page 264) with Sweet Potato–Parmesan Filling (page 266)

Savory Hamantaschen (page 264) with Tomato-Beef Filling (page 267)

PASSOVER

Two years after I moved to Brooklyn, I hosted a Passover seder with my friend Anna. We were recent college graduates with laughably small nonprofit salaries and few resources to pull off one of the Jewish calendar's biggest entertaining holidays. But we were excited anyway.

We invited a scattered mix of friends and friends of friends who needed a place for the seder. Early in the week, we stocked up on boxes of matzo and hit up the farmers' market for ingredients to make vegetarian matzo ball soup, matzo lasagna, and charoset. And for the first time, I attempted my mom's ethereally wonderful chocolate meringues. We laid a bunch of pillows in a circle on the floor and constructed a makeshift seder table out of milk crates draped with colorful tapestries and dotted with tea lights. Anna cobbled together a beautiful homemade Haggadah (the booklet used during the seder) that punctuated the traditional texts with readings by farmers, poets, and activists.

Our guests arrived toting flowers and bottles of wine, and settled in to an evening of telling the Passover story, refilling each other's glasses, and singing until the candles burned low and our voices turned scratchy and hoarse. It was far from my home in suburban Chicago, where I had celebrated nearly every other Passover in my life. But while I missed my family's traditions, I cannot remember another Passover that felt more vibrant or free.

Passover commemorates the Israelites' Exodus from ancient Egypt, and their transition from a life of slavery to one of freedom. It is both a particular and a universal holiday in that the story itself speaks specifically of the Jewish experience, but the larger metaphors of oppression and liberation running throughout the holiday can resonate with almost anyone. As Anna so gorgeously wrote in her Haggadah (I still have a few copies tucked away on my bookshelf): "Mitzrayim [the name for ancient Egypt] means 'narrow places.' Even in our modern context," she asked, "who among us cannot relate to the double pull of freedom versus obligations, or to all the kinds of [metaphorical] slavery we experience—habits, people, food, work, deadlines?" No matter who we are or what our experience, there is always some way that we as individuals, families, and communities seek a greater sense of freedom.

Throughout the weeklong holiday, Jews traditionally abstain from eating *chametz*, which are leavened foods made from wheat, rye, barley, oats, and spelt. Ironically matzo, the unleavened bread eaten on Passover, must be made from one of these five grains. It is done so in a closely supervised environment that ensures it doesn't have time to leaven during the baking process.

Ashkenazi Jews also refrain from eating a category of foods called *kitniyot*—foods like corn, millet, rice, legumes, lentils, and other ingredients that can be used to make bread. These are commonly processed in the same facilities as chametz, or too closely resemble the prohibited grains. Sephardi and Mizrahi Jews do not typically share this additional restriction against kitniyot, and commonly consume rice and legumes throughout Passover.

At the heart of any Passover celebration is the seder. The word *seder* comes from the same Hebrew root as the word "order," and the seder fittingly lays out an ordered script for retelling the Exodus story and asking the question, "Why is this night different from all other nights?" There are fifteen distinct aspects to the seder that get clumped together into four larger sections. Within this structure, there is plenty of room for creativity, interpretation, commentary, and singing. My husband Yoshie's family's seder, for example, regularly features puppetry, skits, and impromptu songwriting.

In the center of the seder table is a seder plate filled with symbolic foods meant to viscerally connect us to the story. They include:

- **Maror—A bitter herb or green, often horseradish or lettuce, that represents the bitter treatment the Israelites faced as slaves.**

- **Charoset—A mixture of fruit, nuts, spices, and sweet wine that symbolizes the mortar used by the Israelites who were forced to build stone storehouses and other structures for the ancient Egyptians.**

- **Karpas—A green vegetable, often parsley, that represents springtime. Passover falls in the spring and is sometimes called *Chag Ha'Aviv*, literally "spring holiday." Before being eaten, the karpas gets dipped into a bowl of salt water, which represents the Israelite's tears and sorrow.**

- **Zeroah—A roasted lamb shank bone, which represents the Korban Pesach, the sacrifice offered by Israelites at the Temple in Jerusalem in ancient times.**

- **Beitzah—A roasted hard-boiled egg, which represents spring and fertility.**

The table also, of course, includes lots and lots of matzo. One highlight from my family's seder growing up was the afikoman, a broken piece of matzo that is eaten as part of dessert. Like mine, many families have a fun tradition of hiding the afikoman from the kids and rewarding the child who finds it with a prize, or having the children "steal" the afikoman from the seder leader, hiding it, and making him or her search for it.

Each of the four seder sections is marked by the pouring, blessing, and drinking of a glass of wine. That ends up being a *lot* of wine. Fortunately, in between the first two cups and the second two, a meal is served. As a holiday that tends to bring families together more than any other, home cooks typically pull out all the stops for the Passover seder by making an array of comfortingly familiar favorites. Here are some suggested seder menus that riff off of traditional fare with a few surprising twists. I also included a menu for vegetarians inspired by the meal Anna and I made for our own seder. And since Passover is a weeklong holiday, I added a weeknight meal menu and breakfast options to keep you going strong after the seder ends.

ASHKENAZI PASSOVER SEDER MENU

Classic Chicken Soup (page 93) with Parsley Matzo Balls (page 148)

Ashkenazi Charoset (page 316)

Gefilte Fish in White Wine–Herb Broth (page 182)

Red Wine and Honey Brisket (page 197)

Savory Matzo Farfel (page 147)

Roasted Cauliflower and Red Onion (page 115)

Passover Pear Cake (page 287)

Coconut Macaroons (page 279)

SEPHARDI PASSOVER SEDER MENU

Tomato-Chickpea Soup with Spinach (page 82; kosher keepers: skip the labneh or yogurt)

Sephardi Charoset (page 317)

Carrot Salad with Mint and Dates (page 58)

Moroccan Chicken with Preserved Lemons (page 186)

Dilled Rice with Lima Beans (page 152)

Jeweled Rice Pudding (page 303; kosher keepers: use almond and coconut milk)

VEGETARIAN PASSOVER SEDER MENU

Rustic Vegetable Soup (page 88; replace Dill Dumplings with Jalapeño-Shallot Matzo Balls, page 149)

Ashkenazi Charoset (page 316) or Sephardi Charoset (page 317)

Heirloom Tabbouleh (page 71; replace bulgur with quinoa)

Spinach-Matzo Lasagna (page 221)

Roasted Broccoli with Shallots and Lemon (page 114)

Caramel-Chocolate Matzo Clusters with Pistachio (page 304)

Chocolate-Almond Meringues (page 274)

PASSOVER WEEKNIGHT MEAL

Grilled Portobellos with Herbs and Mozzarella (page 215; use matzo meal)

Grilled Salmon with Orange and Herbs (page 176)

Chocolate-Dipped Figs (page 308)

PASSOVER BREAKFAST IDEAS

Matzo Granola with Walnuts and Coconut (page 24)

Three-in-One Matzo Brei (page 42)

Apple-Cranberry Chremslach (page 51)

Smoked Salmon Hash with Lemon-Mint Vinaigrette (page 44)

Mozzarella, Tomato, and Basil Frittata (page 41)

Shallot, Leek, and Ginger Omelet (page 40)

SHAVUOT

BEGINS THE 6TH OF SIVAN/MAY OR JUNE

Shavuot, which falls seven weeks after Passover, commemorates the story of God revealing the Torah to the Israelites at Mount Sinai. It marks a monumental turning point in the history of the Jewish people and is, naturally, a major holiday. And like many Jewish holidays, it has an agricultural significance overlaid on the historical one. As one of the Jewish calendar's three pilgrimage festivals (Passover and Sukkot are the other two), it also marks the end of the barley harvest in Israel and the beginning of the wheat harvest. Another name for Shavuot—Hag Habikkurim, or festival of first fruits—speaks to this harvest theme.

Traditionally, people stay up all night on Shavuot studying texts together, which is one way to honor and enjoy the richness of Jewish writing and learning. They also eat a lot of foods made with dairy. In the Ashkenazi world, that means cheese blintzes, cheesecake, and cheesy noodles. Syrian Jews celebrate with sweet cheese-filled pastries called *atayef*. My favorite theory is that one of the psalms refers to Mount Sinai as Har Gav'nunim. The name means something like "mountain of majestic peaks," but sounds similar to the Hebrew word for cheese, *gevinah*. Personally, I am totally on board with the notion of a mountain of majestic cheese.

Several years ago, my friend Avi threw a blintz-making party for Shavuot. He blended up a bunch of batter to make the crepe-like blintz leaves and asked his guests to bring fruit jams, ricotta, Nutella, ginger preserves, pesto, mashed potatoes, and other sundry goodies to fill them. We took turns in front of the stove, swirling batter in the pans, rolling them, and frying the blintzes. Most of us, myself included, had never made a blintz before. But by the end of the evening we were making jokes about opening up a catering business together. Here are two menus to help fortify you for a long night of studying or blintz frying.

SHAVUOT MENU

Classic Challah (page 233) with Vegetarian Chopped "Liver" (page 77)

Romaine Wedge Salad with Buttermilk Dressing (page 60)

Creamy Noodles with Lemon, Mint, and Chives (page 138)

Spiced Lentil Patties (page 210)

Sweet Potato–Scallion Frittata (page 207)

Ricotta–Vanilla Bean Cheesecake with Raspberry Sauce (page 295)

SHAVUOT BLINTZ-PARTY MENU

Orange-Scented Cheese Blintzes (page 49)

Roasted Garlic–Potato Blintzes (page 46)

Roasted Eggplant and Tahini Crostini (page 111)

Red Cabbage and Beet Slaw with Caramelized Walnuts (page 69)

Chocolate Chip Cheesecake with Caramel Whipped Cream (page 300)

Chocolate-Walnut Rugelach (see page 276)

ROSH HASHANAH

BEGINS THE 1ST OF TISHREI/SEPTEMBER OR OCTOBER

Sometime in the late summer, usually when I am planning a trip to the beach or taking a bike ride, the first hint of autumn creeps in. It might come in the form of a cooler-than-usual night, or the spicy scent of leaves blowing through the air. But every year it surprises me, leaving me feeling slightly breathless, wistful, and, out of nowhere, nostalgic. The moment passes quickly and summer resumes in its lighthearted frivolity. But I know in that moment that autumn is on the horizon, and so is Rosh Hashanah.

Rosh Hashanah, which is also known as the Jewish New Year and is considered the spiritual head of the year, launches the Jewish calendar's season of contemplation and introspection. Fittingly, it can feel a little heavy as I pull on my first sweater of the season and look back at the year as it stands. All the missed moments and connections, the opportunities not fully seized, the hurt or harm I brought upon others. And yet Rosh Hashanah is a joyous time, too, filled with family meals and my unblemished hopes for the year to come.

The holiday's many food symbols tend to focus on the positive. It is customary to wish people a sweet New Year on Rosh Hashanah. At the table, that custom translates into a delicious practice: dipping apples into golden honey. It is also customary to eat other foods enriched with honey, including honey cake and the root vegetable and dried fruit stew tzimmes. The challah eaten on Rosh Hashanah, which is typically spiraled into a coil to represent the roundness of the year, also gets drizzled with honey for a maximum dose of sweetness.

Beyond apples and honey, other fruits hold significance. Take pomegranates, with their gorgeous, overlapping layers of ruby-colored seeds. The biblical fruit's many seeds are said to represent the 613 commandments the Jewish people received from God, and therefore tend to show up on Rosh Hashanah tables. (Not surprisingly, pomegranates and apples also come into season right as Rosh Hashanah arrives.)

Some Sephardi communities take the food symbolism a step further with a Rosh Hashanah "seder." While not formal like on Passover, these relaxed seders focus on eating a variety of foods, including pumpkins, beets, fish heads, dates, and leeks, which have a layer of symbolism based on the foods' Hebrew names. Egyptian Jews, for example, make a black-eyed pea dish called *loubia* on Rosh Hashanah, since the Hebrew name for the dish comes from the same root as the verb "to increase" (as in an increase of fortune, merit, and good deeds).

One wonderful thing about the weather turning cooler this time of year is that, after a hot season spent eating ice cream and fresh salads, I finally want to turn on the oven again. The menus that follow take full advantage of apples, honey, and early autumn produce to help usher in a sweet and joyous New Year.

ASHKENAZI ROSH HASHANAH MENU

Classic Challah (page 233) with Rosemary-Roasted Garlic for Challah (page 312)

Classic Chicken Soup (page 93)

Grilled Pear, Fennel, and Toasted Walnut Salad (page 62)

Red Wine and Honey Brisket (page 197)

Apple Cider–Braised Chicken (page 187)

Potato-Leek Kugel (page 127)

Mango-Ginger Tzimmes (page 132)

Honey-Cinnamon Pound Cake (page 286; kosher keepers: use oil)

Maple-Cardamom Roasted Pears (page 307)

SEPHARDI ROSH HASHANAH MENU

Classic Challah (page 233) with Matbucha (page 70)

Tomato-Chickpea Soup with Spinach (page 82; kosher keepers: skip the labneh or yogurt)

Carrot Salad with Mint and Dates (page 58)

Roast Chicken with Fennel and Orange (page 188)

Pomegranate Molasses Meatballs (page 200)

Couscous with Winter Squash and Chickpeas (page 158)

Orange-Glazed Cornmeal Cake (page 284)

VEGETARIAN ROSH HASHANAH MENU

Challah with Sautéed Leeks and Thyme (page 236) with Supremely Creamy Hummus (page 73)

Rustic Vegetable Soup with Dill Dumplings (page 88)

Red Cabbage and Beet Slaw with Caramelized Walnuts (page 69)

Panfried Tofu Steaks with Shallot Gravy (page 224)

Dilled Rice with Lima Beans (page 152)

Puréed Carrots with Orange and Ginger (page 105)

Upside-Down Apple Cake (page 290)

YOM KIPPUR

BEGINS THE 10TH OF TISHREI/SEPTEMBER OR OCTOBER

Some people fast on Yom Kippur, the Jewish day of Atonement; others do not. My family went out for lunch. Somewhere in the middle of morning services, my stomach would start to growl—not because I was so famished, but because I knew we would soon leave and head to the Onion Roll deli to buy their paper-thin slices of briny corned beef. Going out to eat on Yom Kippur is hardly traditional, but for my family, it was our tradition.

A couple of years after graduating college, I tried fasting for the first time. The practice of not eating or drinking during the twenty-five-hour holiday is meant to encourage deeper and more focused prayer. I had always assumed being hungry on Yom Kippur would be a distraction, but the practice is so ancient, I figured there must be something to it. I was also curious to find out if I could physically do it. (For the record, children and people who are physically ill are required *not* to fast.)

I stowed an emergency juice box in a discreet location and gave it a go. That first year, I fasted, except for a few sips of the juice. The following year, I made it the whole way. As the sun set and the final service wound down, I was tired and my stomach growled furiously but I was elated—wowed by the resolve of the human body and spirit, and feeling deeply connected to my tradition and community. And for the first time, I felt the profound rush of gratitude that comes with eating when one is truly hungry.

Yom Kippur is the most sacred day in the Jewish calendar, the high point of the High Holiday season, when Jews ask one another and God for forgiveness. But for a solemn holiday focused on the spiritual realm and *not* eating, Yom Kippur has two surprisingly joyous food traditions. The first is a pre-holiday meal, eaten just before sundown when the holiday begins. It is considered a *mitzvah* (commandment) to feast before fasting. Like gearing up for a long bike ride or run, people tend to load up on carbs. Kreplach, the filled, ravioli-like pasta often eaten in soup, is commonly served, but really anything goes. The most important thing for fasters, I have found, is to drink lots of water in the day or two leading up to Yom Kippur. It makes the day so much easier.

Immediately after Yom Kippur ends, another feast begins: the break fast meal. Just like at a regular morning breakfast, people tend to eat lighter foods such as bagels, lox, and salads, which are gentle on the stomach. Water and juice are also typically available in abundance for people to rehydrate. When I host a break fast meal, I try to serve foods that can be prepared in advance and warmed, or thrown together quickly after the holiday ends.

YOM KIPPUR PRE-FAST MENU

Classic Chicken Soup (page 93) with Beef Kreplach with Ginger and Cilantro (page 145)

Roasted Bell Pepper and Black Olive Salad (page 68)

Chicken Schnitzel with Caper Vinaigrette (page 191)

Toasted Almond Israeli Couscous (page 161)

Chocolate-Almond-Hazelnut Horns (page 271)

VEGETARIAN YOM KIPPUR PRE-FAST MENU

Romaine Wedge Salad with Buttermilk Dressing (page 60)

Baked Ziti with Caramelized Cherry Tomatoes (page 218)

Sautéed Green Beans with Labneh and Sliced Almonds (page 102)

Pine Nut and Scallion Couscous (page 157)

Chocolate-Banana Bundt Cake (page 294)

YOM KIPPUR BREAK FAST MENU

Homemade Bagels (page 240)

Cream Cheese Many Ways (page 314)

Brown Sugar–Citrus Gravlax (page 178)

Avocado–White Bean Salad with Basil-Mint Pesto (page 61)

Sweet Potato–Scallion Frittata (page 207)

Sweet Noodle Kugel with Dried Cherries and Figs (page 139)

Sour Cream Coffee Cake with Pecan Streusel (page 31)

SUKKOT

BEGINS THE 15TH OF TISHREI/USUALLY OCTOBER

I like to think of Sukkot as the Jewish calendar's environmentally-friendly poster child. The weeklong holiday is a harvest pilgrimage that celebrates the bounty that follows a season of growth. Historically it also commemorates the forty years the Israelites spent wandering in the desert after their Exodus from slavery in Egypt.

The primary symbol of Sukkot is an outdoor hut called a *sukkah*, which families traditionally begin building right after Yom Kippur ends. These impermanent structures, which must be covered with tree branches, bamboo, or another natural material, symbolize the temporary dwellings that Israelites built in the desert. They also represent the shelters farmers once built at the edges of their fields during the hectic harvest season. The sukkah offers an incomparable opportunity to dine alfresco throughout the holiday. One of my favorite rules about building a sukkah is that the roof must be woven loosely enough to see the sky through it.

As a kid, my family occasionally built a small sukkah in our backyard. It all depended on the year and how motivated we felt to make a Home Depot run. But every year without fail we would head to our synagogue to help build the communal sukkah they constructed in the parking lot. We would sip apple cider and fan away the curious bees while stringing gourds from the rafters, weaving pine boughs into the walls, and laying bundles of dried corn stalks at the entrance.

Many people would also pick up their *lulav* and *etrog* from the synagogue. On Sukkot, Jews have a custom of waving a bundle of four natural species: fronds from the myrtle, date, and willow trees (collectively called a *lulav*), along with a yellow, lemon-like citron fruit (called an *etrog*). Waving these species together symbolizes Jews' service to God and adds a bit of natural beauty to the holiday.

Unlike most Jewish holidays, Sukkot does not have a lot of specific food traditions—the meals tend to mirror those of Rosh Hashanah, which falls just a couple of weeks earlier. One Sukkot-specific tradition is to eat stuffed foods that represent the season's bounty. Stuffed peppers, the filled grape leaves called *dolmades*, and layered strudel are all tasty examples. And since Sukkot falls on the cusp of autumn, when the season's riot of apples, pears, sweet potatoes, squash, carrots, turnips, and other root vegetables arrive in full force, it is common to find these fruits and vegetables featured at the table. Gastronomically speaking, you could call it the Jewish equivalent of Thanksgiving. Here are some bountiful meal ideas to warm your holiday.

ASHKENAZI SUKKOT MENU

Pumpkin-Apple Challah (page 238)

Butternut Squash and Pear Soup (page 84; kosher keepers: skip the Greek yogurt or labneh)

Mushroom-and-Beef-Stuffed Peppers (page 202)

Rosemary-Maple Roast Chicken (page 190)

Roasted Delicata Squash with Thyme Bread Crumbs (page 108)

Roasted Broccoli with Shallots and Lemon (page 114)

Honey-Cinnamon Pound Cake (page 286; kosher keepers: use oil)

Maple-Cardamom Roasted Pears (page 307)

SEPHARDI SUKKOT MENU

Classic Challah (page 233) with Matbucha (page 70)

Dolmades (page 150)

Tomato-Chickpea Soup with Spinach (page 82)

Roasted Beet Salad with Preserved Lemon (page 67)

Tilapia in Spicy Tomato Sauce (page 174)

Toasted Almond Israeli Couscous (page 161)

Jeweled Rice Pudding (page 303)

Chocolate-Dipped Figs (page 308)

VEGETARIAN SUKKOT MENU

Challah with Sautéed Leeks and Thyme (page 236) with Supremely Creamy Hummus (page 73)

20 Cloves of Garlic Borscht (page 80)

Grilled Pear, Fennel, and Toasted Walnut Salad (page 62)

Porcini-, Tomato-, and Kale-Stuffed Peppers (page 213)

Mushroom–Goat Cheese Tart (page 216)

Butternut Squash Kugel with Crispy Shallots (page 128)

Fig-Ginger Rugelach (page 276)

HANUKKAH

Hanukkah is one of my favorite Jewish holidays. As a child, I loved lighting the candles on the menorah and watching their reflection glint in the kitchen window. And for weeks in advance of the first night, I began to crave the fried potato latkes my mom would fry and dollop with rosy applesauce.

But as an adult, Hanukkah has taken on a deeper significance. The holiday arrives in the darkest depths of winter, when the nights are long and bitter cold. Into that darkness, Hanukkah brings warmth and light. Each night another candle is added, so that by the end of the holiday the menorah glows powerfully—a symbol of hope just when we need it most.

Hanukkah commemorates the rededication of the Temple in Jerusalem after a small Judean army called the Maccabees recaptured it from the Greeks. As the legend goes, the Temple had been knocked into complete disarray, and the Maccabees were only able to find enough oil to light the Temple's menorah for one night. Miraculously, the oil lasted for eight full days and nights, which is why Hanukkah is traditionally referred to as the Festival of Lights.

Compared to major Jewish festivals like Rosh Hashanah, Yom Kippur, and Passover, Hanukkah is considered a relatively minor holiday. And for decades in America, it was hardly observed. But in the early twentieth century, Jewish leaders began to make a push for its celebration, highlighting the holiday's fun, family-centric aspects and positioning it as the Jewish seasonal equivalent of Christmas. As historian Jenna Weissman Joselit writes in her book *The Wonders of America: Reinventing Jewish Culture 1880–1950*, "By the 1920s, [the holiday] began to come into its own as a notable Jewish domestic occasion." The downside to Hanukkah's revitalization in the States is that it has taken on some of the holiday season's consumeristic qualities. And yet, it is lovely to have a midwinter Jewish holiday to celebrate between the long stretch of High Holidays in autumn and Purim in the early spring.

When it comes to food, Hanukkah's primary theme is oil. Jewish cuisines all over the world express this season of fried food in different ways, from the crispy potato pancakes called *latkes* that hail from Eastern Europe to the Sephardi fried leek patties, *keftes de prasa*, and the filled doughnuts called *sufganiyot* that have become popular throughout Israel and, increasingly, in America. Other Hanukkah traditions include eating small, gold and silver foil–wrapped chocolate coins called *gelt*, and spinning a four-sided top called a *dreidel*.

Whenever schedules allow, Yoshie and I like to throw a Hanukkah party. We invite over lots of friends, fry up a bunch of goodies (splattering our kitchen in oil in the process), scatter pieces of gelt all over the table, and toast with sparkling wine. I try to limit the amount of oily foods I consume throughout the year, but Hanukkah is my season of fried-food indulgence. The menu that follows outlines a mix-and-match selection of sweets, salads, and fritters to create a festive Hanukkah cocktail party in your home.

HANUKKAH COCKTAIL PARTY MENU IDEAS

Fried Green Olives (page 126)

Fried Cauliflower with Creamy Cilantro Sauce (page 116)

Beet Latkes with Chive Goat Cheese (page 124)

Sephardi Leek Patties (page 118)

Potato Latkes with Apple-Date Chutney and Cinnamon Sour Cream (page 119)

Red Cabbage and Beet Slaw with Caramelized Walnuts (page 69)

Carrot Salad with Mint and Dates (page 58)

Bittersweet Glazed Sufganiyot with Peanut Butter Cream (page 254)

Fig-Ginger Rugelach (page 276)

SOURCES

Having trouble finding an ingredient in your local grocery store? Harness the powers of Internet shopping and have it delivered right to your door.

PANTRY

BERBERE

The Teeny Tiny Spice Co. of Vermont produces an authentic-tasting version of the traditional Ethiopian spice blend for the Spicy Ethiopian Chicken Stew (page 94). Teenytinyspice.com

CANNED FAVAS

Sahadi brand fava beans make a great, saucy base for Ful Medames with Poached Eggs (page 165). Sayadmarket.com

CRÈME FRAÎCHE

Vermont Creamery makes a rich and delicate crème fraîche to add creaminess to a Sweet Potato–Scallion Frittata (page 207), or to use in place of sour cream. Vermontcreamery.com

GRAPE LEAVES

There are several brands of jarred preserved grape leaves, but Orlando is my favorite in terms of quality. Sadaf.com

HARISSA

Harissa is a Tunisian hot sauce made from a variety of chile peppers. Piquant brand harissa adds flavor as well as heat to North African–inspired dishes, as well as to Creamy Sorrel Soup with Harissa (page 86). Sahadis.com

POMEGRANATE MOLASSES

Used throughout the Middle East, pomegranate molasses, which is essentially pomegranate juice reduced to a thick syrup, adds tartness to a variety of dishes like Pomegranate Molasses Meatballs (page 200). I have never found a pomegranate molasses with a hekhsher (kosher certification), but I have found ones that are made with 100 percent pomegranate, like Mymouné brand. Mymouneusa.com

If you prefer, you can make your own: Boil down 1 cup/240 ml of pomegranate juice in a small pan set over medium heat, until it turns thick and syrupy, 15 to 20 minutes.

PRESERVED LEMONS

The best preserved lemons are the ones you make yourself. Find out how on page 320. Roland also makes a suitable version. Gourmetfoodworld.com

S'CHUG

This Yemenite chile paste is quite spicy, and the perfect condiment to add when you want a lot of heat. Sabra makes versions with both red and green chiles. Aviglatt.com

SILAN

Silan is a sweet and richly flavored syrup made of dates that get boiled down until they reach the color and consistency of molasses. It tastes delicious drizzled on top of Roasted Eggplant and Tahini Crostini (page 111). Aviglatt.com

SUMAC

This Middle Eastern herb is red in color with a tart, lemony flavor. It is often added to za'atar spice mixes, but is delicious on its own as well. Penzeys.com

ZA'ATAR

Za'atar is a fragrant herb that grows in the Middle East, and also the name of a spice mixture that includes that herb, along with sesame seeds, ground sumac, and salt. Teeny Tiny Spice Co. of Vermont makes a great version. Teenytinyspice.com

BAKING

ALMOND PASTE

Almond paste is a thick, sweet mixture of ground almonds and sugar that's similar to marzipan, but a bit coarser in texture. It is the key ingredient in Chocolate-Almond-Hazelnut Horns (page 271). Kingarthurflour.com

BARLEY MALT SYRUP

Eden Organic makes a thick, flavorful syrup from organic sprouted barley that makes the perfect, malty addition to Homemade Bagels (page 240). Edenfoods.com

CAKE FLOUR

King Arthur Flour makes a wonderful unbleached cake flour that is free of any additives or chemicals that other cake flour brands often have. It is the perfect flour for making Honey-Cinnamon Pound Cake (page 286). Kingarthurflour.com

DULCE DE LECHE

This South American confection is made from sweetened milk boiled down into a thick, spreadable caramel. It is delicious used as a cookie filling, or in Chocolate Chip Cheesecake with Caramel Whipped Cream (page 300). Rolandfood.com

LEMON EXTRACT

Made from organic lemon oil, Flavorganic's lemon extract adds bright, lemony flavor to baked goods like Lemon and Rose Water Scones (page 26). Flavorganics.com

PASSOVER CAKE MEAL

Passover cake meal is matzo meal that has been ground super-fine to the consistency of flour. It is great for making Passover-friendly cakes like the tender, moist Passover Pear Cake (page 287), and other baked goods. Aviglatt.com

ROSE WATER

Rose water is used across Middle Eastern cooking to add delicate floral flavor to desserts like Jeweled Rice Pudding (page 303) and other dishes. Be sure to buy regular rose water, not rose oil or rose water concentrate, which are significantly stronger. Sadaf makes kosher certified rose water. Sadaf.com

WHITE WHOLE-WHEAT FLOUR

King Arthur Flour's white whole-wheat flour yields tender baked goods that pack more of a nutritional punch than those made with all-purpose flour. Kingarthurflour.com

MEAT

KOSHER CHORIZO

The kosher sustainable meat company, Grow and Behold, sells mild and spicy versions of chorizo. Jack's Gourmet Kosher offers a spicy Mexican chorizo. Both make great additions to Chorizo, Tomato, and Cabbage Soup (page 91), as well as Spicy Chorizo and Red Pepper Penne (page 199). Growandbehold.com; Jacksgourmetkosher.com

SECOND-CUT BRISKET

A brisket is actually two separate muscles: the first is large and fairly lean, the second is more marbled, which makes it inherently juicy and flavorful. Grow and Behold sells second-cut brisket, which is sometimes referred to as *deckle*. Growandbehold.com

INDEX

Admony, Einat, 64, 126

Almonds
Apple and Honey Granola, 22
Black Pepper and Pistachio Granola, 23
Chocolate-Almond-Hazelnut Horns, 271–72
Chocolate-Almond Meringues, 274–75
Cinnamon-Almond Macaroons, 279
Lemon Cheesecake with Almond Shortbread Crust, 302
Moroccan-Style Charoset Balls, 317
Orange-Glazed Cornmeal Cake, 284
paste, 343
Plum-Almond Cake, 288
Saffron Rice Pilaf, 153
Sautéed Green Beans with Labneh and Sliced Almonds, 102
Sephardi Charoset, 317
Toasted Almond Israeli Couscous, 161

Alpern, Liz, 185

Appetizing shops, 181

Apples
Apple and Honey Granola, 22
Apple Cider–Braised Chicken, 187
Apple-Cranberry Chremslach, 51
Apple-Date Chutney, 119–21
Ashkenazi Charoset, 316
Cinnamon-Sugar Apple Pancakes, 34–35
Pumpkin-Apple Challah, 238–39
Upside-Down Apple Cake, 290–91

Apricots
Bulgur with Walnuts and Pomegranate, 162
Chocolate Cupcakes with Apricot Jam Frosting, 282–83
Chocolate–Poppy Seed Filling, 263
Golden Apricot Filling, 262
Mango-Ginger Tzimmes, 132

Arugula
Carrot Salad with Mint and Dates, 58
Grilled Pear, Fennel, and Toasted Walnut Salad, 62

Ashkenazi Jews, 14, 64

Asparagus, Miso-Roasted, 109

Auster, Louis, 309

Avocado–White Bean Salad with Basil-Mint Pesto, 61

Babka, Chocolate-Raspberry, 250–52

Bagels, Homemade, 240–41

Baharat, 199, 323

Balaboosta, 126

Banana Bundt Cake, Chocolate-, 294

B&H Dairy, 80

Barhany, Beejhy, 94

Barley
malt syrup, 343
Wild Mushroom and Barley Soup, 90

Barney Greengrass, 181

Bars, Rhubarb-Oatmeal Crumble, 280–81

Basil
Basil-Mint Pesto, 61
cutting, 18
Mozzarella, Tomato, and Basil Frittata, 41
Olive-Basil Cream Cheese, 315
Sugar Snap Pea, Corn, and Basil Salad, 55

Beans. See also Chickpeas
Avocado–White Bean Salad with Basil-Mint Pesto, 61
Black Bean–Sweet Potato Chili, 96
canned vs. dried, 18
Dilled Rice with Lima Beans, 152
favas, canned, 342
Ful Medames with Poached Eggs, 165–67
Sautéed Green Beans with Labneh and Sliced Almonds, 102
Vegetarian Chopped "Liver," 77
Vegetarian Porcini Farro and Cholent, 168–69

Beef
Beef Kreplach with Ginger and Cilantro, 145–46
Bukharian Beef and Carrot Rice Pilaf, 154–55
Goulash, 95
Mushroom-and-Beef-Stuffed Peppers, 202–3
Pomegranate Molasses Meatballs, 200–201
Red Wine and Honey Brisket, 197–98
Slow-Cooker Spiced Beef and Chickpea Stew, 170–71
Steak and Za'atar Fajitas, 194–95
Tomato-Beef Filling, 267

Beets
Beet Latkes with Chive Goat Cheese, 124–25
Red Cabbage and Beet Slaw with Caramelized Walnuts, 69
Roasted Beet Salad with Preserved Lemon, 67
20 Cloves of Garlic Borscht, 80

Bell peppers
Matbucha, 70
Mushroom-and-Beef-Stuffed Peppers, 202–3
Porcini-, Tomato-, and Kale-Stuffed Peppers, 213–14
Roasted Bell Pepper and Black Olive Salad, 68
Roasted Red Pepper Cream Cheese, 314
Spicy Chorizo and Red Pepper Penne, 199
Steak and Za'atar Fajitas, 194–95

Berbere, 342

Biscuits, Spicy Cheddar, 28

Blintzes
Orange-Scented Cheese Blintzes, 49–50
Roasted Garlic–Potato Blintzes, 46–47

Borscht, 20 Cloves of Garlic, 80

Bourekas
Butternut Squash and Sage Bourekas, 246
Spinach and Cheese Bourekas, 245

Bread
challah, tips for, 228–31
Challah with Sautéed Leeks and Thyme, 236–37
Classic Challah, 233–35
Fattoush, 72
Homemade Bagels, 240–41
Pletzels, 242–44
Pumpkin-Apple Challah, 238–39
Roasted Bell Pepper and Black Olive Salad, 68
Roasted Eggplant and Tahini Crostini, 111–12
Savory French Toast with Seared Tomatoes and Za'atar Butter, 36
Sourdough Gazpacho, 81

Brisket
Red Wine and Honey Brisket, 197–98
second-cut, 197, 343

Broccoli, Roasted, with Shallots and Lemon, 114

Broths, store-bought, 19

Bukharian Jews, 14, 154

Bulgur
Bulgur with Walnuts and Pomegranate, 162
Heirloom Tabbouleh, 71

Butter
Browned Butter Vinaigrette, 54
margarine vs., 298
Za'atar Butter, 36

Buttermilk Dressing, 60

Butternut squash
Butternut Squash and Pear Soup, 84
Butternut Squash and Sage Bourekas, 246
Butternut Squash Kugel with Crispy Shallots, 128–29
Couscous with Winter Squash and Chickpeas, 158–60

Cabbage
Caraway Cabbage Strudel, 133–34
Chorizo, Tomato, and Cabbage Soup, 91
Red Cabbage and Beet Slaw with Caramelized Walnuts, 69
20 Cloves of Garlic Borscht, 80

Cake flour, 343

Cakes. See also Cheesecakes
Chocolate-Banana Bundt Cake, 294
Chocolate Cupcakes with Apricot Jam Frosting, 282–83
Honey-Cinnamon Pound Cake, 286
Kabocha Squash–Chocolate Chip Cake, 292–93
Orange-Glazed Cornmeal Cake, 284
Passover Pear Cake, 287
Plum-Almond Cake, 288
Sour Cream Coffee Cake with Pecan Streusel, 31–32

Upside-Down Apple Cake, 290–91

Caramel-Chocolate Matzo Clusters with Pistachio, 304–5

Caraway Cabbage Strudel, 133–34

Carrots
Bukharian Beef and Carrot Rice Pilaf, 154–55
Carrot Salad with Mint and Dates, 58
Mango-Ginger Tzimmes, 132
Puréed Carrots with Orange and Ginger, 105

Cauliflower
Fried Cauliflower with Creamy Cilantro Sauce, 116–17
Roasted Cauliflower and Red Onion, 115
Rustic Vegetable Soup with Dill Dumplings, 88–89

Challah
Challah with Sautéed Leeks and Thyme, 236–37
Classic Challah, 233–35
history and ritual significance of, 228
Pumpkin-Apple Challah, 238–39
Rosemary-Roasted Garlic for Challah, 312
tips for, 228–31

Chametz, 330

Charoset
Ashkenazi Charoset, 316
Moroccan-style charoset balls, 317
Sephardi Charoset, 317

Cheese. See also Cream cheese
Baked Ziti with Caramelized Cherry Tomatoes, 218–19
Beet Latkes with Chive Goat Cheese, 124–25
Breaded Eggplant and Tomato Stacks, 206
Butternut Squash and Sage Bourekas, 246
Creamy Noodles with Lemon, Mint, and Chives, 138
Fennel Gratin, 130
Grilled Portobellos with Herbs and Mozzarella, 215
Mozzarella, Tomato, and Basil Frittata, 41
Mushroom-Goat Cheese Tart, 216
Orange-Scented Cheese Blintzes, 49–50
Ricotta-Vanilla Bean Cheesecake with Raspberry Sauce, 295–97
Spicy Cheddar Biscuits, 28
Spinach and Cheese Bourekas, 245
Spinach-Matzo Lasagna, 221–22
Sweet Noodle Kugel with Dried Cherries and Figs, 139–40
Sweet Potato–Parmesan Filling, 266
Sweet Potato–Scallion Frittata, 207

Cheesecakes
Chocolate Chip Cheesecake with Caramel Whipped Cream, 300–301
Lemon Cheesecake with Almond Shortbread Crust, 302
Ricotta-Vanilla Bean Cheesecake with Raspberry Sauce, 295–97

Cherries, Dried, Sweet Noodle Kugel with Figs
and, 139–40
Chicken
Apple Cider–Braised Chicken, 187
Chicken Schnitzel with Caper Vinaigrette,
191–92
Chopped Chicken Liver, 76
Classic Chicken Soup, 93
Gribenes, 318
Moroccan Chicken with Preserved Lemons, 186
Roast Chicken with Fennel and Orange, 188
Rosemary-Maple Roast Chicken, 190
Schmaltz, 318
Spicy Ethiopian Chicken Stew, 94
Chickpeas
Couscous with Winter Squash and Chickpeas,
158–60
Hummus im Basar, 74
Slow-Cooker Spiced Beef and Chickpea Stew,
170–71
Supremely Creamy Hummus, 73
Tomato-Chickpea Soup with Spinach, 82
Chiffonade, 18
Chili, Black Bean–Sweet Potato, 96
Chocolate
Bittersweet Glazed Sufganiyot with Peanut
Butter Cream, 254–55
Caramel-Chocolate Matzo Clusters with Pista-
chio, 304–5
Chocolate-Almond-Hazelnut Horns, 271–72
Chocolate-Almond Meringues, 274–75
Chocolate-Banana Bundt Cake, 294
Chocolate Chip Cheesecake with Caramel
Whipped Cream, 300–301
Chocolate Cupcakes with Apricot Jam
Frosting, 282–83
Chocolate-Dipped Figs, 308
Chocolate Macaroons, 279
Chocolate–Poppy Seed Filling, 263
Chocolate-Raspberry Babka, 250–52
Chocolate-Strawberry Egg Cream, 309
Chocolate-Walnut Filling, 276–77
Kabocha Squash–Chocolate Chip Cake, 292–93
Pumpkin–Chocolate Chip Muffins, 33
Rugelach Two Ways, 276–77
Cholent
Slow-Cooker Spiced Beef and Chickpea Stew,
170–71
Vegetarian Porcini Farro and Cholent, 168–69
Chorizo
Chorizo, Tomato, and Cabbage Soup, 91
kosher, 343
Spicy Chorizo and Red Pepper Penne, 199
Chremslach, Apple-Cranberry, 51
Chutney, Apple-Date, 119–21
Cinnamon
Cinnamon-Almond Macaroons, 279
Cinnamon-Honey Tahini Spread, 313

Cinnamon-Roasted Seitan and Onions, 223
Cinnamon-Sugar Apple Pancakes, 34–35
Coconut
Chocolate Macaroons, 279
Cinnamon-Almond Macaroons, 279
Coconut Macaroons, 279
Matzo Granola with Walnuts and Coconut, 24
Moroccan-style charoset balls, 317
oil, 292
Coffee Cake, Sour Cream, with Pecan Streusel,
31–32
Cohen, Barbara, 185
Concia, 100
Cookies
Chocolate-Almond-Hazelnut Horns, 271–72
Chocolate-Almond Meringues, 274–75
Chocolate Macaroons, 279
Cinnamon-Almond Macaroons, 279
Coconut Macaroons, 279
Rugelach Two Ways, 276–77
Savory Hamantaschen, 264–65
Sweet Hamantaschen, 259–60
Walnut Mandelbrot, 278
Corn
Balsamic-Roasted Mushrooms and Corn, 113
Farro Salad with Corn and Jalapeño, 164
kernels, removing, 18
Sugar Snap Pea, Corn, and Basil Salad, 55
Cornmeal
Mamaliga, 156
Orange-Glazed Cornmeal Cake, 284
Couscous
Couscous with Winter Squash and Chickpeas,
158–60
Pine Nut and Scallion Couscous, 157
Toasted Almond Israeli Couscous, 161
Cranberries
Apple-Cranberry Chremslach, 51
Black Pepper and Pistachio Granola, 23
Cream cheese
Chocolate Chip Cheesecake with Caramel
Whipped Cream, 300–301
Herbed Cream Cheese, 314
Honey-Orange Cream Cheese, 315
Lemon Cheesecake with Almond Shortbread
Crust, 302
Maple-Cinnamon Cream Cheese, 315
Olive-Basil Cream Cheese, 315
Roasted Red Pepper Cream Cheese, 314
Rugelach Two Ways, 276–77
Salmon-Dill Cream Cheese, 315
Shallot-Chive Cream Cheese, 314
Veggie Cream Cheese, 314
Crème fraîche, 342
Crostini, Roasted Eggplant and Tahini, 111–12
Cucumbers
Fattoush, 72

Romaine Wedge Salad with Buttermilk
Dressing, 60
Sourdough Gazpacho, 81
Spicy Dill Pickles, 322
Watermelon Israeli Salad, 57
Cupcakes, Chocolate, with Apricot Jam Frosting,
282–83
Cúrate, 54

Dairy-free desserts, 298–99
Dates
Apple-Date Chutney, 119–21
Carrot Salad with Mint and Dates, 58
Moroccan-style charoset balls, 317
Sephardi Charoset, 317
Deckle, 197, 343
Deep-frying, 122–23
Dill
Dilled Rice with Lima Beans, 152
Spicy Dill Pickles, 322
Dolmades, 150–51
Doro wat, 94
Dulce de leche, 343
Dumplings, Dill, Rustic Vegetable Soup with,
88–89

Egg Cream, Chocolate-Strawberry, 309
Eggplant
Breaded Eggplant and Tomato Stacks, 206
Matbucha, 70
Roasted Eggplant and Tahini Crostini, 111–12
Eggs
Baked Tomatoes and Eggs, 38–39
Ful Medames with Poached Eggs, 165–67
Mozzarella, Tomato, and Basil Frittata, 41
Shallot, Leek, and Ginger Omelet, 40
Slow-Cooker Spiced Beef and Chickpea Stew,
170–71
Spicy Ethiopian Chicken Stew, 94
Spinach Shakshuka, 208
Sweet Potato–Scallion Frittata, 207
Three-in-One Matzo Brei, 42–43
Ephron, Nora, 133
Equipment, 15–17
Escarole
Baked Sole with Bitter Greens, 175
Esther, Queen, 145, 329
Ethiopian Jews, 14, 94

Fajitas, Steak and Za'atar, 194–95
Farfel, Savory Matzo, 147
Farming, Jewish, 85
Farro
Farro Salad with Corn and Jalapeño, 164
Vegetarian Porcini Farro and Cholent, 168–69
Fattoush, 72
Fennel
Fennel Gratin, 130

Grilled Pear, Fennel, and Toasted Walnut Salad,
62
Roast Chicken with Fennel and Orange, 188
Roasted Beet Salad with Preserved Lemon, 67
Rustic Vegetable Soup with Dill Dumplings,
88–89
Figs
Chocolate-Dipped Figs, 308
Fig-Ginger Filling, 276–77
Moroccan-style charoset balls, 317
Rugelach Two Ways, 276–77
Sephardi Charoset, 317
Sweet Noodle Kugel with Dried Cherries and
Figs, 139–40
Tahini, Roasted Fig, and Pistachio Sundaes,
306
Fillings
Chocolate-Poppy Seed Filling, 263
Chocolate-Walnut Filling, 276–77
Fig-Ginger Filling, 276–77
Golden Apricot Filling, 262
Lekvar, 261
Sweet Potato–Parmesan Filling, 266
Tomato-Beef Filling, 267
Fish
Baked Sole with Bitter Greens, 175
Brown Sugar–Citrus Gravlax, 178–80
Gefilte Fish in White Wine–Herb Broth, 182–85
Greek Goddess Salmon, 177
Grilled Salmon with Orange and Herbs, 176
Salmon-Dill Cream Cheese, 315
Smoked Salmon Hash with Lemon-Mint Vinai-
grette, 44
Tilapia in Spicy Tomato Sauce, 174
Flour
cake, 343
measuring, 229
white whole-wheat, 280, 343
Food processors, 16
Frank, Minnie, 278
French Toast, Savory, with Seared Tomatoes and
Za'atar Butter, 36
Frittatas
Mozzarella, Tomato, and Basil Frittata, 41
Sweet Potato–Scallion Frittata, 207
Frosting, Apricot Jam, 282–83
Ful Medames with Poached Eggs, 165–67

Garlic
Garlic-Marinated Zucchini, 100
Roasted Garlic–Potato Blintzes, 46–47
Rosemary-Roasted Garlic for Challah, 312
20 Cloves of Garlic Borscht, 80
Gazpacho, Sourdough, 81
Gefilte Fish in White Wine–Herb Broth, 182–85
Gefilteria, 185
Ginger
Fig-Ginger Filling, 276–77

Mango-Ginger Tzimmes, 132
Rugelach Two Ways, 276–77
Shallot, Leek, and Ginger Omelet, 40
Ginsberg, Stanley, 271
Goldman, Marcy, 304–5
Goldstein, Joyce, 175
Goulash, 95
Granola
Apple and Honey Granola, 22
Black Pepper and Pistachio Granola, 23
Matzo Granola with Walnuts and Coconut, 24
Grape leaves, 342
Dolmades, 150–51
Gravlax
Brown Sugar–Citrus Gravlax, 178–80
lox vs., 178
Greek Goddess Salmon, 177
Gribenes, 318
Grill pans, 16
Grow and Behold, 91

Hamantaschen
fillings for, 261–63, 266–67
Savory Hamantaschen, 264–65
Sweet Hamantaschen, 259–60
tips for, 268, 270
Hamin, 170
Hanau, Naf and Anna, 76, 91, 307
Hanukkah, 122, 340–41
Harissa, 342
Hash, Smoked Salmon, with Lemon-Mint Vinai-
grette, 44
Hathaway, Margaret, 107
Hazelnuts
Carrot Salad with Mint and Dates, 58
Chocolate-Almond-Hazelnut Horns, 271–72
Helou, Anissa, 71
Home Fries with Smoked Paprika, 45
Honey
Cinnamon-Honey Tahini Spread, 313
Honey-Cinnamon Pound Cake, 286
Honey-Orange Cream Cheese, 315
Horseradish Herb Sauce, Creamy, 319
Hummus
Hummus im Basar, 74
Supremely Creamy Hummus, 73

Ice cream
Tahini, Roasted Fig, and Pistachio Sundaes,
306
Indian Jews, 14

Jalapeños
Farro Salad with Corn and Jalapeño, 164
Jalapeño-Shallot Matzo Balls, 149
Jeweled Rice Pudding, 303
Joselit, Jenna Weissman, 340

Kabocha Squash–Chocolate Chip Cake, 292–93
Kale-Stuffed Peppers, Porcini-, Tomato-, and,
213–14
Kasha Varnishkes, 142
Kashrut, 15
Keftes de prasa, 118
Kerouac, Jack, 309
Kitniyot, 330
Kneading, 229–30
Knives, 17
Kosher, keeping, 15
Kreplach, Beef, with Ginger and Cilantro, 145–46
Kugels
Butternut Squash Kugel with Crispy Shallots,
128–29
Potato-Leek Kugel, 127
Sweet Noodle Kugel with Dried Cherries and
Figs, 139–40

Lamb
Hummus im Basar, 74
Pomegranate Molasses Meatballs, 200–201
Lansky, Meyer, 49
Lasagna, Spinach-Matzo, 221–22
Latkes
Beet Latkes with Chive Goat Cheese, 124–25
Potato Latkes with Apple-Date Chutney and
Cinnamon Sour Cream, 119–21
Lebedeff, Aaron, 156
Le Bon Ton, 104
Leeks
Challah with Sautéed Leeks and Thyme,
236–37
Potato-Leek Kugel, 127
Sephardi Leek Patties, 118
Shallot, Leek, and Ginger Omelet, 40
Three-in-One Matzo Brei, 42–43
Lekvar, 261
Lemons
extract, 343
Lemon and Rose Water Scones, 26–27
Lemon-Caper Smashed Potatoes, 106
Lemon Cheesecake with Almond Shortbread
Crust, 302
Lemon-Mint Vinaigrette, 44
Moroccan Chicken with Preserved Lemons, 186
Preserved Lemons, 320, 342
Roasted Beet Salad with Preserved Lemon, 67
Lentil Patties, Spiced, 210
Lettuce
Roasted Bell Pepper and Black Olive Salad, 68
Romaine Wedge Salad with Buttermilk
Dressing, 60
Spring Pea Salad with Browned Butter
Vinaigrette, 54
Liver
Chopped Chicken Liver, 76

Vegetarian Chopped "Liver," 77
Lox, 178

Macaroons
    Chocolate Macaroons, 279
    Cinnamon-Almond Macaroons, 279
    Coconut Macaroons, 279
Machlin, Edda Servi, 100
Mamaliga, 156
Mandelbrot, Walnut, 278
Mango-Ginger Tzimmes, 132
Maple syrup
    Maple-Cardamom Roasted Pears, 307
    Maple-Cinnamon Cream Cheese, 315
Margarine, 298
Marks, Gil, 73, 95
Matbucha, 70
Matzo
    Apple-Cranberry Chremslach, 51
    Caramel-Chocolate Matzo Clusters with
      Pistachio, 304–5
    Jalapeño-Shallot Matzo Balls, 149
    Matzo Granola with Walnuts and Coconut, 24
    meal, homemade, 18
    Parsley Matzo Balls, 148
    Passover Pear Cake, 287
    Savory Matzo Farfel, 147
    Spinach-Matzo Lasagna, 221–22
    Three-in-One Matzo Brei, 42–43
Measuring, 18, 229
Meatballs, Pomegranate Molasses, 200–201
Meringues, Chocolate-Almond, 274–75
Mint
    Basil-Mint Pesto, 61
    Carrot Salad with Mint and Dates, 58
    Heirloom Tabbouleh, 71
    Lemon-Mint Vinaigrette, 44
Mishloach manot, 329
Miso-Roasted Asparagus, 109
Mixers, electric, 16
Mizrahi Jews, 14
Moroccan Chicken with Preserved Lemons, 186
Moroccan-style charoset balls, 317
Muffins, Pumpkin–Chocolate Chip, 33
Murray's Sturgeon Shop, 181
Mushrooms
    Balsamic-Roasted Mushrooms and Corn, 113
    Grilled Portobellos with Herbs and Mozzarella,
      215
    Mushroom-and-Beef-Stuffed Peppers, 202–3
    Mushroom–Goat Cheese Tart, 216
    Porcini-, Tomato-, and Kale-Stuffed Peppers,
      213–14
    Three-in-One Matzo Brei, 42–43
    Vegetarian Chopped "Liver," 77
    Vegetarian Porcini Farro and Cholent, 168–69
    Wild Mushroom and Barley Soup, 90

Nathan, Joan, 320
New Israeli cuisine, 64–65
Noodles. *See* Pasta and noodles

Oats
    Apple and Honey Granola, 22
    Black Pepper and Pistachio Granola, 23
    Rhubarb-Oatmeal Crumble Bars, 280–81
Oils, vegetable, 19
Olives
    Baked Sole with Bitter Greens, 175
    Fried Green Olives, 126
    Olive-Basil Cream Cheese, 315
    Roasted Bell Pepper and Black Olive Salad, 68
    Tomato-Beef Filling, 267
Omelet, Shallot, Leek, and Ginger, 40
Onions
    Cinnamon-Roasted Seitan and Onions, 223
    Roasted Cauliflower and Red Onion, 115
Oranges
    Golden Apricot Filling, 262
    Grilled Salmon with Orange and Herbs, 176
    Honey-Orange Cream Cheese, 315
    Lekvar, 261
    Orange-Glazed Cornmeal Cake, 284
    Orange-Scented Cheese Blintzes, 49–50
    Puréed Carrots with Orange and Ginger, 105
    Roast Chicken with Fennel and Orange, 188
Ottolenghi, Yotam, 64, 71

Pancakes
    Beet Latkes with Chive Goat Cheese, 124–25
    Cinnamon-Sugar Apple Pancakes, 34–35
    Potato Latkes with Apple-Date Chutney and
      Cinnamon Sour Cream, 119–21
Pans, greasing, 18
Parsley
    Heirloom Tabbouleh, 71
    Parsley Matzo Balls, 148
Passover, 287, 330–32
Passover cake meal, 343
Pasta and noodles
    Baked Ziti with Caramelized Cherry Tomatoes,
      218–19
    Creamy Noodles with Lemon, Mint, and Chives,
      138
    Kasha Varnishkes, 142
    salting water for, 19
    Savory Matzo Farfel, 147
    Spicy Chorizo and Red Pepper Penne, 199
    Sweet Noodle Kugel with Dried Cherries and
      Figs, 139–40
Pastry brushes, 17
Pavoncello, Micaela, 104
Peach and Raspberry Tart, 248
Peanut Butter Cream, Bittersweet Glazed Suf-
    ganiyot with, 254–55

Pears
    Butternut Squash and Pear Soup, 84
    Grilled Pear, Fennel, and Toasted Walnut Salad, 62
    Maple-Cardamom Roasted Pears, 307
    Passover Pear Cake, 287
Peas
    Spring Pea Salad with Browned Butter Vinaigrette, 54
    Sugar Snap Pea, Corn, and Basil Salad, 55
Pecans
    Kabocha Squash–Chocolate Chip Cake, 292–93
    Passover Pear Cake, 287
    Sour Cream Coffee Cake with Pecan Streusel, 31–32
Pepitas
    Watermelon Israeli Salad, 57
Pesto, Basil-Mint, 61
Phyllo dough
    Caraway Cabbage Strudel, 133–34
Pickles, Spicy Dill, 322
Pine nuts
    Avocado–White Bean Salad with Basil-Mint Pesto, 61
    Dolmades, 150–51
    Hummus im Basar, 74
    Pine Nut and Scallion Couscous, 157
Pistachios
    Black Pepper and Pistachio Granola, 23
    Caramel-Chocolate Matzo Clusters with Pistachio, 304–5
    Orange-Glazed Cornmeal Cake, 284
    Tahini, Roasted Fig, and Pistachio Sundaes, 306
Pletzels, 242–44
Plum-Almond Cake, 288
Pomegranates
    Bulgur with Walnuts and Pomegranate, 162
    molasses, 342
    Pomegranate Molasses Meatballs, 200–201
    seeding, 162
Poppy Seed Filling, Chocolate–, 263
Potatoes
    Chorizo, Tomato, and Cabbage Soup, 91
    Creamy Sorrel Soup with Harissa, 86
    Goulash, 95
    Home Fries with Smoked Paprika, 45
    Lemon-Caper Smashed Potatoes, 106
    Mango-Ginger Tzimmes, 132
    Potato Latkes with Apple-Date Chutney and Cinnamon Sour Cream, 119–21
    Potato-Leek Kugel, 127
    Roasted Garlic–Potato Blintzes, 46–47
    Rustic Vegetable Soup with Dill Dumplings, 88–89
    Slow-Cooker Spiced Beef and Chickpea Stew, 170–71

Smoked Salmon Hash with Lemon-Mint Vinaigrette, 44
    20 Cloves of Garlic Borscht, 80
    Vegetarian Porcini Farro and Cholent, 168–69
Potato mashers, 17
Pound Cake, Honey-Cinnamon, 286
Prunes
    Lekvar, 261
    Mango-Ginger Tzimmes, 132
Puddings
    Butternut Squash Kugel with Crispy Shallots, 128–29
    Jeweled Rice Pudding, 303
    Potato-Leek Kugel, 127
    Sweet Noodle Kugel with Dried Cherries and Figs, 139–40
Puff pastry
    Butternut Squash and Sage Bourekas, 246
    Mushroom–Goat Cheese Tart, 216
    Peach and Raspberry Tart, 248
    Spinach and Cheese Bourekas, 245
Pumpkin
    Pumpkin-Apple Challah, 238–39
    Pumpkin-Chocolate Chip Muffins, 33
    Purim, 268, 329

Quinoa
    Heirloom Tabbouleh, 71

Raisins
    Apple and Honey Granola, 22
    Black Pepper and Pistachio Granola, 23
    Cinnamon-Sugar Apple Pancakes, 34–35
    Couscous with Winter Squash and Chickpeas, 158–60
    Golden Apricot Filling, 262
    Matzo Granola with Walnuts and Coconut, 24
    Moroccan-style charoset balls, 317
    Pine Nut and Scallion Couscous, 157
    Sephardi Charoset, 317
Raspberries
    Chocolate-Raspberry Babka, 250–52
    Peach and Raspberry Tart, 248
    Ricotta–Vanilla Bean Cheesecake with Raspberry Sauce, 295–97
Ratner's, 49
Raue, Tim, 105
Reed, Lou, 309
Rhubarb-Oatmeal Crumble Bars, 280–81
Rice
    Bukharian Beef and Carrot Rice Pilaf, 154–55
    Dilled Rice with Lima Beans, 152
    Dolmades, 150–51
    Jeweled Rice Pudding, 303
    Mushroom-and-Beef-Stuffed Peppers, 202–3
    Porcini-, Tomato-, and Kale-Stuffed Peppers, 213–14
    Saffron Rice Pilaf, 153

Roden, Claudia, 71, 152
Rome, Jews in, 104
Rosemary
    Rosemary-Maple Roast Chicken, 190
    Rosemary-Roasted Garlic for Challah, 312
Rose water, 343
Rosh Hashanah, 334–35
Rugelach Two Ways, 276–77
Russ & Daughters, 181

Saffron Rice Pilaf, 153
Salad dressings
    Browned Butter Vinaigrette, 54
    Buttermilk Dressing, 60
    Lemon-Mint Vinaigrette, 44
Salads
    Avocado–White Bean Salad with Basil-Mint
        Pesto, 61
    Carrot Salad with Mint and Dates, 58
    Farro Salad with Corn and Jalapeño, 164
    Fattoush, 72
    Grilled Pear, Fennel, and Toasted Walnut Salad,
        62
    Heirloom Tabbouleh, 71
    Matbucha, 70
    Red Cabbage and Beet Slaw with Caramelized
        Walnuts, 69
    Roasted Beet Salad with Preserved Lemon, 67
    Roasted Bell Pepper and Black Olive Salad, 68
    Romaine Wedge Salad with Buttermilk
        Dressing, 60
    Spring Pea Salad with Browned Butter
        Vinaigrette, 54
    Sugar Snap Pea, Corn, and Basil Salad, 55
    Tomato Salad with Fried Capers, 56
    Watermelon Israeli Salad, 57
Salmon
    Brown Sugar–Citrus Gravlax, 178–80
    Greek Goddess Salmon, 177
    Grilled Salmon with Orange and Herbs, 176
    Salmon-Dill Cream Cheese, 315
    Smoked Salmon Hash with Lemon-Mint
        Vinaigrette, 44
Sauces
    Basil-Mint Pesto, 61
    Creamy Cilantro Sauce, 116–17
    Creamy Horseradish Herb Sauce, 319
    Raspberry Sauce, 295–97
Sausage
    Chorizo, Tomato, and Cabbage Soup, 91
    Spicy Chorizo and Red Pepper Penne, 199
Scales, kitchen, 16–17
Schatz, Karl, 107
Schmaltz, 318
Schnitzel, Chicken, with Caper Vinaigrette, 191–92
S'chug, 342
Scones, Lemon and Rose Water, 26–27
Seder, 330–32

Seitan and Onions, Cinnamon-Roasted, 223
Sephardi Jews, 14
Shabbat, 104, 326–28
Shakshuka, 38–39
    Spinach Shakshuka, 208
Shallots
    Shallot-Chive Cream Cheese, 314
    Shallot, Leek, and Ginger Omelet, 40
Shav, 86
Shavuot, 333
Shelsky's Smoked Fish, 181, 276
Siegel, Bugsy, 49
Silan, 342
Slaw, Red Cabbage and Beet, with Caramelized
    Walnuts, 69
Sole, Baked, with Bitter Greens, 175
Solomonov, Michael, 64, 71
Sorrel Soup, Creamy, with Harissa, 86
Soups
    blending hot, 17
    Butternut Squash and Pear Soup, 84
    Chorizo, Tomato, and Cabbage Soup, 91
    Classic Chicken Soup, 93
    Creamy Sorrel Soup with Harissa, 86
    Rustic Vegetable Soup with Dill Dumplings,
        88–89
    Sourdough Gazpacho, 81
    Tomato-Chickpea Soup with Spinach, 82
    20 Cloves of Garlic Borscht, 80
    Wild Mushroom and Barley Soup, 90
Sour Cream Coffee Cake with Pecan Streusel,
    31–32
Sourdough Gazpacho, 81
Spices
    Baharat, 199, 323
    storing, 19
Spinach
    Spinach and Cheese Bourekas, 245
    Spinach-Matzo Lasagna, 221–22
    Spinach Shakshuka, 208
    Tomato-Chickpea Soup with Spinach, 82
Spreads
    Chopped Chicken Liver, 76
    Cinnamon-Honey Tahini Spread, 313
    Herbed Cream Cheese, 314
    Honey-Orange Cream Cheese, 315
    Hummus im Basar, 74
    Maple-Cinnamon Cream Cheese, 315
    Matbucha, 70
    Olive-Basil Cream Cheese, 315
    Roasted Red Pepper Cream Cheese, 314
    Salmon-Dill Cream Cheese, 315
    Shallot-Chive Cream Cheese, 314
    Supremely Creamy Hummus, 73
    Vegetarian Chopped "Liver," 77
    Veggie Cream Cheese, 314
Squash
    Butternut Squash and Pear Soup, 84

Butternut Squash and Sage Bourekas, 246
Butternut Squash Kugel with Crispy Shallots, 128–29
Couscous with Winter Squash and Chickpeas, 158–60
Garlic-Marinated Zucchini, 100
Grilled Zucchini with Balsamic Dressing, 101
Kabocha Squash–Chocolate Chip Cake, 292–93
Roasted Delicata Squash with Thyme Bread Crumbs, 108
Rustic Vegetable Soup with Dill Dumplings, 88–89
Strawberries
    Chocolate-Strawberry Egg Cream, 309
    Three-in-One Matzo Brei, 42–43
Strudel, Caraway Cabbage, 133–34
Sufganiyot, Bittersweet Glazed, with Peanut Butter Cream, 254–55
Sukkot, 338–39
Sumac, 342
Sundaes, Tahini, Roasted Fig, and Pistachio, 306
Sweet potatoes
    Black Bean–Sweet Potato Chili, 96
    Slow-Cooker Spiced Beef and Chickpea Stew, 170–71
    Sweet Potato–Parmesan Filling, 266
    Sweet Potato–Scallion Frittata, 207
    Vegetarian Porcini Farro and Cholent, 168–69

Tabbouleh, Heirloom, 71
Tahini
    Cinnamon-Honey Tahini Spread, 313
    Roasted Eggplant and Tahini Crostini, 111–12
    Supremely Creamy Hummus, 73
    Tahini, Roasted Fig, and Pistachio Sundaes, 306
Tamimi, Sami, 64
Tarts
    Mushroom–Goat Cheese Tart, 216
    Peach and Raspberry Tart, 248
Terracina, Giovanni, 104
Thermometers, instant-read, 16
Tilapia in Spicy Tomato Sauce, 174
Tofu Steaks, Panfried, with Shallot Gravy, 224–25
Tomatoes
    Baked Tomatoes and Eggs, 38–39
    Baked Ziti with Caramelized Cherry Tomatoes, 218–19
    Black Bean–Sweet Potato Chili, 96
    Breaded Eggplant and Tomato Stacks, 206
    Chorizo, Tomato, and Cabbage Soup, 91
    Couscous with Winter Squash and Chickpeas, 158–60
    Fattoush, 72
    Goulash, 95
    Heirloom Tabbouleh, 71
    Matbucha, 70
    Mozzarella, Tomato, and Basil Frittata, 41
    Mushroom-and-Beef-Stuffed Peppers, 202–3

Pomegranate Molasses Meatballs, 200–201
Porcini-, Tomato-, and Kale-Stuffed Peppers, 213–14
Romaine Wedge Salad with Buttermilk Dressing, 60
Savory French Toast with Seared Tomatoes and Za'atar Butter, 36
slicing cherry, 218
Sourdough Gazpacho, 81
Spinach-Matzo Lasagna, 221–22
Sugar Snap Pea, Corn, and Basil Salad, 55
Tilapia in Spicy Tomato Sauce, 174
Tomato-Beef Filling, 267
Tomato-Chickpea Soup with Spinach, 82
Tomato Salad with Fried Capers, 56
Watermelon Israeli Salad, 57
Tools, 15–17
Turnips, Pan-Roasted, 107
20 Cloves of Garlic Borscht, 80
Tzimmes, Mango-Ginger, 132

Upside-Down Apple Cake, 290–91

Varnishkes, Kasha, 142
Vegetable oils, 19
Vegetables. *See also individual vegetables*
    Rustic Vegetable Soup with Dill Dumplings, 88–89
Vegetarian meal planning, 211

Walnuts
    Apple and Honey Granola, 22
    Ashkenazi Charoset, 316
    Black Pepper and Pistachio Granola, 23
    Bulgur with Walnuts and Pomegranate, 162
    Chocolate-Walnut Filling, 276–77
    Grilled Pear, Fennel, and Toasted Walnut Salad, 62
    Matzo Granola with Walnuts and Coconut, 24
    Red Cabbage and Beet Slaw with Caramelized Walnuts, 69
    Rugelach Two Ways, 276–77
    Vegetarian Chopped "Liver," 77
    Walnut Mandelbrot, 278
Watermelon Israeli Salad, 57

Yeast, working with, 229
Yom Kippur, 336–37
Yoskowitz, Jeff, 185

Za'atar, 342
    Za'atar Butter, 36
Zabar's, 181
Zarhin, Shemi, 208
Zucchini
    Garlic-Marinated Zucchini, 100
    Grilled Zucchini with Balsamic Dressing, 101
    Rustic Vegetable Soup with Dill Dumplings, 88–89